OFF THE BOOKS

OFF THE BOOKS

ON LITERATURE AND CULTURE

J. Peder Zane

The University of South Carolina Press

© 2015 University of South Carolina

All the columns in this book originally appeared in the *News & Observer*
of Raleigh, North Carolina, which retains copyright to this material.
They are reprinted by permission of the newspaper.

Published by the University of South Carolina Press
Columbia, South Carolina 29208

www.sc.edu/uscpress

Manufactured in the United States of America

24 23 22 21 20 19 18 17 16 15
10 9 8 7 6 5 4 3 2 1

Library of Congress Cataloging-in-Publication Data
can be found at http://catalog.loc.gov/.

ISBN 978-1-61117-508-0 (paperback)
ISBN 978-1-61117-509-7 (ebook)

This book was printed on recycled paper with
30 percent postconsumer waste content.

To my mother—
that's all.

Contents

Acknowledgments

First thanks belong to my editor at the University of South Carolina Press, Jonathan Haupt, whose sharp eye helped me shape this collection. More important is his vision that the work of newspaper book critics is worth preserving. I am honored to be part of his project.

All of these pieces originally appeared in the News & Observer of Raleigh. I want to thank the newspaper's publisher, Orage Quarles III, who has graciously supported this project. My two main editors at the paper, Suzanne Brown and Felicia Gressette, improved these columns. Copy editors including Eileen Heyes, Nell Medlin and Pam Nelson saved my bacon more times than I like to remember. Book-loving colleagues such as Geoff Edgers, Todd Lothery, Bill Morrison, John Murawski and Dwane Powell made the best job in the world even better.

As the book review editor, I was privileged to work with many talented writers who inspired me through their knowledge—I spent half my day speaking with these brilliant folks—and challenged me to raise my game through the quality of their own work. I especially want to thank Bruce Allen, Ellyn Bache, Sven Birkerts, H. W. Brands, Frederick Busch, Fred Chappell, Michael Chitwood, Peter Coclanis, Rod Cockshutt, Clyde Edgerton, Quinn Eli, Clyde Frazier, John Freeman, Peter Gay, Philip Gerard, Denise Gess, Marianne Gingher, Marvin Hunt, Robert Lalasz, Janet Lembke, Peter Makuck, Phillip Manning, Erin McGraw, Dennis McNally, Herbert Mitgang, Ruth Moose, Louis D. Rubin Jr.,

Michael Skube, John David Smith, Gil Troy, Damon Tweedy, Timothy B. Tyson, Anthony Walton, Steve Weinberg, Roger Wilkins and Tom Wolfe.

Finally, thanks is too weak a word to express my gratitude to my wife, Janine, whose love and support are only matched by her editing chops.

Introduction

Reading the return address on my package, the Raleigh postal clerk asked, "Are you the man from the News & Observer?" I was thrilled. My photo ran with my Sunday books column, but I was hardly even a local celebrity. "I am," I said. Fishing for a compliment, I added, "You like our pages?" She was nonplussed. After an awkward pause, she explained, "You're the one who gets all those boxes."

Guilty as charged. Every day was like Christmas during my 13 years as the book review editor and books columnist. Around mid-morning I'd hear the gray cart's rattling wheels, then I'd see Gus's straining face as he delivered four or five white postal containers stuffed with cardboard envelopes. For the next half hour, I'd valiantly tear them open—paper cuts be damned—organizing my bounty into piles as I once did stocking stuffers. Novels here, biographies there, histories in this stack, memoirs in that.

A few went back in the mail, to the critics from around the country who filled our section. Most wound up in the discount bin, where my colleagues could buy hardbacks for $2 and paperbacks for $1 (the proceeds went to charity). The rest ended up in the four-foot-tall stacks lining the walls of my office; anything higher angered the laws of physics. I didn't see these books as a fire hazard but as windows on the world. From the confines of my Raleigh office, they told me what was going on in America and abroad, in big cities and tiny hamlets, in the minds of the mighty and the many. They were a mirror, reading me as I read them.

I did not come to the Book Review column through the traditional route—I majored in history, not English, at Wesleyan University in

Connecticut. After that, I reported on hard news and cultural issues for various publications in my hometown, including the New York Times.

A confession: I read, but didn't devour, books before moving to Raleigh. Mostly I consumed material that seemed directly relevant to my job of understanding the world around me, especially newspaper and magazine articles. After a few months at the Book Review, I had an awakening. I realized that I had only been skimming the surface, focusing on what was happening but not, in the deepest sense, why it was happening.

I discovered that the novels of Lydia Millet and Thomas Pynchon, the cultural criticism of W. E. B. DuBois, biographies of Alexander the Great and other "irrelevant" works cast brilliant light on the here and now. They reminded me that art is not timeless because it occupies an ethereal realm but because it helps us find meaning in the hurly-burly of daily life. It is not just beautiful and wondrous; it is transcendently useful. When William Faulkner said literature's great subject is "the human heart in conflict with itself," he was urging us to identify the fundamental constants driving our ever-changing universe.

I was not an artist, but a reporter. Books were my beat. Journalism is a craft that rests on curiosity, empathy, honesty and respect. Its practitioners believe that other people have something to teach us. Fortunately, readers have the same attitude. Reading is like a blind date—we focus our attention on others, working with an open mind and generous heart in hopes of forging a connection.

As a books columnist, I had the best sources possible. I used books to do what I always had in my reporting: to get a handle on all around me. I didn't approach them as the works of solitary artists but as cultural artifacts that reveal our present moment as surely as the speeches of Cicero do the crumbling Roman republic. For all the insight and pleasure they provided, books were never an end in themselves. Reflecting my bedrock belief that books are brought to life by readers, I used them as springboards that informed, provoked and challenged my own thoughts to take higher flight. A life spent in books is what prepares us to go off the books in new and stimulating ways.

The columns collected here represent my greatest leaps while working at the News & Observer from 1997 to 2009 (I've spared you my many belly flops). They provide an overview of a period of dazzling, and sometimes lamentable, change. It was an era marked by the rise of the Internet and the confessional memoir as well as the decline of the independent bookstore and the continued marginalization of serious literature and ideas. A time when Oprah Winfrey and Don Imus became literary tastemakers and Harry Potter the world's most famous schoolboy. It was a period defined by the soul-searching fear induced by the 9/11 attacks, the anger of increasingly partisan politics and the renewed hope inspired by the election of America's first black president. It is the past that still shapes us.

With all apologies to Marcel Proust, ideas rather than time drive this collection. The columns are not arranged chronologically, but around general themes, some more focused than others. But even in the looser areas—such as the reviews of nonfiction and the miscellaneous pieces on culture—I've tried, where possible, to organize them so that one piece sheds light on the next one or two that follow, before moving on to something completely different (column writing is a peripatetic pursuit).

The first six sections are devoted to the traditional work of a literary critic: reviews of classic and contemporary fiction as well as works of nonfiction. It also includes profiles of Southern writers and essays on the reading life, columns on the evolving book business and the bedrock book culture. I selected columns that embody my effort to connect books to larger literary and cultural trends. Even as the selections use books to explore the world, they try to convey the sense of discovery, the feeling of joy (and, sometimes, outrage) that books inspire. I would never write a love letter to a single book or author—even as critics seek connection we must keep our distance—but I hope that these pieces, in toto, read like one.

The last six parts feature pieces of cultural commentary. Though rooted in books, these columns are not critiques of specific works. They use a book or group of books to explore trends and ideas. The first section focuses on the changing uses and new abuses of knowledge and language in our high-tech society. I joined other commentators in decrying the dumbing-down of America that continued during this period, but I also tried to explore how this resulted from the grand explosion of information and freedom that loosened the conformist pressures of culture.

I learned long ago that you are what you read and modern literature's strong focus on identity influenced the issues I thought about and how I thought about them. As seen through this lens, my pieces on race, gay rights and 9/11 America revolve around the same core issue: how do we try to understand people who are different from us? These hot-button issues can be minefields, but I've found that readers will listen, if not always agree, to anything so long as the writing is honest and forthright, reflecting an open heart and an open mind.

The final parts offer pieces covering a range of topics, from environmental issues, to changing tastes in baby names and the evolving roles of men and women. They remind us to be highly skeptical whenever historians suggest that certain periods were dominated by a limited number of concerns.

I felt especially privileged to write for the books pages because that station allowed me to address crucial issues too often ignored by the rest of the media. One of the stories I didn't cover during this time was the gradual disappearance of cultural commentators and then cultural reporters at cash-strapped newspapers. The News & Observer, like too many across the country, has abolished the full-time position of book review editor. The postal clerks at Raleigh's downtown station have one less person to wonder about.

These pieces, then, are also historical documents of a vanishing culture, evidence of a time when mid-sized newspapers recognized the value of literature. But, as the French say, *plus ça change*. Despite the assaults, onslaughts and indignities, books remain the vital core of our culture. They are the greatest tool humanity has devised to share deeply felt emotions and profound ideas publicly. They will endure because they are irreplaceable. It is my honor to serve them as they serve me.

BETWEEN
THE COVERS

CLASSIC FICTION

Eudora Welty:
The Writers' Writer

The writer Richard Bausch hit the wall in 1975.

"I began to fear for my sanity; in my then very confused and anxiety-laden head, there convened a judge and jury, which accused me at every turn my mind took. I could not convince myself that my own thoughts, unruly as they were, and often purely crazy, were not evidence of what I feared, that I was losing my mind."

Then he encountered Eudora Welty's shimmering book, "The Ponder Heart," and he bounced back. "Something in that wonderful novel, Edna Earle's attitude about all that, her tolerance of the confusion of mind, the fact that it contains ridiculous and dreadful contradictions—that is how I remember it anyway—something in it caused the judge and jury to be disbanded and I could feel it dispersing, adjourning, as I read on. I remember more the feeling of having been healed, reading that book, than very many of the details of the book itself."

Bausch's poignant essay is one of 22 tributes that grace "Eudora Welty: Writers' Reflections Upon First Reading Welty." To call these pieces marking the Mississippi writer's 90th birthday appreciations is to underestimate the power and the glory of Welty's gently fierce pen. Instead they read like testimonials by devotees waist-deep in a nourishing spring, challenged, comforted, awed and emboldened by her glorious short stories and novels.

These heartfelt essays are especially welcome when the celebration of literature seems like an endangered species. For decades scholars have deconstructed "texts," coldly dismembering them to discover hidden agendas. There is no meaning, they declare, but meanings, discernible only through suffocating layers of theory.

Bang! goes their sniper's rifle, aimed at the emotional experience of art.

Thus, criticism in the academy—admittedly, often piercing—has largely become the study of power. But the real power grab is by the scholars themselves who, like waves that would rule the oceans, assert that it is the interpreters, rather than the creators, who hold the keys to literature.

Thud! falls their now lifeless prey, prepared for autopsy.

By contrast, the exuberant essays in "Eudora Welty" are weighty yet roiling with life. Lee Smith, Fred Chappell, Louis D. Rubin Jr. and the other contributors offer thoughtful shouts of praise that reclaim literature for those who make and serve it.

The pieces suggest the humble traits that made Welty an extraordinary writer. The poet William Jay Smith imagines a youthful Eudora, "watching the children eat at recess (you knew their sandwiches)." When she writes, he asserts, "the stories come to the tips of your fingers while you listen."

Elizabeth Spencer adds, "her sensitivity takes the form of feeling for the other person. She can guess what is going on in that mind and heart."

Welty knows what to look for, writes Doris Betts: "[Her] photographs constitute a metaphor for her story method, since it was at the camera she first learned 'to wait' for 'the moment in which people reveal themselves.'"

The essays also note the gargantuan empathy that enabled Welty to reveal the remarkable in the unremarkable. They remind us of the courageous clarity she brought to hot-button issues, especially race. And we can marvel at her poetic language: "He could not hear his heart—it was as quiet as ashes falling."

Best of all, they address the mystery that envelops us as we read her deceptively straightforward works: How does she get so much out of so little? Simple, says George Garrett, providing a penetrating description of art. In Welty's stories and novels, Garrett notes, there is almost always "a totally inexplicable moment of pure unadulterated and inimitable magic. I mean real magic, because there is no technical or mechanical explanation for it . . . From Eudora Welty, you learn to believe in magic."

Welty's magic, "the very personification of the nature of art," Ellen Douglas writes, is at once ineffable and familiar as suggested by this passage from Welty's transcendent story of a black musician, "Powerhouse": "Then he took hold of the piano, as if he saw it for the first time in his life, and tested it for strength, hit it down in the bass, played an octave with his elbow, lifted to the top, looked inside, and leaned against it with all his might. He sat down and played it for a few minutes with outrageous force and got it under his power—a deep bass and coarse as a sea net—then produced something glimmering and fragile, and smiled."

Douglas concludes, "This is 'Powerhouse.' It's also Eudora Welty, who produced a body of work as deep and coarse as a sea net—and then produced something glimmering and fragile. Whose piano is our language and our lives. Who hands us the gift of her work and smiles."

June 13, 1999

John Fante:
What the Boys Read

Like a great old song or Proust's madeleine, "Ask the Dust" transported me back to a time when novels did not just impress or enthrall but spoke for me.

As John Fante's splendid 1939 novel detailed the dreamy flights (and flutters) of a writer seeking love and glory in Depression-era Los Angeles, I remembered my years on the cusp of manhood, when I was awash with dawning dreams and dusky doubt.

Back then I was topic A, B & C. Yet I lacked the insight to understand B or C (much less D-Z) about myself. Then I encountered three books—"Hunger" by Knut Hamsun, "Women" by Charles Bukowski and "A Fan's Notes" by Frederick Exley—and saw myself in their pages.

I wasn't unique. It seemed like all my buddies were devouring those books, whose mix of self-aggrandizement and self-degradation captured our young man minds. Now I can add Fante's novel to the list of what I call Boy/Man Books—with a twist.

Discovering "Ask the Dust" as a mature adult gave me two reading experiences: As I re-experienced the woosh of recognition, the "yes,

yes, yes" that had defined my relationship with the earlier books, I was also able to look back—aha!—at the person who had been so moved by "Hunger," "Women" and "A Fan's Notes."

Like those three, "Ask the Dust" is an autobiographical novel narrated by a writer whose literary gifts are awaiting discovery. (Once upon a time I was certain that Faulkner and Hemingway would be revealed as "poetasters"—man, I used to love that word—once my genius bloomed.)

Fante's novel reminded me of the power of first-person narration to erase the line between writer and reader. Reading "Hunger" et al, I knew the narrators were talking about themselves; I also knew they were me, talking about myself. Their utter self-absorption—the novels are less concerned with story than their protagonists' wishing wells of consciousness—reflected my state of mind.

As a young man, I envisioned a spot on Johnny Carson's couch: "How do you do it? Really, how do you do it?" "Well, Johnny . . . ."

Fante's alter ego, 20-year-old Arturo Bandini, sees himself in even better company: "A day and another day and the day before, and the library with the big boys in the shelves, old Dreiser, old Mencken, all the boys down there, and I went to see them," he confides. "Hya Dreiser, Hya Mencken, Hya, hya: there's a place for me, too, and it begins with B, in the shelf, Arturo Bandini, make way for Arturo Bandini, his slot for his book."

It's not all peaches and cream for Bandini. As with the protagonists of those other novels, and little me, the real world counters his dreams with humiliation.

Often out of cash, Bandini lives off bags of oranges, which he sucks down in his dingy room in the Alta Loma hotel. He has enjoyed some success—a magazine published his story, "The Little Dog Laughed"—but he is often wracked by doubt. "You haven't any material, your talent is dubious," he scolds himself, "your talent is pitiful, you haven't any talent, and stop lying to yourself day after day."

Girls are also problematic. "Afraid of a woman!" he tells himself. "Ha, great writer this! How can he write about women, when he's never had a woman?" He falls hard for a waitress named Camilla, but her heart belongs to a creep who only gives her the back of his hand.

As it progresses, this short novel assumes near-epic scale. Bandini's pursuit of literature and love become part of a larger, more universal quest: the transition all boys must make into the frightening and mythic world of manhood.

Most any adolescent boy can tell you that being a man means leaving a mark. It is about heroism, strength and startling accomplishments. Greatness is the only option. To join the company of men, you must imagine yourself to be better than every other man. Bandini does not hope simply for publication; he knows his books will be acclaimed as the "finest written."

Yet he throbs with impulses that would declare all that bunk: "Scared of high places too, and blood, and of earthquakes," is how he describes himself, "otherwise, quite fearless, excepting death, except the fear I'll scream in a crowd, except the fear of appendicitis, except the fear of heart trouble, even that, sitting in his room holding the clock and pressing his jugular vein."

Reading that passage today, I admire Fante's complex exploration of manhood. But I know my younger self would have read right past those insights, just as I had the similarly painful passages of "Hunger," "Women" and "A Fan's Notes."

Back then, the dream was all. And the lesson I took from those books was the books themselves. Despite it all, the authors had triumphed; their victory was in my mitts. They were me; what's theirs would be mine!

Life seemed easier then, even if it was harder.

December 10, 2006

Knut Hamsun:
Risking a Literary Friendship

When it comes to books, my only question is: What's next?

So much spine-tingling greatness, so little time. So many gaps—"The Man Without Qualities," "The Decline and Fall of the Roman Empire," "Eloise." So much guilt.

Despite the onward march, old books are like old friends. Those we encounter in youth stand out more than the rest, crystallized by feeling memory. I met Knut Hamsun (1859–1952) in college. After devouring "Hunger," I quickly moved to his other psychological masterpieces, "Mysteries" and "Pan," then "Growth of the Soil," "Victoria," "Rosa," "Under the Autumn Stars" and "Dreamers." Rationally, I knew many other writers were at least the Norwegian's equal. But Hamsun became my spirited answer to: "Who's your favorite writer?" Each new girlfriend received a crisp copy, followed by a measuring discussion.

I valued him so, made him mine, because he didn't seem to belong to anyone else. "Knut who?" others would say—to my delight—of the man who had won the Nobel Prize for literature in 1920. Elitism, snobbery, call it what you will, but my love of Hamsun told me something about myself at that young age that was forcefully affirming.

Learning why his reputation had fallen into eclipse—he had supported Germany during World War II—I took pause, wrestling for the first time with the tension between politics and art. I saw that he was no fascist on the page and, quite honestly, he meant too much to me to cast away.

Through the years, his totemic stature grew in my mind while his books gathered dust on my shelf as I continued to ask: What's next? So it was with some trepidation that I recently came across Sverre Lyngstad's definitive new translation of "Hunger." Did I dare? What if, almost two decades later, the prose seemed flat and irrelevant? For us common readers do not assess books with the cold eye of learned judgment but fuse with them through the idiosyncratic lens of emotional self-definition. Could I relinquish my generous dear friend?

Ah, what the heck.

"Hunger" (1890) now seemed a subtly different book to me. It is indeed the story of a nameless young writer failing to eke out a living, a plotless, stream-of-consciousness work about a man "too feeble to steer or guide myself where I wanted to go." For several months he roams the streets of Kristiania (now Oslo), cursing God, berating strangers, fomenting ludicrous run-ins with prostitutes, sailors, blind men and editors. All the while he imagines composing world-shaking newspaper articles—"[I] decided upon a three part monograph about philosophical cognition. Needless to say, I would have an opportunity to deal a deathblow to Kant's sophisms"—that might secure him pocket change for bread. To little avail. "I swallowed my saliva again and again to take the edge off, and it seemed to help."

Introspective but not analytic—the action in "Hunger" pivots on the whirligig fluctuations of the narrator's mind: suicidal one moment, joyful the next, angry, heartbroken, proud, malicious, pretentious, polite, petty, perplexed, generous, hilarious, warped, inspired seemingly all at once. "I give a hoarse scream of terror and clutch the bed. How wonderful it was to feel safe again as I clapped my hand against that hard bunk bed. This is what it's like to die, I said to myself, and now you're going to die. Then I sit up in bed and ask sternly, 'Who said I was going to die?'"

In memory, "Hunger" was the story of a heroic man, lonely, frightened, unappreciated, yelling "take notice" at a deaf and dumb world upon which he will, make no mistake, impose himself. That so much of the work was based on Hamsun's experience, that the starving young writer willed himself into a Nobel laureate, transformed "Hunger" in my mind into a semi-autobiographical work of my own fears and desires.

So it remained.

Rereading "Hunger" as I hurtle toward middle-age, I was more impressed by the great degree to which the world, whether it be other people or his own swirling consciousness, imposes itself upon the narrator. "However estranged I was from myself in that moment," he tells us, "so completely at the mercy of invisible influences, nothing that was taking place around me escaped my perceptions."

As the narrator learns, the world is fair and unfair, just and unjust. But it is not easily fled or transformed. It exacts its price as it takes our measure. This, of course, is a much harder lesson. But, for me, the great achievement of "Hunger" is that even as its words stay bound to the page, it keeps speaking to whirligiging me. It's a friend indeed.

June 6, 1999

Georges Simenon: Rediscovering
a Literary Phenomenon

The New York Review of Books is more than a leading journal of ideas. It is also a literary miracle worker. Since 1999 it has brought dead books back to life through its Classic series.

Its latest Lazarus is the work of Belgian writer Georges Simenon (1903–89). It is a sign of fame's fleeting nature that he would need the New York Review's magic. Simenon, a phenomenon of 20th-century letters, published almost 400 books under at least 18 different pen names—including 40 books in 1929. His works have sold more than 500 million copies worldwide. He claimed to have used half a million pencils while at work, and to have slept with 10,000 women when he wasn't.

Best known for his series of Parisian mysteries featuring Inspector Maigret, Simenon produced superb prose at a torrential pace. "He reckoned to complete a novel in five, or six, or at most eleven days," the novelist Anita Brookner has observed, "and to this end would labor in an almost fetishistic trance: his sweat-soaked lumberjack's shirt would be laundered every night, ready for him to wear the following morning, and so on until the brief spasm was over."

It was during such literary fevers that Simenon crafted the seven accomplished novels that the New York Review has returned to print. Like all of the nearly 200 titles in the Classic series, the Simenon volumes include appreciations by distinguished writers. One measure of this commercial writer's skill is the elite roster of authors who gush about it: Brookner, Joyce Carol Oates, Larry McMurtry, P. D. James, William T. Vollmann, Luc Sante and Norman Rush.

As with P. G. Wodehouse, another prolific 20th-century genius, there is a satisfying sameness to Simenon's oeuvre—his novels were known across Europe as "simenons." Where Wodehouse was the master of gentle comedy, Simenon excelled at brisk tales of existential angst and hard-boiled fatalism.

Oates notes: "A 'simenon' may or may not be a crime/suspense novella, but it will always move swiftly and with seeming inevitability from its opening scene to its final, often startling and ironic conclusion. . . . [T]he quintessential 'simenon' . . . is a sequence of cinematic confrontations in which an individual—male, middle-aged, unwittingly trapped in his life—is catapulted into an extraordinary adventure that will leave him transformed, unless destroyed."

If two quotes could capture a life's work, it would be these. In "The Man Who Watched Trains Go By" (1938, translated from the French by Marc Romano), Simenon defines the predicament into which he drops his characters: "For all these years it had been a strain playing [his] part, and watching himself incessantly to make sure that he didn't say or do the wrong thing. Now all that was ended."

In "Red Lights" (1953, translated from the French by Norman Denny) he gives a glimpse of the tenuous peace they might achieve: "He had the feeling that, for the first time since they had known one another, there was no deception between them any longer, nothing more than, nothing as thick even as a veil, to prevent them from being themselves face-to-face."

Simenon's books fall into three general categories: mysteries, what he called "*roman romans*" (or novel novels) and the series the New York Review is focusing on, his "*romans durs,*" or hard novels. Hard here does not mean complicated—Simenon prided himself on writing smart books for common readers. Instead, they revolve around characters facing trials of the soul as they try to connect with their authentic selves.

"Red Lights," for example, depicts the simmering rage of a frustrated man as he and his wife drive to Maine to pick up their children from summer camp.

"Three Bedrooms in Manhattan" (1946, translated from the French by Romano and Lawrence G. Blochman) focuses on a wounded couple who come together in the bars of New York. Simenon displays his gift for compression in describing their budding relationship: "And gradually, this silent nighttime walk took on the solemn aspect of a wedding march. Both knew that from now on they'd cling to each other even harder, not as lovers, but as two creatures who'd been alone and at last, after a long time, had found someone to walk with."

His masterpiece, "Dirty Snow" (1948, translated from the French by Romano and Louise Varese), features one of literature's most despicable characters: a young man who murders, rapes and steals just to feel something. But like all Simenon characters, he yearns for something more.

"Dirty Snow" was so raw that I had to put it down momentarily to escape its nihilistic landscape. Yet like Simenon's other books, it was thoroughly absorbing.

These novels are dated—in ways that illuminate our contemporary world. For much of the 20th century, Simenon and other artists focused on the individual's relationship to society. They saw our greatest challenge as finding ways to realize our true selves despite the iron grip of culture and the state.

That theme has all but disappeared from literature, film and the other arts, which now cast problems in largely personal terms. As our ties to the larger community have frayed, our relationship to ourselves, our family, friends and co-workers has taken center stage.

Of course, society is still potent; it still twists and shapes us. As Simenon grabs us with his compelling stories, he also shakes us to recognize and confront its force.

July 23, 2006

Walter Brooks: The World According to Freddy the Pig

If children's literature has an answer to William Faulkner, it is Walter R. Brooks. While the sage of Oxford was imagining the complex world of Yoknapatawpha County, Brooks, a staff writer for the New Yorker who died in 1958, was detailing the rich life on the Bean farm in upstate New York. Instead of Compsons, Sutpens and Snopeses, Brooks gave us Freddy the Pig, Jinx the Cat, Mrs. Wiggins the Cow and a host of other clever, lighthearted animals as endearing and loquacious as his most famous creation, Ed the talking horse (of course, of course).

Although the 26 Freddy the Pig novels that Brooks wrote between 1927 and 1958 enjoyed healthier sales than Faulkner's works, they were out of print by the 1970s. Now the Overlook Press is living up to its name by republishing all of them in handsome hardcover editions with Kurt Wiese's beautiful illustrations.

Their reissue couldn't be timelier. In an era when young adult literature is dominated by raw tales of dysfunction, Brooks offers beautifully written works light on topical concerns but rich in the wonders of life and the power of imagination. Instead of trauma and pain, we find kindness, humor and respect.

It is as easy to be drawn into Brooks's world as it was for Alice to tumble down the rabbit's hole into Wonderland. The best point of entry is through "The Freddy Anniversary Collection," which includes the first three novels in the series: "Freddy Goes to Florida," details the gang's effort to migrate south for the winter; "Freddy Goes to the North Pole" recounts their trip to the home of Santa Claus; and "Freddy the Detective," like most of the subsequent novels, describes the intrigues and adventures the animals gin up for themselves in their upstate New York home. Along the way they outwit alligators and pirates, burglars and "bad men with mustaches." They meet U.S. senators, discover jewels and gold, and ride on Santa's sleigh.

As the series progresses Brooks develops strong and consistent character traits for his animals. Jinx is brash, Freddy is smart but dreamy (he is a poet, after all), Mrs. Wiggins is slow but terribly kind. Like all accomplished writers, Brooks respects his creations. Sure, his animals talk and read and write poetry—Freddy's ode to the North Pole begins: "O Pole, O Pole, O glorious Pole! / To you I sing this song, / Where bedtime comes but once a year, / Since the nights are six months long." But they are not people with snouts and beaks. Instead, Brooks imagines what it's like to be a rooster, crow, dog or goose, allowing readers to observe their habits and hear their thoughts. Charles the Rooster, for instance, is not too keen on having to rise before everyone else to cock-a-doodle in the morning for Mr. Bean. "Doesn't matter how cold and rainy it is, it has to be done. And if I miss a morning, what do I get? I get fricasseed, that's what!"

We see the spider, Mr. Webb, in his morning ritual: "He took a long drink of fresh cold water from a raindrop, and then strolled along over the pine needles."

This same sense of wonder informs Brooks's descriptions of the natural world. His sun doesn't simply rise; it comes "up from the other side of the world, where all night long it had been shining on Chinese pagodas and the Himalayas and jungles in Africa and all the queer places where people work and play while we are sound asleep."

Every paragraph seems graced with such wisdom and inventiveness. There are no pauses or dead passages. Like Rumpelstiltskin's wheel, Brooks's mind tirelessly spins literary gold.

The two great themes of the series are friendship and respect. The animals stick by one another through thick and thin, all helping out the best way they can. Mr. Webb, the tiny spider, is an expert spy. The mice Eek and Quick and Eeny and Cousin Augustus save the day by using "their sharp little teeth to nibble holes through the hard rubber tires" on the car driven by bad men chasing the animals. And when the group needs to attach a rope to the carriage carrying the treasure they found under an ant hill, they turn to Jinx the Cat because "all cats are good at tying knots. The stupidest cat can tie forty knots in a ball of yarn in two minutes—and if you don't believe it, ask your grandmother."

I've never lived in the country or befriended a talking pig, but Brooks's novels evoked a rich emotion in me that I can only describe as nostalgia. Like the Jeeves novels of P. G. Wodehouse, Brooks created a universe so palpably benign and full of good cheer that it reaches deep into the recesses of our memories to rekindle our child's eye view of the world. As he delights and entertains, Brooks rekindles our ability to see the world as we once did, as a place full of wonder and love.

April 9, 2003

Robert Penn Warren—
A King Restored: Round Two
for an American Classic

Sensitive consumers are rising up against business's influence on culture. They want the unfiltered, the authentic, the pure. They want to experience art unadulterated by Big Business. And Big Business is happy to oblige. There's a booming little trade in "uncut," "uncensored," "director's cuts" of movies. Record stores are filled with expensive box sets offering five discs documenting the making of a single record.

Publishers have also gotten into the act. The last two years have brought us handsome editions of the pre-edited or pre-revised texts of Thomas Wolfe's "Look Homeward, Angel" (titled "O, Lost"), F. Scott Fitzgerald's "The Great Gatsby" ("Under the Red, White, and Blue"), Benjamin Franklin's "Autobiography" ("Franklin on Franklin") and Walt Whitman's "Leaves of Grass" ("Walt Whitman, Selected Poems, 1855–1892").

These books, movies and box sets are fascinating documents, providing illuminating peeks into the creative process. In most cases—especially for Wolfe and Fitzgerald—the "official" work is far stronger than the "original," but in art there is only one rule: More is better. In time, consumers will decide which "version" is better.

The latest entry is the "restored edition" of Robert Penn Warren's classic novel "All the King's Men." Editor Noel Polk, a professor at the University of Southern Mississippi who has "restored" works by William Faulkner, compared Warren's original typescripts with the text published in 1946. He makes a convincing case that commercial concerns and aesthetic myopia led Warren's editors to weaken his work. "At nearly every point where editors intervened," Polk writes, "what Warren wrote is all but demonstrably superior to the editor's revisions."

That sounds like a broad claim, but Polk also acknowledges that a general reader would be hard-pressed to identify his changes. Polk undid scores of mostly minor alterations.

The editors—presumably with Warren's consent—toned down the book for public consumption. For example, they changed Warren's phrase "callous-assed" to "callous-rumped." They deleted a paragraph that referred to condoms and several others that reflected the deep anger of the narrator, Jack Burden, including one in which he daydreams about drowning a woman.

Unfortunately, Polk's most obvious restoration is also the most problematic. Warren had called the novel's Huey Long-inspired political leader Willie Talos. Talos has resonances in Greek mythology but it also sounds Greek, which makes it an odd-sounding name for a Southern politician. Warren's editors rightly felt that the name got in the reader's way and insisted on something more American. Reluctantly, Warren acceded to Stark.

It was the right call.

But Polk's greatest contribution may lie in the place where art and commerce meet. By giving the publishers a profit motive for republishing Warren, Polk prompts readers to reconsider a work many of us haven't read since high school. And what I found is that Warren's masterpiece is one of the most misunderstood books in the American canon.

ETERNAL TRUTHS

Critics routinely describe "All the King's Men" as a political novel. The dust jacket of the restored edition tells readers: "Set in the 1930s, it traces the rise and fall of Willie [Stark] Talos, a fictional Southern politician who resembles the real-life Huey 'Kingfish' Long of Louisiana."

In fact, "All the King's Men" is no more a story of politics than "Hamlet" is a play about the Danish court. Governor Talos's rise and fall is one of the most compelling threads of this novel, but this book is not his story. It is, instead, the saga of the governor's assistant, Jack Burden, a tortured man who, like Prince Hamlet, describes and contemplates a vast range of human thought, emotion and experience as he tries to find a basis for action.

The novel does provide vivid insights into how a gullible public is often manipulated and betrayed by cynical politicians, but this is not its main concern. Politics serves as backdrop for Warren's far more ambitious effort of questioning whether the eternal verities—honor, nobility, goodness and free will—still have a place in the modern world.

The result is the rarest of books: a philosophical potboiler. Deeply imagined, beautifully written, it is both a reckoning with the deepest forces of life—how Time and History shape our destinies—and an edge-of-your seat page-turner. Like the greatest works of literature, Warren brilliantly details a vision of man's fate, one that is unrelentingly pessimistic. Like the juiciest best seller, the story is propelled by a series of startling revelations involving love, lust, betrayal, tragedy, suicide and murder.

Our narrator is part detective, part confessor. Jack combs the past to find the hidden patterns, the logic and meaning that must reside within the raw jumble of experience. He describes his pilgrim's progress in a hardboiled voice, filled with anger, irony and reflection—a cross between Raymond Chandler's Philip Marlowe and Faulkner's Quentin Compson.

Jack was born into a little Eden in the Southern hamlet of Burden's Landing. He was a child of privilege, though his life was disrupted when his father up and left one day. But his mother was devoted to him, and the kindly Judge Irwin served as a beloved surrogate father. He swam and played tennis with his two close companions, Adam Stanton, who would become a renowned surgeon, and Adam's sister Anne. Anne was Jack's first and true love—a long, complicated relationship that Warren draws with exquisite sensitivity.

His inability to consummate their relationship is the first sign that all is not well with Jack. "I lacked," he explains in retrospect, "some essential confidence in the world and in myself." They part. Eventually he enters graduate school, studying history. His dissertation concerns the life of Cass Mastern, a Civil War-era relative of Jack's whose relationship with his best friend's wife spawns an unending string of tragedy. (Warren's long, absorbing account of Mastern's tortured life is one of the book's many triumphs.)

Jack wants to be noble and good, not in a heroic but an everyday sense. Yet it remains beyond him. His life becomes an act of self-abnegation, a slow drift from the values he cherishes. He becomes a newspaper reporter, covering Willie's early campaigns. Eventually he goes to work for the man, using his investigative skills to dig up dirt on his boss' adversaries—a dishonorable job that disgusts his friends and family.

One of those adversaries turns out to be Judge Irwin. When the boss orders him to rake the Judge's muck, Jack says he knows the man is spotless. Willie responds with one of the novel's most famous lines: "Man is conceived in sin and born in corruption and he passeth from the stink of the didie to the stench of the shroud. There is always something."

And he's right. The dark secret Jack learns about the Judge and Anne and Adam's father makes Jack, like Cass Mastern before him, the agent of irrevocable ruin for everyone he knows and loves.

The essential point is that all the characters have something in common: Each is shown to have existed in a state of grace, and all suffer falls of biblical proportions because of sin—committed either by themselves or someone they trusted.

ARCS OF RUIN

One of Warren's great achievements is that he has managed to write a novel of ideas—the characters and events are focused on developing the book's philosophical concerns—while preserving the basic humanity and individualism of his players, a feat Don DeLillo, Thomas Pynchon, Richard Powers and our other modern meganovelists routinely fail to achieve. In fact, one of the reasons that "All the King's Men" is described as the story of Willie Talos is that Warren paints such a rich portrait of this character.

Yet in the larger context of the book, Willie's life is just one of many arcs of ruin. When Jack meets him, Willie is a teetotaler; a one-woman farm boy who enters politics to do good. His early speeches are full of facts, figures and high-minded programs that might make a real difference in the lives of his downtrodden constituents. Instead, he only bored them.

"They don't give a damn about [your plans]," Jack tells him. "Hell, make 'em cry, or make 'em laugh, make 'em think you're their weak and erring pal, or make 'em think you're God-a-Mighty. Or make 'em mad. Even mad at you. Just stir 'em up, it doesn't matter how or why, and they'll love you and come back for more. Pinch 'em in the soft place. They aren't alive, most of 'em, and haven't been alive in twenty years."

It takes a while, but Willie takes this cynical advice to heart. He becomes a new man: a boozing philanderer and a down-and-dirty demagogue, beloved and feared by all. "The Boss isn't interested in money," Jack tells us. "He's interested in Willie. Quite simply and directly. And when anybody is interested in himself quite simply and directly the way Willie is in Willie you call it genius."

It is tempting to say Willie's corruption is a product of free will, that he chose to surrender to his demons. But the fact that every character in the book suffers a similar fate makes such a reading impossible. Instead, Warren offers a dark vision in which History and Time—Warren always capitalizes these terms to underscore their overwhelming power—are forces that grind people down, agents of doom.

Live long enough, you'll be stepped on, too.

In many ways, "All the King's Men" is a product of its times. It is the creation of a man deeply influenced by the crushing carnage of two world wars, by William Faulkner's dark view of history, and existentialist critiques of human freedom. Fifty-five years later, Warren's view seems unrelentingly bleak. In these more comfortable and, relatively speaking, more peaceful times, it is hard to accept his notion of inescapable ruin. And yet, we might also note that his pessimism was hard-earned.

But even if we might feel alienated from Warren's philosophy, his artistry is absorbing. This meticulously crafted book, with sentences, paragraphs and chapters resonating with all that came before them and all that will follow, is a literary tour de force. It is so good it can sour you on other novels, almost all of which pale in comparison.

Noel Polk and the publishers at Harcourt Brace should be commended for this "restored edition" of Warren's great novel. By repackaging "All the King's Men" they have used the most powerful force in American life, the marketplace, to prompt us to reread, and re-evaluate, a great book.

December 23, 2001

Thomas/Tom Wolfe:
The Man Who Cried Wolfe

My mailbag isn't as overstuffed with dispatches from famous writers as you might think. Truth be told, when the return address says "Don De-Lillo," "Toni Morrison" or "Jackie Collins," I feel a tingle of anticipation as I watch one of my many assistants reading said letter to determine whether it is worth my while.

Most, alas, are not.

However, a recent missive was so astounding, its contents at once posing, then solving, the greatest mystery in literature, necessitating nothing less than a complete reconsideration of 20th-century American letters, that I must reprint it in full.

Dear Mr. Zane,
It is with the deepest gratitude and most heartfelt humility that I wit-ness folks in my native North Carolina and others across the country and around the world mark the centennial of my birth. To be read is all that a writer can ask. To see that he is also admired and loved is

beyond category. To be 100, that's no picnic. Just the other day I was trying to reach my "primary care physician" when . . . but I digress.

I am writing to you because I find it rather aggravating that all of the centennial celebrations are focusing on my early work, such as "Look Homeward, Angel," with nary a mention of my path-breaking journalism from the 1960s or my more recent novels such as "The Bonfire of the Vanities" and "A Man in Full." Nowadays any undergraduate will tell you that "Thomas Wolfe and Tom Wolfe are the same guy," and yet the literati honoring me seem oblivious to this fact.

As I shall explain presently, I am partly to blame for this confusion. But, let me ask you, can any truly sensitive reader assess the work of Thomas and Tom and not see that we are no different than Samuel Clemens and Mark Twain, Mary Ann Evans and George Eliot, Walker Evans and Walker Percy?

This identity crisis is particularly annoying because I have never received proper credit for my work. It all began during my "first career," when Maxwell Perkins was my editor. Sure, Max sharpened my prose. But the legend that I needed a truck to deliver my draft of "Look Homeward, Angel," a mountainous mess of material alchemized by Max's glistening genius, is twaddle (by the by, I have it on very good authority that Margaret Mitchell did indeed find "Gone With the Wind" in an attic trunk, but that's another story for another day).

Though hailed by critics, my early books were, admittedly, tough on the townspeople of my native Asheville. When I realized that I really couldn't go home again, I slipped into the sloughs of despond. Reeling, I took rash action: In 1938 I faked my death (a singer friend of mine, let's call him EP, later tried the same thing and, except for a few sightings at the 7-Eleven—he loves their Big Gulps—he has pulled it off).

I led a buried life during the 1940s and '50s. But even as I ached to escape my past, I burned to be my one true self.

It was the wild and wooly 1960s, that radical period of unfettered reinvention, which offered me a new start. After a few fruitful visits to that gifted plastic surgeon, Dr. Dan D. Whitesuit, I shortened my name, moved to New York and started writing for newspapers.

To anyone familiar with my work, this was a logical move: I had never been a novelist of the imagination; my best early work was largely autobiographical. Once bit, twice shy, they say, so I moved away from the personal stuff. What to write? Thomas Wolfe needed the material only a reporter like Tom Wolfe could dig up.

But I was always a novelist at heart. So I fused my art and my craft. People hailed this as the New Journalism. Tom Wolfe became as big a star as Thomas Wolfe ever was. At first I delighted in this charade—Pynchon told me it was "mucho postmodern," though you'll notice he always stuck with Thomas. Still, I craved a fuller recognition of my achievements. I began leaving clues. I started writing books again, such as "The Electric Kool-Aid Acid Test" and "The Right Stuff."

Sure enough, people began confusing Thomas and Tom. Almost there, I thought. However, cruel fate and Dr. Whitesuit's expertise—I'm 100 and still don't have a double chin!—led most critics to seize on this popular observation as evidence of literature's decline.

So I upped the ante once more. I returned to writing novels in 1987, enjoying stunning success with "Bonfire." Maybe critics failed to connect the dots because my earlier work was, perhaps, more poetic. But hey, how many 87-year-olds do you know who can even write a 700-page book?

As a last-ditch effort, I titled my last book "A Man in Full" in order to force critics to recognize my literal dilemma. No dice. Today, I am the victim of my own success. My ruse has overwhelmed my muse.

Yet, even as my brilliant career continues, I am also an old man who hears the ticking of the clock. Through this letter I hope to tear off the mask, to come clean, to finally get what's coming to me.

Sincerely,
T. Wolfe

October 1, 2000

Ralph Ellison:
Popeye vs. The Invisible Man

Popeye said it best, "I yam what I yam."

Sure, I'm a *who,* different from you. But fight and scorn it, I am also a *what:* a comfortable 37-year-old American white male with a wife and two (adorable) children. My assumptions, the details of my conformity, are as different as can be from those of a modern-day Iranian or one of Caesar's Romans. My choices are made from the menu of possibilities offered by my world.

That sounds extreme, but my mind is reeling, as it often does when I'm under the influence of a provocative book. On the occasion of the posthumous publication of his second novel, "Juneteenth," I opened myself to Ralph Ellison's classic novel "Invisible Man" (1952). It is, as so many others have noted, a near-perfect work of literature—its use of symbol and metaphor and its depiction of a single mind is a high point of American letters. As I read this powerful story of a man subconsciously struggling with his "who" and "what," I was energized by the narrator's quest for self-determination and overwhelmed by the barriers mounted against him.

"Invisible Man" is the first-person story of a college-age black man who yearns for acceptance. Tracing the unnamed narrator's passage from the Deep South to Harlem, where he becomes a community leader, the novel depicts a character who realizes that blacks, whites and the world only countenance him on their terms.

"I am an invisible man," he states. "No, I am not a spook like those who haunted Edgar Allen Poe; nor am I one of your Hollywood-movie ectoplasms. I am a man of substance, of flesh and bone, fiber and liquids —and I might even be said to possess a mind. I am invisible, understand, simply because people refuse to see me."

Through 572 violent, angry, tragic, optimistic and poetic pages, Ellison presents the black experience as a surreal series of soul-sucking dead-ends; its loftiest dreams are "boomerangs" that soar then zing back to clobber us. Incest, murder, riots and high-blown speech form the backdrop for the manipulative characters the narrator encounters. They include a corrupted black college president who uses separate but equal to his advantage; white benefactors whose philanthropy is a vehicle to assuage their guilt and maintain control; a Marcus Garveyesque black nationalist who foments racial hatred to seize power; white communists who hire the narrator to organize blacks but admonish him, "you were not hired to think"; and countless sharecroppers, prostitutes, vagabonds, criminals, drunks, nymphomaniacs and bullies who seem like denizens of a dark planet to our well-educated and ambitious hero.

It is a bleak world of realpolitik, where people are human resources to be cultivated, extracted and used for personal aggrandizement. Paradoxically, it is also a nightmare world of illusion, as Ellison suggests how reality conflicts with the higher truth of human potential.

Frighteningly, Ellison imparts a sense of doom to the reader as the narrator evidences resilient hope. Time and again, the hero is duped. Time and again he picks himself up, ready to be duped again. Running in place in a futile world marked by the repetition of scarring moments rather than forward movement, he remains a man without quit, an anti-Quixote, running from the illusions of circumstance and history to the clear light he can barely imagine.

At the book's end, the narrator has holed himself up in a basement. Confined underground, he has found true freedom. No longer seeing himself through other people's eyes, "my world has become one of infinite possibilities."

Yet, even as he argues for autonomy, Ellison recognizes the need for collective action. He calls for a revolution not of arms but of minds. The destiny of all Americans, he asserts, is as bound together as hydrogen and oxygen in a drop of water. But we are also as separate as oil and water. By forging unity through our diversity, creating a politics of "love" instead of antagonism, we might realize the free and sublime America of the dream. "Our fate is to become one and yet many."

It is a beautiful vision. But it also suggests a final paradox. Though Ellison rails against conformity, he also understands its necessity. For what is conformity but the values, judgments and standards we all agree to live by? Can we do without them? How else can we avoid a world in which David Duke is as respected as Rosa Parks?

The problem, Ellison shows, arises when we conform to a corrupt system. In its place, he offers his own ideology. Ellison sees no way to dissolve the timeless tension between freedom and community. There will always be a reality that imposes itself on us. But to be truly human we must never stop confronting that world, never stop asking the six questions: who? what? when? where? how? and why?

June 20, 1999

Nadezhda Mandelstam: Spanish Wine and Oranges

The irony of our Age of Irony is that irony is dead. Though we wear the mask of hip cynicism, affecting a clued-in, above-it-all detachment from mass society, we are, in truth, about as conformist as they come.

Bill Gates, Rupert Murdoch, Michael Eisner and other moguls shape our culture, making billions by telling us the Internet is the future and that "Star Wars" matters. Our celebrity-obsessed, gossip-rich media have become marketing arms—convincing us that anointed movie stars and CEOs deserve more than all the rest of us. Instead of rebelling, we blithely suck down another un-cola with our Happy Meals.

The trouble is that this is perfectly normal. Though we fancy ourselves free-thinkers, people are by nature go-along, get-along creatures. We adapt instead of confront, accede rather than challenge. Despite the illusion of freedom, we are formed by our times, largely assuming its assumptions, making choices from the limited menu we are offered. As Nadezhda Mandelstam asks in her brilliant 1970 memoir "Hope Against Hope," "Can a man really be held accountable for his own actions? His behavior, even his character, is always in the merciless grip of the age."

Recently restored to print in a beautiful translation by Max Hayward, "Hope Against Hope" is an especially penetrating description of how people adapt to their culture because of its extreme context: Stalin's Russia in the 1920s and '30s. The wife of the great poet Osip Mandelstam (1891–1938), who was among the millions murdered by the dictator, she details both her husband's suicidal allegiance to poetic resistance and the accommodation so many of their contemporaries made to terror.

The Mandelstams' world was forged by Stalin's paranoia. "We all felt we were constantly exposed to X-rays," she writes. "The penetration of the world at large by the secret police was organized on a grand scale."

In a land where every friend could be a foe, where complaint meant death, where the "members of the exterminating class" lived by the credo, "Give us a man, and we'll make a case," Russians were forced to wear a mask of contentment. "The mask was taken off only at home, and then not always—even from your children you had to conceal how horrorstruck you were; otherwise, God save you, they might let something slip in school."

From our own comfortable seat, we might recoil at this weakness—just as we are sure that we would have opposed slavery had we lived in the Old South, and opposed Hitler had we lived in Nazi Germany. That, of course, is wishful nonsense.

Mandelstam's book is especially chilling in its depiction of how ordinary people normalized their insane world. "Some people," she writes, "had adapted to the terror so well that they knew how to profit from it—there was nothing out of the ordinary about denouncing a neighbor to get his apartment or his job."

As countless innocents were rounded up, she and her husband never asked, " 'What was he arrested for?' but we were exceptional. Most people, crazed by fear, asked this question just to give themselves a little hope; if others were arrested for some reasons, then they wouldn't be arrested, because they hadn't done anything wrong."

She adds, "After each show trial, people sighed, 'Well, it's over at last.' What they meant was: Thank God, it looks as though I've escaped. But then there would be a new wave, and the same people would rush to heap abuse on the 'enemies of the people.'"

Sadly, heroically, her husband believed his words were "vows," that poetry was not a tool for "propagating predigested notions" but a stimulus to question, to think. This made him a marked man. "People sensed the dynamic strength fermenting in him and knew that he was doomed." By the late 1920s no one would publish his poems, and the translation work he depended on had dried up. Still his fate was not sealed until 1934 when an informer, probably a close friend, told the authorities about his unpublished poem on Stalin and its lines, "All we hear is the Kremlin mountaineer / the murderer and peasant slayer."

The Mandelstams were exiled for three years. Freed, they were forced to beg their bread from other writers who had secured steady supplies of "Spanish wine and oranges" by toeing the party line. Mandelstam does not condemn them: "Those who had tasted the delights of heaven had no wish to be cast down into the pit. Who can blame them?"

Blindly, tellingly, even the Mandelstams convinced themselves that the worst was over. They were wrong. In 1938, Osip was arrested again for his previous "crimes." This time Stalin decided that Osip should die.

For the next few decades Nadezhda feared the knock on the door, worked menial jobs and remembered: "I kept myself awake by muttering [Osip's] verse to myself. I had to commit everything to memory in case all my papers were taken away from me." Somehow, she stayed alive, long enough to ensure that the memory of her husband and her times and the truth their story tells of human nature will live forever.

In one sense, "Hope Against Hope" is an affirming book: We could have greater problems than "Star Wars" hype. But it is also a warning against complacency, a reminder of how willing we are to trade our freedom for Spanish wine and oranges.

May 23, 1999

BEYOND THE COVERS

CONTEMPORARY FICTION

E. L. Doctorow:
The Civil War in All Its Raging Glory

Memorable novels declare themselves from the start, their first few sentences reading as rich distillations of all that will follow: "Anna Karenina" will concern an unhappy family; "Moby-Dick" will explore our quest to name and thereby control ourselves and the world.

Here is the opening sentence of E. L. Doctorow's superb new novel, "The March": "At five in the morning someone banging on the door and shouting, her husband John, leaping out of bed, grabbing his rifle, and Roscoe, at the same time roused from the backhouse, his bare feet pounding."

Notice what Doctorow establishes in that short sentence. Through the frantic pace, he tells us that this will be a novel of action. By introducing four people—the wife; her husband, John; Roscoe; and the person banging on the door—he signals a tale filled with characters. Then there is the fifth, unseen character who has sparked all the activity in this Georgia home: Gen. Sherman's Union army, which is blazing across the South in the Civil War's endgame.

Finally, notice the implied silence, the vanquished early morning calm, which tells us that change will be a major theme of this splendid novel.

Recipient of a National Book Award, two National Book Critics Circle awards and the Pen/Faulkner award, Doctorow has established himself as a master of historical fiction through such novels as "Billy Bathgate" and "Ragtime." "The March" is another beautifully realized work full of pathos and drama that allows us to look anew upon one of the most exhaustively documented periods in our nation's history and literature.

"The March" follows Sherman's army across Georgia and the Caro-linas, and one of its great accomplishments is how Doctorow tailors his story to his subject matter. An Army on the move is not the story of one man, one battle or one emotion, but a sprawling behemoth that sucks in and spits out everyone and everything before it, revealing the range of human potential in the process.

Doctorow suggests that the battlefield is war's least interesting the-ater. Military tactics take a back seat to the stories of those swept up by war: freed slaves, orphaned children, newly minted widows, surgeons and nurses, wounded soldiers, devastated civilians, bloodthirsty generals and fed-up deserters.

The novel has no protagonist save the war itself. Characters we meet early on disappear by the book's middle, slowly replaced by others swept up by Sherman's all-consuming march. To some extent, all are devices Doctorow uses to explore facets of war: the hope that overcomes or is snuffed out by the weight of conflict; the enduring need for love; the inexorable power of hatred and self-interest. Yet he so skillfully brings each to life in a few sentences that we feel their pulse on the page.

Consider the husband, John Jameson, introduced in the first sen-tence. He is a smart and wealthy Georgian who had the foresight to send his valuables to a protected warehouse. Soon the insanity of war destroys his mind. Having lost his reason, he waves a paving stone while cursing a Union soldier. His wife, Mattie, describes what happens next: "And I watched my husband of nineteen years, who married me when I was a girl and took me to live on his plantation, drop like a tree felled, all the sense blown from him on the blood sprung from his poor head."

Doctorow also uses Mattie to convey the difficulties of processing the vast changes wrought by war: "She knew, of course, that there might never again be slaves, but she couldn't quite see how anything could be done without them. And so when she imagined the war over and a return to their home, as often as not in her imagination the slaves would still be there. . . . She worried about her sons going off to battle, but at the same time she couldn't imagine them not coming back or, when they did come back, being any older or different from when they went away."

The novel is filled with moments of near photographic intensity—indelible snapshots of soldiers wading through blood-soaked swamps;

of freed slaves banking on the war's promise; of children abandoned by those they trusted; of wounded men choosing death over life; of men and women doing what they must for love or safety.

Through these gorgeously crafted, psychologically intense scenes, Doctorow's chronicle of war becomes a commentary on the novel and life.

We watch an illiterate young slave named Pearl become a freed-woman, then a nurse, then a wife; we hear her language change from Uncle Remus-type dialect to standard English as she learns how to read. We watch an imprisoned Confederate deserter become a Union soldier, then an ambulance driver, then a photographer and finally an assassin. Doctorow reminds us that life is a constant flux that our minds and art freezes at certain moments so that we might assign meaning to experience.

"The March" is a deeply imagined, tremendously satisfying novel that seems to pack all of life into 373 pages. Through rigorous yet effortlessly rendered research, Doctorow thrusts us back into the waning days of the Civil War while showing us—through the universal emotions he conveys—the timeless march of the human animal.

October 23, 2005

Richard Slotkin:
11 Openings to Abe Lincoln

We read against the infinite canvas of our imagination. We write in a tight space. How does one even begin to tell another about the thoughts, feelings and ideas a good book has kindled?

How should I start?

I

Richard Slotkin's novel "Abe" is a great American novel. Imagining Abraham Lincoln's first 22 years (1809–31), from his hardscrabble beginnings in the Kentucky frontier to his initial emergence as a leader in New Salem, Ill., "Abe" convincingly and entertainingly depicts the crude landscape and heroic dreams that produced our revered leader.

2

I confess: Strive as I might for passionately dispassionate objectivity, it is hard to read some books apart from our historical moment. I admit: My disappointment in two unremarkable men, Al Gore and George W. Bush, fueled my enthusiasm for "Abe." It was exhilarating to read about a political figure whose character is best revealed by asking: How did he become a great person?

3

We live in an age without heroes, which makes real ones all the more appealing. That's why I loved "Abe." Slotkin, a professor of American Studies at Wesleyan University and a two-time finalist for the National Book Award, sees Lincoln as a man to whom everything came easily. Born a genius, he was smarter, wiser, more focused and more ambitious than anyone around him. Best of all, he could whip any man in a fight.

4

"Huckleberry Finn" is often called the great American novel. So it is fitting that Richard Slotkin uses it for the basis of his stirring novel about our greatest President. Like Twain's classic, "Abe" is a tale of race and power told through a boy's coming-of-age. With a brilliant eye for the details of Lincoln's life and times, Slotkin also raises deep moral questions about how one should live in a flawed society by transforming a boat trip Lincoln took down the Mississippi in 1828–29 into a profound test of Lincoln's feelings toward slaves.

5

We're armed. Our prisons are packed tighter than boxes of popcorn. This land of plenty is one of the most violent nations on Earth. How come? Richard Slotkin suggests that part of the answer can be found in the rough, tough world of inexorable conflict that made Abraham Lincoln.

Born on the Kentucky frontier in 1809, Lincoln and his family were in constant fear of attacks from Indians and bears. They killed them all and most everything else in their way. But nature offered every resistance:

"Cut 'em down all you like," Slotkin writes, "girdle 'em till they rotted standing, or burn 'em like injuns at the stake, but the trees kept coming at you."

Disease, like the mysterious "milk-sick" that cut down Lincoln's beloved mother in 1818—"she fell on her side and her body snapped like a whip and she barked and strangled and blew puke out all over"—struck without warning or remedy.

Imagine a gaunt, too-tall 20-year-old with jug ears planted on "a coarse ugly face, ratty thatch of hair, ragged clothes, no shoes." He is expert with a knife but unacquainted with the fork. He makes money splitting rails, slaughtering pigs and steering a flatboat. He makes friends by telling crude stories. When you look at him he hears you thinking, "You ain't got the clothes for it" and "No-account father's no-account son." What you're really thinking is "white trash."

Now place him on his huge carved throne in Washington because that's where he belongs. His name is Abraham Lincoln.

6

The pivotal scene in Athol Fugard's play, " 'Master Harold' . . . and the boys," comes when the white South African boy reaches the age when he can no longer have an equal relationship with his family's black servants.

Lincoln's life was transformed by a similar moment. Though he was white, Lincoln was also poor and when he was old enough to be paid for his work, Abe's cold and unambitious father started hiring his son out to the families of Abe's former playmates.

"He didn't love the work itself," Slotkin writes, "but he didn't hate it. It was the way that Pap hired him out that graveled him." Thomas Lincoln would describe his son as "Horse-high, bull-strong and hog-tight." To Abe's ears he sounded "like a man selling a horse."

7

The key to understanding Abraham Lincoln is in appreciating the difference between compassion and empathy. Lincoln was raised in a profoundly racist society. However, as a poor outsider with few apparent opportunities, he did not simply feel pity for blacks and other victims but was able to identify with them. In a stirring finale, this empathy is tested by the fate of a slave Lincoln has befriended, but that's getting ahead of the story.

8

Lincoln was a boundlessly ambitious man whose grand dreams for himself were driven by his hatred for his father. While eschewing psychohistory for clear period prose, Slotkin writes, "He wanted to not be anymore the one that rules and orders was laid on by everyone else, especially Pap. He wanted to make his own rules for his own self. There were men that did that . . . Moses . . . Washington . . . the [Founding] Fathers."

9

Debunk, demythologize, deconstruct. Those are the intellectual values of our age. How quickly would we try to disabuse and wise-up some poor kid without access to good schools who tells us in his fractured English that "any man that larns to make sense when he talks can go as far as he likes in this country . . . All a boy had to do was learn to speak like a republican man, and there wasn't anything he couldn't be or do."

Then what would Abraham Lincoln have done?

10

William Faulkner said that the way to become a writer was to "Read, read, read. Read everything." Another great American writer, Abraham Lincoln, might dispute that. Growing up poor with little formal education, Lincoln cultivated his native genius for language and his innate moral purpose by poring over, again and again and again, the few books that came his way: the fables of Aesop, the plays of Shakespeare, the poetry of Burns and, above all, the Bible. "Abe," Slotkin writes, "worked as hard at books as some men . . . worked at farming—harder."

11

Richard Slotkin's novel "Abe" is such a rich and beautiful portrait of Abraham Lincoln that I barely know where to begin. So I'll just say this: Read this book.

April 2, 2000

Dan Brown: I've Cracked the Code
of 'Da Vinci Code' Hypomania

During her keynote address at the N.C. Festival of the Book, Barbara Kingsolver articulated one of the great riddles of literature: When she writes nonfiction readers think she's spinning the facts, but when she writes fiction they believe she's telling the truth.

Kingsolver's insight is particularly relevant as the movie version of "The Da Vinci Code" comes to theaters Friday. Dan Brown's novel has sold more than 40 million copies worldwide becoming the best-selling work of adult hardcover fiction in history in no small measure because many readers believe it reveals secret truths about Christianity.

Although Brown's publisher claims the thriller is based on "meticulous research," it owes far more to fantasy than fact: "The Da Vinci Crackpots" would have been a more accurate title. Yet the book draws from so many deep wells—including ancient conspiracy theories and modern scholarship—that it can help us clarify mysteries about faith, literature and truth.

Opening with a murder at the Louvre, "The Da Vinci Code" follows two main characters, Harvard art historian Robert Langdon and French cryptologist Sophie Neveu, as they seek to decipher ingenious clues left by the victim. During the next 24 hours, while fleeing the police and an albino assassin, the pair untangles a serpentine web of puzzles and codes to discover a truth that the Catholic Church has long suppressed.

In a nutshell (pun intended) they learn that Jesus had been married to and had children with Mary Magdalene (His DNA is still out there!). This fact, Brown's book maintains, was covered up by the Church because it proved that Jesus was not divine but an inspired man. In addition, Brown asserts, Jesus had wanted his wife to lead his church. To disciples like Peter, this was anathema. After the crucifixion, they forced Magdalene to flee to France and erased the central role of women—what Brown and others call the "sacred feminine"—in Jesus's teachings.

But Magdalene's story was not lost. She kept a diary, and others chronicled her life. These secret teachings, revealing the duplicity and misogyny of the church, were safeguarded through the centuries by a series of famous figures—including Sir Isaac Newton, Sandro Botticelli, Leonardo da Vinci and the murder victim—who belonged to the mysterious Priory of Sion.

While waiting until humanity was ready to hear the truth, these men left tantalizing clues about the relationship between Mary and Jesus, the most famous of which are those hidden in da Vinci's "The Last Supper."

There's much, much more. And despite the frequent insistence of Brown's characters that this history is well documented, almost all of it is bogus. Indeed, the success of "The Da Vinci Code" has inspired scores of debunkers including "Truth & Error in the Da Vinci Code" by Mark L. Strauss, "Da Vinci Code Decoded" by Martin Lunn and "Secrets of the Code," edited by Dan Burstein. It's hard not to conclude that the only thing Dan Brown got right was the spelling of his own name.

Of course, "The Da Vinci Code" is a novel. But it raises the question of what responsibility works of historical fiction have to the known record. My rule of thumb: The better known the subject, the more liberties the author may take. A novel about an obscure figure—which may largely shape our memory of the person—must hew closely to the facts.

When the figure is a titan like Jesus, all bets are off. True, readers may be misled by "The Da Vinci Code." But they can easily avail themselves of works that get the story right. Because of this vast literature, Brown's arguments will never become mainstream. Their impact will always be minimal.

In fact, Brown's conspiracy theories can be portals to knowledge. Before "The Da Vinci Code," the general public had little interest in the legitimate historic actors and events Brown mangles and misconstrues, including the Council of Nicea in 325 and medieval phenomena such as the Priory of Sion, the Knights Templar and quests for the Holy Grail. Numerous books and Web sites about them have been produced since the novel's publication in 2003. Just as Brown captures readers by convincing them they're hearing a dangerous truth, these sources are especially exciting as they reveal the truth Brown won't tell us.

The novel correctly observes that the early church was riven by theological debates. Scholarly works such as "Beyond Belief" by Elaine Pagels of Princeton University and "Lost Christianities" by Bart Ehrman of

UNC-Chapel Hill discuss these early Christian writings—known as the Gnostic Gospels—that were denounced as heretical by the Church 1,600 to 1,800 years ago.

A similar ancient document, "The Gospel of Judas," was released last month to great fanfare. In portraying Judas as Jesus's favorite disciple, it clashed with many other biblical accounts, most notably the earlier gospels of Matthew, Mark, Luke and John. It also highlighted the problem with many such texts composed long after Jesus's death, raising red flags about its knowledge of secret communications between Jesus and Judas.

Nevertheless, truth is a complicated matter. Although unacquainted with facts, "The Da Vinci Code" has become a phenomenon because it encompasses so many larger truths. Its discussion of the "sacred feminine," for example, taps into widespread dissatisfaction with the church, especially its treatment of women. It also prompted millions of women who do not ordinarily read thrillers to purchase "The Da Vinci Code."

At a time when many fiction writers confront important but small bore questions of identity, Brown's satisfy our hunger for big ideas. At play is nothing less than the greatest story ever told.

Brown's book also reflects a yearning for faith. True, "The Da Vinci Code" challenges the Catholic Church. But in its way, it allows skeptical Americans a chance to reconnect with Jesus, whose greatness Brown never disputes.

Most intriguing is the fact that almost none of the theories Brown spouts are his own—though he does a fine job bringing them together. Brown's Web site (www.danbrown.com) lists 27 source texts, including "The Templar Revelation: Secret Guardians of the True Identity of Christ" by Lynn Picknett and Clive Prince, "Rosslyn: Guardians of the Secret of the Holy Grail" by Tim Wallace-Murphy and Marilyn Hopkins, "The Goddess in the Gospels: Reclaiming the Sacred Feminine" by Margaret Starbird and "Holy Blood, Holy Grail" by Michael Baigent, Richard Leigh and Henry Lincoln, who recently lost a British lawsuit charging Brown with plagiarism.

These modern works are part of a rich tradition, as old as Christianity itself, of voices unsettled by questions of faith. It is easy to dismiss many of them as goofy and harebrained, but they lead us to a central fact: The mind craves certainty. Lacking solid information, it seizes on speculation. We know so little about the life of Jesus and the inner workings of the Catholic Church that it is small wonder so many wild ideas have flourished around them (and I'm not even talking about the virgin birth).

Make no mistake, "The Da Vinci Code" is a piece of pop culture schlock. Yet like great literature, it reflects our longing to apprehend truths beyond our grasp.

May 14, 2006

Haruki Murakami: A Writer Who Takes on the World

No contemporary writer has impressed me more than Haruki Murakami. In "The Wind-Up Bird Chronicle" (1997), "South of the Border, West of the Sun" (1999), and now, "Norwegian Wood," the Japanese novelist has proved himself a master of word, image and story. But it is not so much his technical virtuosity but the moral vision he brings to modern culture that elicits my deep response to his work. His books offer an insightful and eloquent repudiation of the heart- and head-numbing irony that overwhelms popular culture.

His work is so vital because he confronts irony—that dismissive pose that suggests nothing is worth fighting for or caring about—on its own turf. Murakami embraces the postmodern concepts that have fueled irony's rise: the dislocation and alienation caused by contemporary life, the suspicion of authority and all systems of belief. His novels are filled with baffled characters spiraling through a chaotic world.

Yet, he rejects the idea that this maelstrom frees us from responsibility to ourselves and to others. Murakami accepts that there is no absolute Truth but suggests that we must strive to be honest about our own thoughts and feelings. Morality may lie in the eye of the beholder, but to be fully human we must consciously try to determine the right thing to do.

Murakami kindles these arguments and more in "Norwegian Wood," his 1987 novel just translated by Jay Rubin. This complex coming-of-age story is narrated in poignantly spare language by Toru Watanabe, a 37-year-old looking back 20 years to the late 1960s. "My memory is growing ever more distant," he confides, " . . . from the spot where my old self used to stand."

As Watanabe shares his story of love, loss and confusion, Murakami creates a tale fueled by the struggle between life and death—which he explores not only as physical cessation, but death caused by forgetting, by the end of relationships, by the continuous process whereby experience distances us from our old selves, and most importantly, by the choice we have to engage life, complicated and bedeviling though it may be, or to commit a kind of suicide by withdrawing from it.

The plot is triggered by the decision of Watanabe's best friend, Kizuki, to kill himself at age 17. A year later, while attending college in Tokyo, Watanabe bumps into Kizuki's girlfriend, Naoko. Chance is a signature theme of Murakami's fiction, in which characters are remade by unexpected events. "I realized that if I hadn't run into Naoko on the train that Sunday in May, my life would have been very different from what it was now," Watanabe explains. But he also wants to believe that there is some sense, some design, to life: "But then I changed my mind; no, even if we hadn't met that day, my life might not have been any different. We had met that day because we were supposed to."

Watanabe is an observant, well-read but aimless young man; "there was nothing I wanted to be." Still, he seeks some order in life: "I don't mind ironing at all. There's a special satisfaction in making a wrinkled shirt smooth."

Naoko is more deeply troubled. Overcome by grief and other difficulties of her past, she enters a sanitarium, sheltered deep in the mountains. There she rooms with Reiko, a former piano prodigy whose life was shattered first by a freak injury to her hand and later by a 13-year-old lesbian's seduction. "That's why I can't leave this place," Reiko explains to Watanabe during one of his visits. "I'm afraid to leave and get involved with the outside world. I'm afraid to meet new people and feel new feelings."

Watanabe falls in love with Naoko. But in the complicated outside world, he befriends another troubled and spirited young woman, Midori, who delights in detailing her strange pornographic fantasies to him.

Gradually, and against his wishes, they also fall in love—which Watanabe feels honor-bound not to act upon.

The book's moral center does not revolve around monogamy, but our obligations to ourselves, to others and to life. Murakami drops his narrator into a labyrinthine world—his college campus is filled with oddballs, reactionaries and revolutionaries who are at least as puzzling as Watanabe's love interests and his own heart—and pushes him to make choices. Murakami offers no easy answers. Four characters commit suicide, an act that comes across as one option in the face of life's confusion. Similarly, Watanabe' safest course might have been to knit a psychic cocoon and flee from his troubled friends. But, he explains, "I don't feel it's O.K. if nobody understands me. I've got people I want to understand and be understood by. But aside from those few, well, I figure it's kind of hopeless."

Finally, the 37-year-old Watanabe narrating the story could have chosen to bury his past by forgetting it, rather than dredging up his painful and mystifying memories. Where other characters opt for various modes of death, Watanabe chooses life.

In "Norwegian Wood," Murakami gives us a powerful and mature moral vision. He lays outs life's complications and conundrums, admits there is equal reason to engage or dismiss it, and then has his protagonist make the affirming choice to submit to it head-on, to take the risk and hurl himself into the maelstrom.

October 8, 2000

Lydia Millet: A Daring Tale of a Lonely Heart

Lydia Millet is one of America's most daring writers. While reading her second novel, "George Bush, Dark Prince of Love," which details a dangerously kooky woman's obsession with the 41st president, I found myself repeatedly turning to the author's picture to see the face behind these bold visions. I was doing the same thing while reading her third novel, "My Happy Life," in which she harnesses the power of her quirky imagination to reinvent one of the most popular themes of contemporary literature—abuse.

In "My Happy Life," Millet has created one of the most pathetic, strange and lonesome victims in American letters.

The unnamed narrator was abandoned on the street at birth, in a shoe box "marked Brown Ladies narrow 8." Her childhood was marked by frightening stays in dangerous foster homes where she was repeatedly raped, beaten and told, "You are extra. Nobody needs you."

Unschooled and unskilled, she later works as a housekeeper for a disturbed woman who lashes her with tongue and fist. When the woman's husband has the narrator sent away, she repairs to a tree in the park. She considers it her happy home until an older man, named Mr. D., offers her a warm room. They have a baby together, which Mr. D. swipes. Heartbroken, she spends years in feckless pursuit of her child. "I felt his absence for longer than I had known him," she says. "I thought it was possible, although very faintly, that if I never gave up I would be forgiven."

Eventually, she is sent to a mental hospital, where her misery reaches new depths. The institution is slated for demolition; everyone else has been removed. Locked in her room, she spends her days trying to dig a hole in one part of the wall while scratching her memoir upon another part of it.

Given our heroine's suffering, "My Happy Life" seems an ironic title. But Millet's novel is extraordinary because her narrator uses it sincerely. Remember, this is a novel: No real-life human being could face such harm with such optimism. But in creating a pathological literary character, Millet allows us to see past the abuse to encounter an artistic vision of the need that propels so many people to endure it. Like others who are unable to take control of their physical circumstances, her narrator adopts extreme attitudes and forges understandings to make her horrors bearable.

The world treats her heroine as an object to act upon, without human rights or dignity. Yet, she hungers for human connection. In her case, it trumps all because her greatest source of pain is her loneliness. "Like all people," she says, "I was quite imaginary when I was alone. And alone we were all of us ghosts."

So she describes her rape this way: "He pulled me down onto the ground and draped himself over my person. . . . Initially I was confused, but then at last I understood the boy was removing all the space between us. And I thought of all the good and wise other people that he could also have chosen for this, and saw that he must be a new friend."

In a brilliant stroke, Millet gives her heroine a child's eye and voice. Children are the most dependent creatures, and hence the most trusting. They can cling to and love the most awful people because they must. They also tend to see life in uncomplicated, yet fundamental, terms, in truthful ways unvarnished by the complexities of adulthood.

This narrative strategy allows Millet to write about abuse from arresting angles, with poignancy and humor. She can have her heroine see her mother in the sky: "She was a coat that covered the earth and made the sun feel softer. And she said, You are not extra, no. You are good and useful."

Without a hint of meanness she can say a picture of Mr. D's wife reminded her "of an eminent person. . . . His name was Winston Churchill."

And when the lonely heroine holds conversations with the weeds in the yard and the linoleum in her hospital ward—activities that pass as normal in children—we see this technically insane behavior as a powerful coping mechanism.

One of the book's great triumphs is Millet's ability to show how the most sophisticated forms of thought are connected to the thoughts and feelings of children. In her simple voice, Millet's narrator evokes the ecstatic visions of Walt Whitman and the existential philosophy of Jean-Paul Sartre. Desperate for connection, she sees herself as part of the unity of all life: "The world is full. It is teeming with us." Yet she also recognizes her own inconsequentiality: "I could simply disappear and nothing would have changed. And when I saw this, I laughed in the dark and felt happier than ever."

"My Happy Life" is a dark and rich work that reminds us of the power of fiction. Millet reimagines the world to reveal deeper truths of reality that strict realism would be hard-pressed to match.

Lydia Millet is a true original.

January 20, 2002

Nicholson Baker: Bomb-Throwing Book Against Bush Fizzles

'I'm going to assassinate the President. . . . I'm going to do it today." The target is not Lincoln or Kennedy but the man now sitting in the White House: George W. Bush.

This is the premise of Nicholson Baker's 10th book, "Checkpoint," a novel that promises to be not just interesting but revelatory, not simply controversial but dangerous.

"Checkpoint," alas, is a bore.

At a time when U.S. politics is filled with anger, Baker throws down the trump card, giving voice to a man who wants to do far more than criticize Bush for the war in Iraq. Instead of rising to the challenge by creating an artistic work of high moral seriousness, Baker serves up a sensationalistic piece of gimmickry unworthy of its explosive premise.

Many people will be repulsed by this storyline, but the problem is that Baker does not go far enough. Unlike Don DeLillo's novel "Libra" or Eudora Welty's short story "Where Is the Voice Coming From?" which boldly explored the seductive logic of the men who assassinated JFK and Medgar Evers, respectively, Baker fails to illuminate the darkest intersections between psychology and culture. He's like a tightrope walker who demands that the wire be strung to record heights and lengths and then loses his nerve with the first step.

Set in a Washington, D.C., hotel room, "Checkpoint"—like Baker's notorious phone sex novel, "Vox"—consists of the conversation between two people: Jay, a middle-age man who plans to assassinate Bush later that day, and Ben, who tries to prevent his longtime friend from executing his plan.

Much of the dialogue is devoted to Jay's somewhat comic anger at Bush. He disparages the president in language that would make Michael Moore proud—Jay calls him "George W. Tumblewad," "this unelected [expletive] OILMAN" and a "Texas punk, who can't even talk, with his drugged-out eyes." The vice president fares no better: "Dick Cheney! Oh, he's hunched, man, the corruption has completely hunched and gnarled him."

Jay repeatedly asserts that the president is a murderer for prosecuting an unnecessary war whose innocent victims include frightened Iraqi girls killed by U.S. soldiers when they fail to stop at a roadside checkpoint. Jay says: "I can't understand why this outlaw, this FELON, who's killed something like twelve thousand people, should be alive when those girls are dead."

When Ben says that assassinating Bush is hardly an appropriate response, Jay counters: "By causing a minor blip of bloodshed in one human being I'm going to prevent further bloodshed."

Jay's critique of Bush and the war will be familiar to anyone who takes a newspaper or watches the evening news. Since Baker does not provide his would-be assassin with novel reasons for killing the president, he ought to show us why this man is prepared to cross a line millions of like-minded people will not. He doesn't. All we can guess is that Jay is angrier than everybody else.

Baker draws so heavily on common arguments that it is tempting to believe he is engaging in a rear-guard action, subtly lampooning liberal attacks on Bush. However, he (and Ben) seem wholly sympathetic to the thrust of Jay's argument. They never challenge Jay's opinions or emotions, only his murderous intentions. Which makes the reader wonder: What's the point? Whom is Baker addressing? Our era stands in stark contrast to the 1960s; no one is calling for insurrection. The story of our times is that our flaming passions have not produced a Lee Harvey Oswald—or a Jay.

Baker's lack of courage is the novel's fundamental weakness. His central choices seem designed to protect himself from his novel's dangerous implications instead of allowing him to run with them.

Baker's timidity is evident in the book's first line. "Testing, testing," Jay says into a microphone he will use to record his conversation with Ben. This device weakens the story because it fixes Ben's mind on the fact that he could be considered an accessory to the crime. He cannot speak or think freely, cannot push Jay to develop his arguments or be seduced by his logic. He is not trying to explore the situation—which is what literature does; he (and Baker) want to put Pandora back in her box.

The most egregious example of authorial self-protection comes early, on page 14, when Baker assures us that his killer is no threat at all. How will Jay kill Bush? "I've got some radio-controlled flying saws," he says. "They look like little CDs but they're ultrasharp and they're totally deadly, really nasty. . . . I've got a huge boulder I'm working on that has a giant ball bearing in the center of it so that it rolls wherever I tell it to." Later he says he might use special "programmable bullets."

Such nonsense is totally out of character for Jay. He is bent, but not delusional. He's a broken man—divorced, out of work—but self-aware. Of his failed marriage, he says, "I just wore Lila out. You know? With me, everything's political."

It is hard not to conclude that Baker betrays his character and makes Jay's assassination plots so foolish for fear that some fool might take his book seriously.

"Checkpoint" reminds me of Napoleon's famous quotes: "If you're going to take Vienna, take Vienna." Baker barely makes it out of Paris. He established his reputation as a miniaturist, able to craft highly imaginative stories about the most mundane aspects of daily life (e.g. "The Mezzanine" and "A Box of Matches"). In "Checkpoint" he is unable to work a larger canvas. Instead of illuminating the American mind, he reveals the limits of one American author.

August 15, 2004

Don DeLillo's Sound and Fury

Don DeLillo is one of the most acclaimed writers of our time. He is also a second-rate novelist.

DeLillo's seminal works crackle with observations about consumer culture ("White Noise," 1985), terrorism ("Mao II," 1991) and post-war America ("Underworld," 1997). His new novel, "Cosmopolis," suggests interesting notions about modern capitalism and the post 9/11 world. But it is hard to find a flesh-and-blood character in any of his 13 novels. DeLillo isn't interested in people; they are merely vessels for his ideas.

This is a fundamental flaw for a novelist, whose basic mission is to bring ideas and emotions to life through compelling human dramas.

Historians have offered more insight into the South than William Faulkner, psychologists have probed the human mind more deeply than Fyodor Dostoevsky, but their ideas resonate because they explored them through surpassing stories.

DeLillo's decision to write as a novelist allows him to comment on contemporary life without having to think as rigorously as, or endure the scrutiny of, a nonfiction writer.

Set in contemporary Manhattan, "Cosmopolis" follows Eric Packer, a 28-year-old private investor, through one momentous day. Suffice it to say "Cosmopolis" does not bring to mind "Mrs. Dalloway" or "Ulysses."

Eric is ridiculously rich—a self-made billionaire, he lives in a 48-room triplex worth $104 million but spends much of his time in a white stretch limousine with Carrara marble floors and a bathroom (a metaphor, perhaps, for how he tries to close himself off from the world).

Eric is ridiculously smart. When he was 4 years old, he figured out how much he would weigh on each planet. Now he reads science and poetry, Freud and Einstein in German. "He liked paintings that his guests did not know how to look at."

Eric is ridiculously arrogant and predatory. He is so selfish and self-absorbed he believes that "when he died he would not end. The world would end."

Thus Eric joins the long list of DeLillo's cartoon creations. He is not a man, but a sledgehammer symbol of the author's beliefs about the dehumanizing effects of America's money culture.

On this day, Eric is trying to divine the movements of the Japanese yen, on which he has risked his entire fortune (we're supposed to believe that the ridiculously smart Eric has ridiculously bet the farm because he is so ridiculously numb that he can only generate feeling *in extremis*).

Eric also needs a haircut. As he inches his way through hellish traffic in his limousine, he holds cryptic conversations with various employees who speak in bloodless aphorisms. "The yen is making a statement. Read it. Then leap," and, "Any assault on the borders of perception is going to seem rash at first."

The soulless Eric often sounds like a mystic. For him, "data itself was soulful and glowing, a dynamic aspect of the life process. This was the eloquence of alphabets and numeric systems, not fully realized in electronic form. . . . Here was the heave of the biosphere. Our bodies and oceans were here, knowable and whole."

This is an intriguing perspective, which, as a novelist, DeLillo sees no reason to elaborate on or defend. His books are full of such intellectual shock and awe, a mish-mash of ideas that hypnotize readers through their lack of clarity and precision. He's so obscure, he's got to be smart.

Without rhyme or reason, Eric keeps bumping into his wife of 22 days, a poet and heir to a great European banking fortune. They say things like, "Your eyes are blue. . . . You never told me you were blue-eyed." Their non-relationship may suggest the breakdown of the family and of intimacy. But DeLillo paints them with such a broad brush—without the subtlety and nuance of real life—that they become silly caricatures.

Much more is going on this day—there are riots in the streets, three world leaders are assassinated, and Eric's life is threatened by a downsized employee. DeLillo portrays the world as a dark and grim place where safety and order are anachronisms. It might be frightening, instead of laughable, if he didn't lay it on so thick.

DeLillo also tries to make an argument about history. In a nutshell, he holds that the capitalist system Eric represents is so concerned with the future, with creating new markets, new opportunities, new technologies, that it has destroyed the past.

For DeLillo, the past is the reservoir and wellspring of our humanity; the future promises only one thing: death.

DeLillo isn't saying anything we haven't heard before. But his thoughts might have moved or changed us if he had brought them to life through believable characters. Instead they remain pulseless abstractions.

The irony is that DeLillo is at heart a humanist. Like many of his previous works, "Cosmopolis" is concerned with the ways that modern life pushes us from the thoughts, feelings and ideas that make us fully human. It is a powerful message. Unfortunately, DeLillo hasn't mustered the artistic imagination to deliver it compellingly.

April 20, 2003

Tom Wolfe:
Far from Empty, Not Quite Full

Fearless, remorseless, unfamiliar with the notion of limits, Tom Wolfe has always been a man full of himself.

From hippie culture to Radical Chic, from the Me Decade to the greed and fear that fueled the Reagan era, no subject has been too big, no subject too powerful to daunt his withering pen.

At a time when most writers work in miniature, boring in on the small worlds of smaller subjects, Wolfe, 68, still chases the Zeitgeist. Fusing novelistic techniques with old-fashioned reporting into an amalgam called "the new journalism," he captured America's soaring pulse and contradictory impulses in such high-octane works as "The Electric Kool-Aid Acid Test" (1968), "The Right Stuff" (1979) and his first novel, "The Bonfire of the Vanities" (1987).

Wolfe's latest dispatch, "A Man in Full," may not be the book of the decade, but it is certainly the book of the moment. A comically bittersweet novel of desire and loss set in contemporary Atlanta, it has 1.2 million copies in print and is one of five finalists for the 1998 National Book Award. It is also vintage Wolfe: fat (742 pages that took 11 years to research and write), ambitious (encompassing modern banking and real estate, the penal system and race relations, football, trophy wives and Stoic philosophy) and flawed (the novel sports one of the worst endings in modern American literature).

Like all of Wolfe's work, it demands attention like a jackknifed tractor-trailer. It is also his most deeply felt, most unabashedly literary book, imbued more with compassion than satire.

In its grand scope and overarching themes, "A Man in Full" continues Wolfe's self-appointed role as the savior of American letters. The problem, he told me last week in a phone interview from his Manhattan apartment, is that most of today's fiction writers don't work the way he does.

"Most people become writers because they have a certain musical ability: They can make words sing," he said. "They think talent is 95 percent genius and 5 percent material. Actually, it's about 40/60, and most writers don't get that. What I do is go out and find material, find my story, report my story and then write it."

Written in Wolfe's typically addictive, desperate-to-please style—with a lifetime's worth of italics, exclamation points and onomatopoeia—"A Man in Full" tells three interconnected stories. The central plot revolves around Charlie Croker, a 60-year-old Atlanta developer who is the "King of the Crackers." A former football star at Georgia Tech—"a man in full, he had a back like a Jersey bull"—Croker rose from humble beginnings to become a multimillionaire. He has a stately mansion, a 29,000-acre quail plantation called "Turpmtine," several airplanes and a 28-year-old second wife who has a "slow, voluptuous way of crossing her legs and letting a half-slipper dangle on her toes."

And he may lose it all. His great monument to himself, Croker Concourse, is a bust, and his creditors are squeezing him for the $800 million he owes. Throwing a bone to the bankers, Croker fires 15 percent of the employees at a food warehouse he owns in California. The second plot revolves around one of his victims, Conrad Hensley, a 23-year-old working stiff with an unhappy wife, a shrewish mother-in-law and two children. Hensley is Wolfe's most likable and honorable fictional character—make that his only likable and honorable character—and his pink slip leads him to prison and, ultimately, to Croker.

The third plot line focuses on Georgia Tech's star black tailback, Fareek "The Cannon" Fanon, "225 pounds of attitude" who may have raped the white daughter of one of Atlanta's leading citizens, the billionaire businessman Inman Armholster. The complaint is being kept quiet, but the city's black mayor fears a racial bonfire. So he calls an old classmate from Morehouse College, Roger White II—nicknamed Roger "Too White" because of his conservative beliefs—to craft a solution.

As the novel barrels forward, these three strands remain separate until the final chapters: Eventually, White promises Croker, who has fallen under the spell of Hensley's "stoic" philosophy, that he will fix his money problems if Croker tries to persuade the white establishment to lay off Fanon.

"A Man in Full" touches on so many themes that it is not surprising that reviewers have varying takes on the book. Writing in the New

Yorker, John Updike said "Wolfe has attempted a Great Black Novel." In the New York Times Book Review, Michael Lewis said that the book's great theme "is the decline of Old South agrarian values—or, at any rate, the New South's idea of Old South agrarian values."

Such readings are problematic. Wolfe's earlier works set in New York City, especially "Radical Chic" and "Bonfire," mercilessly depicted the disquieting racial views of Northerners. In "Bonfire," for example, he allowed readers to become flies on the wall to hear how Northern Jews, Gentiles, blacks and whites talk among themselves in all their raw and unguarded ugliness. But in his new book, perhaps because he is a Southerner writing a book about Southerners, Wolfe is less confrontational and less telling.

None of the black characters are drawn in full. Roger "Too White," Fareek Fanon and the city's mayor seem more like caricatures than three-dimensional people. They don't have enough bite to leave a lasting impression. In the novel's haunting prison scenes, blacks are anonymous voices of muscular pathos that we see and hear but never understand. It is a harrowing portrait, but more an indictment of a penal system that warehouses blacks than a portrait of its victims.

Croker treats his servants at Turpmtine—obsequious lawn jockeys who call their boss "Cap'm Charlie"—with genteel paternalism. But he seems less hateful than sadly out of touch.

Though Croker's attitudes may suggest some malignant residue of the Old South, he is not a symbol of that world's endurance but its decline. In modern Atlanta, the past is as dead as Stonewall Jackson. It is money, not family, that counts. Arrivistes such as Croker have replaced the planter aristocracy and are welcomed into the upper echelons of society as long as they can foot the bill.

Wolfe is less concerned with traditional Southern values than enduring notions of manhood—of physical strength and macho braggadocio. But rather than burying or debunking this concept, he suggests that it is still the path for achieving the single greatest value in this world: climbing the ladder and staying on top.

The novel's great theme is vulnerability. Wolfe has long plumbed the distinction between class and status. "It's very hard to speak of class in America," Wolfe told me, "because the concept is rooted in nobility. In

England, for example, no matter how far you rise or low you fall, you are still generally a member of the class to which you were born. In America, we tend to cluster around other people who have a mutual conception of where they stand in the world."

It is this fragile basis of American identity—the way we often define ourselves by how others see us rather than by who we actually are—that Wolfe depicts so convincingly in "A Man in Full."

For starters, there is the book's cover, which has a peephole with an eye watching us. Wolfe sets the novel in the American city most concerned with how the rest of the world sees it. And though Wolfe always dresses up his books with precise details of what his characters wear, own and drive, the descriptions here have a life of their own. Rather than simply signifying wealth, they are living and breathing embodiments of identity. Croker's plantation, his Gulfstream Jet, his $500 sheets and his trophy wife are not simply goods he has acquired but items without which he would not know himself: "In an era like this one, the twentieth century's fin de siècle, position was everything, and it was the hardest to get. Once you had position . . . there were innumerable places to go for . . . life's merely carnal delights."

As a result, every character seems absolutely and utterly alone. No one has anyone to confide in or trust. Every social interaction—whether it is with spouses, lovers, colleagues or adversaries—is a calculation. For instance, as Croker anguishes late one night in bed, he realizes that if he were still married to his first wife, "he could have reached over to [her] and shaken [her] by the shoulder and she would have put up with it and asked him why he couldn't sleep. Your first wife married you for better or for worse. Your second wife . . . she married you for better."

Finally, there is the wrenching humiliation that suffuses the book: Croker's fall, Hensley's tumble, Roger Too White's lust for acceptance. In a series of heartbreaking scenes, Wolfe follows Croker's first wife, Martha, as she bumps into old "friends." Each looks right past her, silently moving on. Without Croker, she is nobody.

It is the deft and compelling psychological insight that gives "A Man in Full" its literary weight. While his previous novels were rich with surface details that created memorable scenes of people living in a particular moment, here Wolfe assays something more timeless and resonant: the human heart. He does not simply skewer his characters but empathizes with them.

Nevertheless, "A Man in Full" is not a great book. With a tacked-on ending that subverts his book's message, Wolfe loses control of his story. Though his characters, as a group, suggest the tenuousness of modern life, none of them is fully drawn. Like cogs in a great machine they serve a single purpose—acting and doing to keep the pages turning. None of them has the nuance, the ambiguity that is the foundation of great literature.

But it is Wolfe's ambition that is most memorable. He is one of the few contemporary writers willing to wrestle with our world. It is not his material that stops him from pinning his prey but the limits of his own considerable talent.

November 15, 1998

Thomas Pynchon: Another Monument in Pynchonland

Great literary achievement is marked not by nouns but adjectives. Many American writers have earned lasting fame, yet only a handful have produced work of such originality, force and influence that their names represent visions of art and life.

Jamesian, Faulknerian and Hemingwayesque refer to signature styles as well as specific bodies of work. Similarly, Pynchonesque encompasses the postmodern pyrotechnics, madcap playfulness and high-low hijinks that distinguish Thomas Pynchon's novels—and also his legions of acolytes.

A new novel from Pynchon, then, is no ordinary literary event. "Against the Day" is at once a magnificent book and another gleaming skyscraper in Pynchonland, whose spires include "The Crying of Lot 49" (1966), "Gravity's Rainbow" (1973) and "Mason and Dixon" (1997).

Pynchon, who published his first novel, "V," in 1963, came of age when Americans were breaking with tradition. A dazzlingly learned writer, he stares down the great forces of history and fate and gives them a rousing Bronx cheer. His characters battle history and fate, but their goals are personal. Untethered to community or custom, these free agents seek a whiff of freedom in a madcap world that is more carnival than proving ground. Instead of mythic pathos, they evince seat-of-the-pants striving in struggles hard to define.

"Against the Day" is vintage Pynchon, a riotous and intricate work. Spanning 30 years, it deploys scores of characters across almost every continent and unmapped places to explore central problems of human existence—including the tension between light and dark, knowledge and intuition, carnal pleasure and idealism, self-interest and the common good.

Yet Pynchon is also aware of life's supreme paradox: the importance we attach to ourselves and our cosmic insignificance. He frames this probing, philosophic novel as the latest adventure of the Chums of Chance, a Tom Swift-like group whose swashbuckling adventures aboard the airship Inconvenience have been chronicled in a series of books including "The Chums of Chance at Krakatoa" and "The Chums Search for Atlantis."

In a nod to Freud's belief that people are governed by two competing instincts, one craving life, the other death, Pynchon opens with the Chums flying over the Chicago World's Fair of 1893, a gleaming White City promising a better tomorrow. He ends with them aloft after Western civilization has tried to commit suicide during World War I.

Between these symbolic events, Pynchon unlooses characters stamped by their epoch's promise and march toward death. They fall into two broad groups. First are the forces of the day—pitiless champions of status quo. Their leader is Scarsdale Vibe, a ruthless industrialist who murders and exploits others in his coal mines and railroads as he pursues a vicious vision of progress. "We will buy it all up," Vibe declares, "all this country. Money speaks, the land listens."

Opposed to Vibe are inconvenient dreamers standing "against the day"—who seek to fly above or transcend his rapacious world and the even crueler force of time, which eventually claims us all. They terrify Vibe because they refuse to accept the world as it appears.

Some try a direct approach, using dynamite to destroy Vibe's power to define reality. Others adopt more esoteric approaches to escape the world or cheat death: tarot cards, stage magic, narcotics, Christianity and shamanism, the dark arts of alchemy, time travel and astral projection. They believe in the afterlife, in better worlds beneath the sea (Atlantis) or under the desert (Shambhala), and in the potential for math and science to provide access to other dimensions and universes.

The efforts of anarchists with utopian dreams are secondary to those of individuals seeking sanctuary. As Pynchon has found refuge through imagining fantastical literary worlds, his characters also realize their dreams—they speak with ghosts, travel through time, discover Shambhala and cross into the fourth dimension. But like the author, all eventually find themselves back in the Day. Their struggle is not futile. It is noble and necessary because, Pynchon suggests, it is the only option.

The novel explores these themes through two braided plotlines. One is set in a world being destroyed by modernity—the Wild West. In the mining towns of Colorado, Vibe has Webb Traverse, aka the Kieselgurh Kid, murdered for his pro-Union bombings. We then follow Webb's four grown children—Reef, Kit, Frank and Lake—as they seek vengeance while resisting Vibe's efforts to co-opt them.

The other story is set in the world being born, the modern landscape of scientific and mathematic breakthroughs that could produce a new day for humanity, or terrible weapons that would destroy it. The beautiful bisexual Yashmeen Halfcourt, who befriends Kit Traverse and marries Reef, the male prostitute/spy Cyprian Latewood, members of the mystical T.W.I.T. society (The Worshippers of the Ineffable Tretractyls)—they and others seek transcendence across Europe and Asia and in mystical lands while trying to avoid Vibe and associates who want to commodify the wisdom they seek.

This might be heavy sledding but for Pynchon's crazy wit. The novel is full of bad puns, silly songs, offbeat allusions and bathroom humor. Perverse sexual acts—I mean REALLY perverse—imaginative characters (a dog who reads Henry James, giant talking fleas) and surreal scenes (including strange doings at the Museum of Mayonnaise) keep things humming.

For all his imaginative brilliance, Pynchon is often criticized for being cold, skilled at juggling ideas, unable to create characters readers care about it. Despite touching and heart-rending moments, his canvas is so vast, his characters so multitudinous, that it is hard to develop deep emotional attachments to them.

Yet few of the emotional roller coasters that cram our bookshelves contain the scope, the originality, the seriousness, playfulness and wit of "Against the Day." Pynchon makes great demands but he rewards our efforts: Keep turning the 1,085 pages, resist the temporary confusion of information overload, and all becomes clear. His gem of a novel has innumerable facets. All reveal aspects of a single stone: the struggle between grubby reality and transcendence.

Funny, brilliant and gorgeously written, "Against the Day" is a soaring addition to Pynchonland. It is another monument to a writer whose gifts are so rare and wide that they can only be described as Pynchonesque.

December 24, 2006

Norman Mailer
Celebrates Himself, Again

Norman Mailer is the Richard Nixon of American letters, a figure so gifted yet regrettable, so encompassing yet divisive, so insistently in your face.

Now 75, Mailer has decided once again to celebrate himself with "The Time of Our Time," a collage of his writings that presents a social and cultural interpretation of post-war America from his first sensational novel, "The Naked and the Dead" (1948), to his latest disappointing one, "The Gospel According to the Son" (1997).

It is a sign of how much we still care about Mailer, how he stokes rushes of emotion no other writer can, that when I told colleagues and friends about the anthology they expressed not simply disinterest, but near-violent and principled revulsion—not "ohs," but "yecchs."

Of course, there are many reasons to condemn Mailer—his egregious misogyny and homophobia, his successful efforts to free Jack Henry Abbott and abdication of responsibility when Abbott subsequently committed murder, his unquenchable ego and testicular bombast. Yet, this animus has deeper roots that are, intriguingly, nourished by his sublime gifts.

Mailer is a first-rate, second-tier novelist, ambitious and talented yet lacking the ability of a Conrad or Faulkner to create new worlds that illuminate our own. But, he is also the most audacious reporter of his generation, singularly skilled at applying the novelist's imagination and technique to find the truth beyond the truth that reveals the deeper meanings of our politics and culture.

While fiction provides the reader a certain safe distance, Mailer's best work, such as "The White Negro," (1957) "The Armies of the Night" (1968) and "Miami and the Siege of Chicago" (1968), forces us to confront our delusions, hatreds and hypocrisy, exposing and challenging our conflicted feelings about sex, class, race and God with raw, uncompromising insight. He is fearless and disconcerting in the extreme.

The best understanding of Mailer and of Mailer-haters can be found between the lines of his greatest work, "The Executioner's Song" (1979). This "nonfiction novel" tells the story of Gary Gilmore, the execrable hood who became the first person executed in the United States after the death penalty was reinstituted in 1976.

Through spare and riveting prose that plumbs the human condition through the accumulation of brilliantly chosen detail, Mailer follows the 35-year-old Gilmore as he leaves an Oregon prison to live with family members in Utah. An unremarkable ex-con, Gilmore is an impulsive alcoholic and pill popper who spends his liberty shoplifting beer, hustling money from relatives and chasing women.

Soon he sets his sights on Nicole—a 20-year-old waif with two children and three marriages—and a used white truck that he can't afford. He robs a gas station, firing two bullets into the head of the night attendant who lies on the floor. The next night, Gilmore knocks over a motel, killing the manager after he had handed over the money.

Hours later Gilmore is captured. After a quick trial he is sentenced to death. He waives his right of appeal and insists that the state kill him. "Let's do it, you cowards," Gilmore taunts.

Among the book's many triumphs are Mailer's portrait of the selfish, manipulative yet strangely principled Gilmore as he fights to die while seducing Nicole to commit suicide so he can possess her in the afterlife. Equally striking are the chilling parallels Mailer draws between Gilmore's violent impulsiveness and the unreflective behavior of defense attorneys, law enforcement officials and the media who do what they feel they must, wantonly oblivious to the human tragedy fueling their efforts.

"He had never felt any moral dilemma in carrying out Gary's desires," Mailer writes of Gilmore's lawyer on his client's final day. "In fact, he couldn't have represented him if he really believed the State would go through with it all. It had been a play."

Most impressive is the way Mailer depicts Gilmore's world as it expands geometrically, from a small coterie of family and friends to the entire world. Through his murderous acts and unrepentant death wish— through his breach of society's most sacred rules and conventions—this ignoble man commanded the world's attention, forcing it to confront the darkest questions of crime and punishment.

And it is here we find the nexus between Mailer and Gilmore. Outlandish and confrontational, buttonholing us at every turn, forcing us to think hard about uneasy truths we would rather ignore, Mailer demands that we notice him and listen to what he says about us.

He is so unlikable because he is so admirable.

June 28, 1998

Philip Roth for MVP

Do you hear the trumpet's fanfare? It's sounding for Philip Roth, the new King of the Litterati. In reviews of Roth's latest work, "The Dying Animal," two of our most respected critics, Gail Caldwell of the Boston Globe and Michael Dirda of the Washington Post, hinted at the coronation. Caldwell wrote: "Sometimes I think he's the best and most infuriating writer in America." Dirda mused: "Is Philip Roth now our finest living novelist?" Then, in its July 9 issue, Time magazine crowned Roth "America's best novelist."

Roth is on a roll. During the last decade he is the only writer who has snagged all four of America's top literary prizes: the National Book Award for "Sabbath's Theater" (1995), the Pulitzer Prize in fiction for "American Pastoral" (1997), a National Book Critics Circle Award for his memoir "Patrimony" (1991) and two PEN/Faulkner Awards, for "Operation Shylock" (1993) and "The Human Stain" (2001).

But do those honors mean he is our best writer? If our most honored writer isn't our best, then who is, and why? Hey, wait a minute. Isn't Saul Bellow our most honored writer?

Anyway, part of me pooh-poohs literary lists, but I also love the parlor game "who's your favorite author?" Through years of play, I've noticed two basic approaches: Some people assess writers like baseball players, while others rate them as we do military commanders.

Performance over the long haul, that's the ballplayer's measure. A career is not assessed by its heights but its averages: lifetime batting mark, total number of home runs, final won-loss record. If a player has only one phenomenal season, it's called a fluke.

Philip Roth is a ballplayer's writer. Listen to how Paul Gray described him in Time: "Solely on the basis of his output over the past 10 or so years . . . Roth, 68, would win much support as America's best working novelist. Who else during the same period published so much of such consistently high quality? Even more remarkably, Roth has maintained this elevated standard for 40 years, a creative marathon that totals 20 books of fiction. Not all of these are masterpieces, but all are unfailingly ambitious, the products of a mature, demanding artistic conscience."

Notice the longitudinal language—"consistently high quality," "elevated standard" and "creative marathon." There's no claim that Roth transformed the novel, just the well-earned recognition for constant excellence. Except perhaps for Updike and Bellow, it is hard to think of another author who has written so much so well for so long.

The other approach takes its cue from military history buffs, who often rate commanders on how they responded in the decisive moment of a crucial battle. Its proponents value the big bang; the author of one truly great book has it all over writers who have crafted a dozen first-rate works. That might sound extreme. In fact, it is a generous measure.

Ralph Ellison published only one novel in his lifetime, but it was a great one, and so he is remembered as a great writer. Much of Herman Melville's later work is, to my taste, unreadable; if he were a ballplayer, I shudder to think how much "The Confidence-Man" would have brought down his lifetime average. Instead we remember him as the great author of "Moby-Dick." Similarly, I keep my lather low whenever the Hemingway estate spits out another work that the author had wanted buried with him: A dozen failures like "True at First Light" cannot dim the brilliance of stories such as "A Clean, Well-Lighted Place," or its author.

Which approach is better? Breaking out the broad brush, we can split the difference: Our baseball analogy works best for the living, the military one is just right for the dead. In the here and now, we value writers like Roth who keep giving us wonderful books. It's the constancy of the pleasure he provides that places us in his debt, which we repay with honor. But when his day is done, we'll ask another question: As his books lose the excitement of the new, as we stop comparing them with contemporary works but against all that has been written, how will he stack up?

Time for a pop quiz.

Name a great book—not fine or excellent but a GREAT one—by each of the following writers: 1) Mark Twain, 2) William Faulkner, 3) F. Scott Fitzgerald, 4) Philip Roth.

The first three are no-brainers, but Roth? Maybe "Portnoy's Complaint" or "Sabbath's Theater." But are those or any of his others in the same league with "Huckleberry Finn," "The Sound and the Fury," or "The Great Gatsby"? Can you say with certainty that any of his books will be discussed 50 or 100 years from now? I can't. By contrast, contemporary readers of Twain, Faulkner and Fitzgerald would have had no trouble speaking up for their guy.

In fairness to Roth, it is hard to name many contemporary works that are indisputable classics—"Gravity's Rainbow" by Thomas Pynchon leaps to my mind. In this context, Roth's anointment is more than just a parlor game. It alerts us to an idea: We are living in an age of very good but not great literature. This is not too surprising. The 20th century was marked by such breathtaking invention in nearly every art form, as modernism and postmodernism moved the goal posts of human consciousness. The works of Marcel Proust, James Joyce, Virginia Woolf and Ernest Hemingway led readers to believe that true originality and incessant change were the norms—just as the bold efforts of Louis

Armstrong, Miles Davis, John Coltrane and others spoiled jazz aficionados. No major art form—film, literature, music, visual art—feels as vibrant in America as it was during the 1950s or '60s.

Perhaps we are in a transitional period, catching our breath after the last revolution, revving up (hopefully) for the next. In an era marked by excellence rather than mind-blowing greatness, Philip Roth has as much claim to the Litterati's crown as anyone.

July 15, 2001

SOUTHERN
WRITING LIVES

David Sedaris:
Him Write Pretty

For Mark Twain, it was piloting riverboats down the mighty Mississippi. For Ernest Hemingway, it was driving ambulances across the blood-soaked fields of World War I. For David Sedaris, the formative experience that propelled him to the top ranks of American letters was working as an elf at Macy's. Before elfdom (BE), Sedaris was a recovering drug addict working odd jobs as his mind spun fantasies of fame and fortune.

After elfdom (AE), he achieved success beyond his wildest hopes.

The abracadabra moment that turned a 35-year-old elf into a major writer occurred in the wee hours of Dec. 23, 1992. That's when the NPR program Morning Edition broadcast "SantaLand Diaries," his comic essay about Christmas at Macy's.

Through finely crafted sentences that articulated a gentle, self-deprecating wit, the piece contrasted the high hopes Sedaris had carried to the city of dreams with bracing reality. "I am trying to look on the bright side," he explained. "I figure that at least as an elf I will have a place; I'll be in Santa's Village with all the other elves. We will reside in a fluffy wonderland surrounded by candy canes and gingerbread shacks. It won't be quite as sad as standing on some street corner dressed as a french fry."

"SantaLand Diaries" was the most popular segment in the show's history, and Sedaris became a star. A publisher asked him to write a book of stories, "Barrel Fever" (1994). In the 11 years since, he has produced four more collections of comic personal essays, often focusing on the outsized personalities of his parents and five siblings. His latest work, "Dress Your Family in Corduroy and Denim," debuted in June 2004 atop the New York Times best-seller list. A contributor to NPR, the New Yorker and

Esquire, he has earned critical acclaim as well as the most prestigious prize for American humor writing, the James Thurber Award.

Since seeing Sedaris perform at N.C. State University last spring, I've happily immersed myself in his work, tearing through his five collections, avoiding minor traffic accidents while absorbed in the audio versions. As my jaw and stomach ached with laughter, I encountered a virtuoso whose work encompasses the past and present of literary humor. His soaring imagination echoes James Thurber in full Walter Mitty flight. His kooky self-awareness reads like vintage Woody Allen. The pitch-perfect ear he uses to craft beautifully modulated sentences is reminiscent of the 20th century's greatest comic writer, P. G. Wodehouse.

Yet Sedaris is also an original. His paradoxical style—ironic yet earnest, cruel yet kind, self-absorbed yet empathetic—has influenced a new generation of writers such as Sarah Vowell, Neal Pollack and Dave Eggers. His adventures in the land of creative nonfiction have shown that memoir does not always require self-immolation, that it is possible to write about pain and dysfunction with a wry smile.

On paper, it is easy to divide Sedaris's life and work into two neat segments: BE and AE, as though his life had been changed—poof!—by elfin magic. But no writer's life is a jagged edge; it is always a flowing river.

This is especially true for Sedaris, who continually draws from the waters of his youth in Raleigh to nourish his mature work. Through a close reading of his books, we can develop a Unified Theory of David Sedaris, one that merges his pre- and post-elf periods, to shed light on the wellsprings of his prose and his rare ability to enlarge his essays into commentaries on modern America.

KNACK FOR NEATNESS

"It's important to have clean money—not new, but well maintained"—from "Naked"

The first thing you notice is that Sedaris has always played to his strengths, even when those gifts were not so obvious.

In the beginning, Sedaris was a neatnik. As a child, he asked Santa for a vacuum cleaner. He prohibited his siblings from "crossing the threshold" of his room, for fear they might bring disorder to his "immaculate . . . shrine." As a famous writer visiting one sister's unkempt apartment, he fights the urge "to get down on my knees and scrub until my fingers bleed."

As a youth, this need for order expressed itself more darkly through the obsessive-compulsive behavior he describes in the story "A Plague of Tics." The short walk between his school and home—"no more than six-hundred thirty-seven steps"—might take an hour as he paused "every few feet to tongue a mailbox or touch whichever single leaf or blade of grass demanded my attention. . . . It might be raining or maybe I had to go to the bathroom, but running home was not an option. This was a long and complicated process that demanded an oppressive attention to detail."

When Sedaris tells us he often made his living as a rent-a-maid during his pre-elf days, we can only conclude: Sweating the details is exactly what he should be doing.

Then we reread the sentences he has crafted to document himself: "I could be wrong, but according to my calculations, I got exactly fourteen minutes of sleep during my first year of college. I'd always had my own bedroom, a meticulously clean and well-ordered place where I could practice my habits in private. Now I would have a roommate, some complete stranger spoiling my routine with his God-given right to exist."

Notice the brisk pace and perfect rhythm, the precise details that flow effortlessly to the unforced punch line. This is the hallmark of Sedaris's writing style—clean, taut, measured. Never slack or lazy, it reflects tremendous care. His prose is as polished as his old bedroom.

SLAP OF REALITY

"[My parents] always knew how special I was, that I had something extra, that I would eventually become a big celebrity who would belong to the entire world and not just to them"—from "Barrel Fever"

Despite Sedaris's best efforts to bring order to the world, reality never quite measured up to the meticulously constructed images that filled his young mind. He seems to have spent most of his pre-elfin life concocting elaborate fantasies of celebrity. He imagined himself as a famous artist, a famous writer of daytime dramas and the famous star of a prime-time program featuring him and a pet monkey named Socrates.

Sedaris gave full flight to these dreams in his first collection, "Barrel Fever," which consists almost entirely of fantasy stories. The opening line reads, "I was on 'Oprah' a while ago, talking about how I used to love too much. Did you see it?" Through this voice, he not only articulates his interior life but also gently mocks modern America, where all are assured that they are gifted, talented, unique.

In "Don's Story," he satirizes this self-important standpoint—and himself—with subtle brilliance. The semi-autobiographical tale features a man who believes his unexceptional life is riveting. Lo and behold, so does the rest of the world when he comes to Hollywood and makes a movie about himself that wins best actor, best director and best picture.

In one passage, studio honcho Brandon Tartikoff introduces Don to Barbra Streisand. "Brandon told Barbra Streisand that my name was Don and that I used to wash dishes at K&W Cafeteria and, ha, ha, I tell you, Barbra Streisand just couldn't ask enough questions.

"'A dishwasher! Tell me, was it a conveyor run-through Waste King Jet System or a double hot sink layout? What detergents did you use? At what temperature does a drinking glass become quote unquote clean.' She took my arm and led me into the house, which was just absolutely teeming with celebrities."

"Naked" (1997), the collection that followed "Barrel Fever," opens with more fantasy: "I'm thinking of asking the servants to wax my change before placing it in the Chinese tank I keep on my dresser." But then he makes a crucial turn. By page four, the character's mother is assailing him for "yammering on" about nonsense. "Find your father," she orders. "If he's not underneath his car, he's probably working on the septic system."

This quick slap awakens reality, and it begins to dominate Sedaris's work. Instead of creating fictional characters, he makes characters of those around him. Rather than yammering on about a world that doesn't exist, he details his own life—his obsessive-compulsive behavior and addiction to methamphetamine; his painful realization that his homosexuality might make him an outcast; his years of struggle in New York, his salad days in France; his relationship with his family and his longtime partner, Hugh.

From now on, his fantasies give way to measured self-awareness.

DARING EMPATHY

"In imagining myself as modest, mysterious, and fiercely intelligent, I'm forced to realize that, in real life, I have none of these qualities"— from "Me Talk Pretty One Day"

In a typical story, his subject starts not with a dream but a mindset, a set way of looking at the world. Along the narrative arc, the hammer drops and the character is forced to see more broadly. Many critics have characterized these reality checks as moments of humiliation, arguing that Sedaris's comedy of manners revolves around embarrassment. This misreading robs his work of its intellectual nuance and depth.

Consider his story from "Me Talk Pretty One Day" (2000) about the time Sedaris took guitar lessons from a midget. "Not a dwarf," he writes, "but an honest-to-God midget. . . . His arms were manly and covered in coarse dark hair, but his voice was high and strange, as if it had been recorded and was now being played back at a faster speed." He uses this fact to one-up his siblings, who also were forced to take music lessons. "With a midget," he boasts, "I'd definitely won the my-teacher-is-stranger-than-yours competition."

Nevertheless, Sedaris comes to trust this object of ridicule enough to reveal his secret passion: singing commercial jingles for Oscar Mayer Weiners or Raleigh's Cameron Village in the voice of Billie Holiday. "The Excitement of Cameron Village Will Carry You Away." (Funny enough on the page, yet hearing Sedaris croon it on the audio version of "Me Talk Pretty" is beyond category.)

The guitar teacher cuts short his performance.

"'Hey guy,' he said. 'You can hold it right there. I'm not into that scene. . . . There were plenty of screwballs like you back in Atlanta, but me, I don't swing that way.'"

Typically, Sedaris does not analyze this remark, or ponder it, or wrestle with its clear implication. No doubt the teacher's response embarrassed him, but that is not the central point, which is tolerance—the notion that when you look under the hood, we're all a little strange. At its best, his work embodies this daring empathy that recognizes differences, sometimes ridicules them, but ultimately accepts them with a playful shrug.

Sedaris is not only a gifted writer but also an important one in large part because of his ability to both mock political correctness and reinforce it at its most profound level.

POIGNANT FLAWS

"[My sister Tiffany] later phoned my brother, referring to me as Fairy Poppins, which wouldn't bother me if it weren't so apt"—from "Dress Your Family in Corduroy and Denim."

In a recent New York Times article, the humorist P. J. O'Rourke said there are two major themes in American comedy: The "What a fool am I" tradition and the "What a fool are you" approach.

Sedaris is part of a Third Wave that says: Oh, what fools are we all, and isn't it great?

He can be cruel, as he was to his guitar teacher. Southerners, whom he loves to portray as daffy yokels, are favorite targets of derision. Here's how he describes one co-worker: "One look at his teeth, and you could understand his crusade for universal health care."

Disabled people are a steady source of laughs, and so are black people. In the story about how the Dutch believe that "Six to Eight Black Men" help Santa dispense presents, he writes: "This, I think, is the greatest difference between us and the Dutch. While a certain segment of our population might be perfectly happy with the arrangement, if you told the average white American that six to eight nameless black men would be sneaking into his house in the middle of the night, he would barricade the doors and arm himself with whatever he could get his hands on."

That comment may test the bounds of politeness. But it loses its harsh edge in the larger context of Sedaris's work.

In one story, the writer tells us his father kicked him out of the house when he learned his son was gay. In another, we watch his brother, Paul, introduce him to his baby daughter as "Uncle Faggot."

All of this becomes water under the bridge. The father and son quickly reconcile, David brushes off his brother's remark. Whether he is describing his family members or passing acquaintances, the aha! moment does not occur when someone's failings are revealed but with the recognition that we're all flawed, all traveling down the same river in the same boat.

This quality also answers one of the central riddles surrounding his work: How can someone who writes so frequently and openly about homosexual desire sell millions of books?

Sedaris is not a gay writer, but a writer who is gay. He does not politicize his homosexuality; he humanizes it, enabling readers to do the same.

However, he makes it easy for the reader's tolerance to end at his shore.

PROSE PORTRAITIST

"My father favored a chair in the basement, but my mother was apt to lie down anywhere, waking with carpet burns on her face or the pattern of the sofa embossed into the soft flesh of her upper arms"— from "Dress Your Family in Corduroy and Denim"

Comedy often challenges the audience—think of Lenny Bruce or Richard Pryor. Sedaris is more interested in making them feel comfortable. His humor never implicates readers, never directly forces them to consider their own thoughts and actions.

This approach does not seem calculated; it's how Sedaris's mind works. He is, at heart, a portrait painter, a master of the character sketch who can make people pulse with life on the page.

His mother "was the sort of person who could talk to anyone, not in the pointed, investigative manner that the situation called for, but generally, casually. Had she been sent to interview Charles Manson, she might have come away saying, 'I never knew he liked bamboo!'"

His father, "a tight man with a dollar," would never "buy anything not marked REDUCED FOR QUICK SALE. Without that orange tag, an item was virtually invisible to him."

His sister Lisa "is a person who once witnessed a car accident, saying, 'I just hope there isn't a dog in the back seat'"—and that's all we need to know.

But Sedaris also has an advanced case of tunnel vision. He seems unwilling or incapable of larger connections. He makes readers feel they are on a first-name basis with the family members: his father, Lou, and late mother, Sharon; his siblings, Gretchen, Lisa, Amy, Tiffany and Paul;

and his partner, Hugh. Yet we almost always see them in isolation. We know each of the Sedarises, but can't quite grasp the family dynamic.

His books contain many vivid portraits of Lou, the no-nonsense IBM engineer, and Sharon, the witty, slightly desperate housewife, but they never make clear what made these two very different people click as a couple. We know about David's achievements and those of his sister Amy, an actress who co-writes plays with him, but don't quite grasp how the Sedaris home produced such daring and imaginative children. Rather than bringing order to the entire house in one manic swoop, Sedaris polishes his sterling silver memories, one piece at a time.

The book on David Sedaris is far from closed. Although my Unified Theory of David Sedaris argues for a deep continuity between the writer's pre- and post-elfin life, his work is far from static. While he is often pigeonholed as a one-trick pony, the master of the humorous personal essay, his work displays a brisk evolution from the straight comedy of "Barrel Fever" to the deeply nuanced memoir "Dress Your Family in Corduroy and Denim."

It appears that David Sedaris has not finished reinventing himself—even as he stays true to himself, playing to his considerable strengths.

July 24, 2005

Jonathan Miles:
Author Keeps the Tales Pouring

Alcohol has been very, very good to Jonathan Miles.

The ecstasies and sorrows of drink are at the center of the 37-year-old's first novel, "Dear American Airlines." The darkly funny, achingly poignant portrait of a recovering alcoholic trapped at Chicago's O'Hare Airport received a warm review from Richard Russo on the cover of last Sunday's New York Times Book Review.

As he worked on the novel, Miles began writing his Sunday column on cocktails, Shaken and Stirred, for the Times.

During the 1990s, he wooed his wife, Catherine, now a wine importer, from his favorite barstool at the City Grocery restaurant in Oxford, Miss., where she worked as a manager.

His writing life began in the early 1990s when he befriended novelist and legendary drinker Larry Brown. "I couldn't ask for a better education than driving around Mississippi, drinking beer and talking about books and writing with Larry," Miles said.

Booze even gave him his name. After World War II, his Polish grandfather was sitting with his brothers at a Cleveland pub trying to come up with a last name that sounded more American than Mozelski. They couldn't agree on anything until someone noticed the bar sat on Miles Road.

"I've been around alcohol my whole life," Miles said by phone from his upstate New York home. "I'm fascinated by all its facets, especially how it can enhance life so beautifully and destroy it so completely. That's one reason I like to hang out in bars: You see people *in extremis,* at their happiest and saddest."

Miles has done far more than warm barstools. The college dropout has enjoyed tremendous success since becoming a freelance writer in 1994. He has written for Esquire, GQ, Food & Wine, Sports Afield and Men's Journal, where he writes a column on books. His articles have been included in the 1997, 1999 and 2000 editions of "The Best American Sports Writing" and the 2005 edition of "The Best American Crime Writing" series.

With that track record, it seems only natural that Houghton Mifflin would make his first novel its lead fiction title this summer, sending him on a 17-city tour.

MESMERIZED IN MISSISSIPPI

His life only seems as smooth as 12-year-old Scotch; it is more akin to the colorful drinks served in coconut shell with paper umbrellas and spears of fruit. Miles was reared in Cleveland and Phoenix, where his father worked at various jobs and his mother was a homemaker who loved popular fiction.

"I was such an avid enough reader growing up that I'd go to Walden Books at the mall and shoplift Louis L'Amour books," Miles remembers.

A science fiction fan, he exhibited the freelancer's crucial networking skills at a tender age when he wrote Isaac Asimov to see if they might become pen pals. "He balked at the long-term thing but gave me the only advice that matters: 'Read as much as possible; write as much as possible.'"

Still, music was his first love. After graduating from high school in Phoenix, he returned to Cleveland, living with one of his two sisters, playing blues guitar at local clubs. On Sundays he'd sit in with Robert Jimmy Lockwood, stepson of blues legend Robert Johnson, who mesmerized Miles with stories of the Mississippi.

"I'd already discovered Faulkner, so I just had to see this place," Miles said. Without ever having crossed the Mason-Dixon line, he applied to the University of Mississippi in 1989.

Miles's tenure at Ole Miss was short-lived, but he fell in love with Oxford. He lived in a $30 a month "Unabomber type" shack, worked at a series of "boy jobs: bus boy, lawn boy, bag boy at the grocery store" and became part of the town's close-knit community of writers and musicians.

"I just met Larry Brown at a bar one night," Miles recalled. Many drinks led to dinner, which became memorable when Brown spotted a banker who'd turned him down for a loan. The well-lubricated novelist mounted the man's table "and did this slow twist," Miles said, laughing. "He finished the whole song with his boots in the banker's meal and I'm thinking, yeah, I'm going to hang out with this guy a lot." Brown, who died in 2004, would became a "second father" to Miles, who dedicates his novel to him.

NO AUTOBIOGRAPHY HERE

As he worked on his fiction, Miles became a reporter at the Oxford Eagle in 1994. All was well until he added what he considered an essential fact to an already edited obituary: The deceased had been Faulkner's bootlegger.

His angry boss told Miles the paper did not print people's crimes in their obits. "I told him," Miles recalled, " 'Bootlegging is not a crime, it's a service.' That was my last day at the paper."

It was the start of his freelance career, writing for the locally published national magazine, the Oxford American, and pitching stories about Mississippi to New York-based publications. He was still living in his primitive shack when an editor at GQ, Will Blythe, gave him some invaluable advice: "If you're thinking about doing this for a living, you might want to invest in a phone."

As his journalism career took off, Miles continued to write fiction. He spent years writing more than 700 pages of a novel about "my great love for Mississippi" before realizing he could never finish it. When his agent asked him how it was going, he said "great."

This was only a half-lie. Miles was expanding an old short story based on a personal experience: a Memphis-Chicago-New York flight he'd taken that had been forced to land in Peoria. Miles and the other passengers were bused late at night to Chicago's O'Hare where he slept under a restaurant table. He was furious, until he considered that he was only going to New York to meet friends for drinks. "I started looking around thinking someone is missing something important, something essential. What would that fury be like?"

That thought gave birth to his novel's protagonist, Bennie Ford, a failed poet and translator of Polish novels who is trying to get to Los Angles to attend the wedding of his estranged daughter. In a drunken life where most everything's gone wrong, he was hoping to do one thing right: walk his daughter down the aisle.

Through delays and cancellations, American Airlines has denied him that chance at redemption. The letter he writes while stuck at O'Hare demanding a refund becomes a 180-page examination of his hopes and failings.

"I'm happy to say there's not a shred of autobiography in this novel," Miles said. "Bennie is a nightmare of what I could have become, of what I've seen other people become."

June 8, 2008

Jonathan Williams:
Nosing Out Talent

"Always on the go, always on the look-out"

Jonathan Williams,
Blues and Roots, Rue and Bluets

In a house fashioned from native woods nestled in the mountains of Western North Carolina, scores of poets, novelists, painters, photographers, publishers and longtime neighbors are planning to gather this afternoon to celebrate the life of Jonathan Williams.

His given name was only one of the monikers this accomplished man of letters went by during his 79 colorful years. Others included: Lord Stodge, Lord Nose, Big Enis, Cap'n Butch, Dr. Strange Glove and Big J. Mac-Sanders.

And yet, those and his many other playful aliases couldn't begin to encompass the innumerable passions and pursuits that defined this native Tar Heel before his death in March.

Where to begin?

A tall, imposing man with a deep-rich voice, he was a brilliantly understated poet whose lines were funny: "It was morning / and lo! Now it is evening // nothing memorable / accomplished."

And inspiring: "You have eyes / outside / and eyes / inside // your heart / is full / of eyes // to communicate / you put the two / together / amen!"

And tenderly erotic: "My lips in / your flowers."

Williams was also an accomplished photographer whose images of writers, artists, gravestones and natural landscapes are housed at Yale University.

He ran also one the nation's great small presses. The Jargon Society, which he founded as a 21-year-old, published 113 books during his lifetime. Guided by his quixotic mission, "To keep afloat the Ark of Culture in these dark and tacky times," it spotlighted talented but neglected poets, writers and artists, including Charles Olson, Denise Levertov, Guy Davenport, Louis Zukofsky, Paul Metcalf, Mina Loy and Lorine Niedecker.

He was "the truffle-hound of American poetry," critic Hugh Kenner said in describing Williams's ability to unearth unheralded genius. He was "our Johnny Appleseed," added the visionary architect and writer Buckminster Fuller, referring to the decades Williams spent crisscrossing America in a Volkswagen stuffed with Jargon titles, spreading the good news about avant-garde art to bookstores and university campuses.

Distinguished publisher, poet and photographer those were only Williams's better-known identities. He was also an expert on Chinese porcelain and Japanese poetry, the music of Brahms and Mahler, Doc Watson and Earl Scruggs; a sports nut, lover of fine cigars and single malt whiskey; a connoisseur of barbecue and French cuisine; a collector of outsider art; an indefatigable hiker who conquered 1,400 miles of the Appalachian Trail and a tireless correspondent who wrote up to 40 letters a day; a gay man who lived with poet Tom Meyer for 40 years; a conscientious objector during the Korean War and an irascible, opinionated curmudgeon who celebrated talent but rarely suffered fools.

I am, Williams once said, "easily satisfied by the very best."

Chapel Hill poet Jeffery Beam put it differently last week: "He was interested in everything that came in front of him, especially if he thought people were ignoring it."

Durham poet Michael McFee, who counts Fred Chappell and Robert Morgan among his mentors, described Williams as "the most unique man of letters North Carolina has ever produced. He was a polymath who seemed to know everything and everybody. I feel like I'd have to go to four or five people to get all he had in one person. He is irreplaceable."

TRUST IN HIS JUDGMENT

Jonathan Chamberlain Williams was born in Asheville in 1929, the only son of Thomas Benjamin and Georgette (Chamberlain) Williams. His family soon moved to Washington, D.C., where his father made a comfortable living providing office systems to the federal government and his mother exercised what Meyer called her "exquisite taste" as an interior designer.

In 1942, his parents built a home they called Skywinding Farm near the Macon County town of Highlands. The teenage Williams loved spending summers in the surrounding woods, painting waterfalls, collecting minerals and arrowheads.

"We still have those minerals, which were the first of many collections," Meyer said. "Jonathan was interested in things of great value that were hidden in plain sight."

As an adult he championed outsider artists including Howard Finster. He "found" poems in the language of everyday people, such as

"Aunt Dory Ellis, of Penland, Remembers When She Fell in Her Garden at the Home Place and Broke Her Hip in 19 and 56": "the sky was high, / white clouds passing / by, I lay / a hour in that petunia patch / hollered, / and I knew I was out of whack."

Dividing his time between Highlands and a 17th century cottage in rural England, he abhorred the pace and pretense of urban culture. He wrote: "I hear the hornets buzzing, get on with it, get on with it. But, you do not hurry in Appalachia. It is considered uncultivated. I have stood for many an hour while my neighbor, Uncle Iv Owens, prognosticated tomorrow's weather. Why not? Old Walt told us: 'Loaf, and invite the Soul.'"

After graduating from St. Albans prep school in Washington, he dropped out of Princeton. At 19, he recalled, "I had made the choice to betray the Middleclass in favor of something called art."

After a stint at Chicago's Institute of Design, he landed at Black Mountain College near Asheville, a hotbed of experimental art. Its faculty and student body included some of America's most influential artists, musicians, dancers and poets, including Robert Rauschenberg, John Cage, Merce Cunningham and Charles Olson.

It was here, Williams said, that the poet Olson gave him advice that would inform the rest of his life: "Don't ever be intimidated by the disdain or disinterest in the world. Get yourself some type, get yourself some paper, and print it."

In the decades that followed Williams used a small inheritance, the support of wealthy patrons and his keen eye (he bought art low and sold it high) to, as Meyer put it, "live exactly the life he wanted."

His resume included a Guggenheim fellowship and NEA grants, but "neglected" was the adjective most often used to describe him. He was frustrated by the shallow nature of mainstream American culture. "Boobus americanus and the barbarians are way past the gates, my friend," he wrote. "They are on the third floor breaking down the attic."

Still, he persevered, confident in the value of the work.

A few years ago, Jeffery Beam asked Williams what he'd like his epitaph to be. Williams said the one he wrote for his Uncle Iv Owens:

"he done
what he could
when he got round
to it"

June 1, 2008

Reynolds Price:
Rooted in His Native Soil

Durham—For five decades, visitors both famous and plain have climbed the steep dirt driveway up to Reynolds Price's home. Set by a pond in a dense forest, the great writer's small, wooden house looks remarkably ordinary.

But its doors open to a magnificent world: Sculptures of angels float along walls that are covered with works of fine art, including exquisite golden paintings of Jesus and the Virgin Mary. They cast a spell that is broken only when Price rolls forward in his wheelchair and says in his rich, folksy baritone, "Thanks for comin' by, buddy. Have yourself a seat."

These contrasts, the earthy and the ethereal, the high-minded and low-key, are entirely consistent with the man. His life and work have revolved around the symbiotic relationship between the everyday and the extraordinary.

Price will mark two milestones this week. From Thursday to Saturday, Toni Morrison, Richard Ford, Josephine Humphries, Charlie Rose and other luminaries will gather in Durham to commemorate Price's 50th year of teaching at Duke University. And on Friday he will celebrate his 75th birthday.

Many people mark birthdays and are saluted for long service. But these events take on a miraculous quality when Price explains that it is only through blood oaths and divine interventions that he is around to enjoy them.

Seventy-five years ago in Macon, N.C., a doctor told Price's father that his wife and first-born might not survive the difficult labor. A bereft

Will Price repaired to a barn and made a pact with God: Allow them to live, he beseeched, and I will quit drinking. Mother and child pulled through.

That's not the only time, the writer says, that he was saved by a higher power.

In 1984, suffering with the spinal cancer that cost him the use of his legs, Price had surrendered hope. Then one morning he saw himself lying by a lake that he recognized as the Sea of Galilee. A man he knew to be Jesus began pouring water over Price's surgical scar.

"Your sins are forgiven," Jesus told him.

Price wanted more. "Am I also healed?" he asked.

"That, too," Jesus answered.

FROM COMMON TO COSMIC

The literal truth of these events, which Price firmly embraces, is at least as important as what they reveal about his great gift: the ability to see the eternal workings of the cosmos in the common events of life: in birth, sickness, love, sex, family and death.

This understanding has informed his 37 books—novels, memoirs, plays and short story and poetry collections. Just as his unassuming home contains wonders, his writing often reveals how the deepest forces of life and nature unfold in humble lives.

As the eponymous narrator of Price's 1998 novel "Roxanna Slade" put it: "If you can tell the absolute truth about five or ten moments that mattered in any one life, then you'll have shown how every life is as useful to the world and to the eyes of God as any president's or pope's."

This grounding of the extraordinary in the ordinary also helps resolve a central paradox about Price. He is an erudite man of the world, an acclaimed writer and Rhodes scholar, an authority on Milton and a leading theologian. He is also a serious student of music, travel and fine art whose friends have included the writers Eudora Welty, W. H. Auden and Sir Stephen Spender and the opera singer Leontyne Price.

"Given his interest in art and travel and European culture, you would think someone like that would be living in London, New York or Rome," said James Schiff, a former student who has published two books on Price's work.

Yet Price is deeply rooted. He has chosen to live all but four of his years in North Carolina. Since 1958, he has inhabited the same patch of land in Durham. He has had only one main employer, Duke, and one major publisher, Atheneum/Scribner.

He has traveled the world, but he has set the vast majority of his books in his native state, including "A Long and Happy Life" (1962), his Mayfield Trilogy (1975–95) and "Kate Vaiden" (1986), which won the National Book Critics Circle prize for fiction.

Asked why he has hewed so close to home, Price replied, "I just love this place." Pressed for more detail, he lets a flicker of frustration tinge his voice.

"How can I put this? What do you love about your wife? It's just the whole thing, the land, the people, the food. I even love the climate, though I'm thankful for air conditioning."

There are other ties that bind.

A close look at Price's life suggests how family, teachers and faith helped him become a man whose feet are planted on the ground as his eyes look up.

'THIS IS WHAT I KNOW'

In his 1989 memoir, "Clear Pictures," Price wrote that his bond with his parents was so close that it felt like they were married.

"We were three people who'd trust each other for good," he wrote, "and that trust would last on every side." The feeling did not change with the arrival of brother William when Reynolds was 8.

His mother, Elizabeth, never felt so secure. Her parents died when she was young and she was reared by a loving older sister.

"Though she wasn't a self-pitying woman," Price recalled, "she did have a bit of a sense of being an outcast. I don't know if that had anything to do with her habit of walking into my bedroom and saying, 'Son, pack up your comic books. We're going to move to the other side of town.'"

The Prices lived in 11 different homes during his first 13 years in the rural towns of Macon, Roxboro and Warrenton as his mother and father, an appliance salesman, tried to inch ahead. Perhaps all that moving made him happy to stay put as an adult, Price said.

The love of his parents and a large extended family gave Price more than self-confidence. Though Tolstoy suggested that happy families are boring, Price has devoted much of his career to excavating, reimagining and taking inspiration from his childhood memories.

Price said the writer's job is "to get as close to the bone of your own life and your own knowledge as possible. This is what I know."

He was an observant child who could sit for hours on the porch and in the kitchen, listening to family lore. He was also a solitary boy who loved to draw and read.

His father gave him his first book, an illustrated version of the Bible, when he was 3. He moved on to "Robinson Crusoe" and "Gone with the Wind," then the novels of Tolstoy and Flaubert.

In his curiously vivid mind, young Price saw the universality of human experience. One day when he was 6 or 7, he had a vision in the woods: A "great wheel of nature" told him that everything he was aware of "was all one thing."

THE WRITER'S JOURNEY

Great teachers bridged the path from the visionary child to the Rhodes scholar.

His eighth-grade teacher in Warrenton, Crichton Davis, recognized his writing talent. Phyllis Peacock, his 11th-grade English teacher at Broughton High School in Raleigh, took him on his first trip to New York. She sent a a paper he'd written on "Hamlet" to Laurence Olivier, and the actor autographed it. "I nearly fell out of my britches."

He added: "What her actions told me was that serious people would take a serious interest in me."

Though no one in Price's immediate family had gone to college, Peacock prodded him to apply for a scholarship at Duke University, which he won. In Durham the legendary English professor William Blackburn took Price under his wing. Over a barbecue sandwich, he suggested that Price apply for a Rhodes scholarship.

"Well, honest to goodness, I barely knew what a Rhodes scholarship was," Price said. "Certainly no one in my family, loving as they were, would have known what it was. . . . So Blackburn got me thinking gosh, perhaps it would be interesting to go to graduate school in England."

A confident sense of self and place anchors Price the writer.

"He works out of a sense of conviction, even when it has been inconvenient," his Duke colleague Victor Strandberg said.

When Price came on the scene in the early 1960s, his style of fiction —Tolstoyan novels set in the South—was falling out of favor. In a scathing New York Times review in 1975, Richard Gilman dismissed "The Surface of the Earth" as a "great lumbering archaic beast."

His crimes?

First, the novel, set in rural North Carolina and Virginia between 1903 and 1944, might be classified as Southern fiction, which "only has the most marginal place in general consciousness now," Gilman wrote. And second, Price eschewed the "cool, ironic" approach of Thomas Pynchon, Donald Barthelme and other celebrated postmodern writers to tell a story about "love, its difficulty and rarity."

A lesser artist might have bowed to fashion. But, Strandberg said, Price was always committed to the classic tradition of character-based novels exploring humanity's greatest moral challenges, and our obligations to one another and ourselves.

Similarly, Price has written openly and honestly about his Christian faith at a time when most intellectuals have moved away from open declarations of belief or sectarianism.

While faith informs most of Price's writing, he has addressed the issue most directly in works of nonfiction. His 2006 book, "Letter to a Godchild: Concerning Faith," emphasized how his faith connects him to larger, timeless aspects of existence.

Price, who said he has never had a moment of serious doubt in his entire life, is surprised by the way many nonbelievers casually dismiss a notion that about "80 percent of the greatest minds of Western civilizations have devoted themselves to trying to understand."

DESTINED FOR DUKE

On a January afternoon in the living room of his Durham home, Price reflects on the powers of fate and Duke University that brought him and kept him here.

He was none too happy in the spring of 1957. His three years at Oxford were ending and the budding writer dreaded the idea of "having to write 10,000 letters" in search of a job.

His future revealed itself in a letter postmarked Durham, N.C. The chairman of Duke's English department was wondering if he was interested in teaching.

"I thought, 'Oh, my God, would I,'" Price recalled with a laugh. "'Now I don't have to write those 10,000 letters.'"

That was the first of four occasions when Duke would cement Price's ties to his alma mater, where his students would include the budding novelists Anne Tyler, Josephine Humphries and David Guy.

Three years after he arrived, the department chair said Price's fiction was so strong that he didn't need a Ph.D. to be considered for tenure. In 1966, after the success of his first novel, "A Long and Happy Life," the school allowed him to teach half time for half pay. And in the mid-'70s came one last arrangement. Price would receive full pay for teaching one semester. In exchange he would give Duke his most valuable possession: his papers.

"Duke has been a real peach of a place to work, a wonderful employer from the very beginning," Price said. "Fate may have planned all that, but Reynolds Price didn't."

In this room where images of angels and Jesus watch over him, Price said he is leading a life with few regrets.

"I try to tell as many people as possible that breadth of experience is hugely to be sought and desired," he said. "I've had that breadth of experience living here. I would have to say there's nothing I regret about living the last 50 years in Durham and Orange County."

January 27, 2008

Eudora Welty's Passing:
A Death in the Family

Eudora Welty never married, but she had dozens of children. And all of them were writers. In North Carolina alone her progeny includes

Elizabeth Spencer and Reynolds Price, Lee Smith and Kaye Gibbons, Clyde Edgerton, Fred Chappell, Allan Gurganus, Jill McCorkle and Louis D. Rubin Jr.

Miss Welty's death Monday at age 92 occasioned mourning across America and around the world. But the sadness ran deeper, the loss felt more personal, like a death in the family, here in the South, where the Mississippi writer's brilliant prose and generous spirit had nurtured several generations of writers.

"She was the last representative of that older generation of masters, William Faulkner, Katherine Ann Porter, Robert Penn Warren and Tennessee Williams, who created Southern literature," said Reynolds Price, whose close friendship with Miss Welty began in 1955. "But she was also an approachable genius who opened herself to others and could make you fall out of your chair laughing at the marvelous remarks she would make about a writer you liked or hated or the waitress walking across the dining room."

Miss Welty's influence on Southern—and American—literature would have been indelible even if she had lived as a hermit in Jackson, Miss., where she was born, lived and died. Through five novels and scores of short stories, including "Why I Live at the P.O.," "Powerhouse" and "A Worn Path," she displayed a technical and imaginative virtuosity that drew comparisons not only to Faulkner, but also to Anton Chekhov, Marcel Proust and James Joyce. Her honors included the Pulitzer Prize, the American Book Award, the National Books Critics Circle Award, several O. Henry Awards and the Gold Medal of the American Academy and Institute of Arts and Letters. She was also inducted into the French Legion of Honor.

"As only the very greatest writers can, her work conveyed the clarity and power of universal emotions," said Louis Rubin, an essayist and critic who was an early champion of Miss Welty's writing. "She wrote of ordinary people loving and hating, of solitude and community, time and art all set against a background of the ultimate questions of human existence."

Miss Welty's genius made her prose the literature of the world, but her impact on Southern writers was especially deep because it was their world, their experience, their people that she alchemized through the thunderclap of higher consciousness into great art. "What she taught me and countless other Southern writers," Rubin said, "was that the place we grew up in and knew, the things that we did and the people we talked with were worth writing about, were as worthy of being captured in language as castles in Spain."

To begin to understand her influence on so many Southern writers, you have to appreciate the deep identification those authors have with their region and the fellowship they share. To a much greater degree than writers in Manhattan, the Midwest and the West, Southerners identify themselves with their region and they tend to work out of a tradition defined by the achievements of Miss Welty and other titans.

"Faulkner and Flannery O'Connor and Miss Welty seemed to me to purify the drinking water," said the novelist Allan Gurganus. "It meant that you did not want to publish a book until you could come up with something worthy of being on the same shelf with them, which is one reason why I didn't publish my first book until I was 42."

As Kaye Gibbons put it, "Those writers set a standard so high that every page and every paragraph and every line had to be the very best it could be."

Miss Welty's influence was particularly deep because it extended beyond her work.

"The number of really good Southern writers is relatively small," Gurganus said. "And she seemed to know all of us. We are members of this little tribal community. She was the beloved favorite aunt, the genius fifth-grade teacher who could have run GM but chose instead to stay home and write."

Miss Welty brought attention to many talented writers, including Spencer, Gibbons and Price. But her effect on them was more personal than professional, hinging on her spirit rather than her connections. It is hard to find a Southern author of note who has not sipped Maker's Mark bourbon with Miss Welty at her Jackson home.

"What I remember most of the times I spent with her is the laughter," said Lee Smith, echoing the comments of other writers. "She was so social. She really loved people and gossip and talk, and it was just really fun to talk with her. Her writing was grounded in the everyday and so was her conversation. We didn't talk too much about literature, but she liked to tell stories about things. She had tons of snake stories and dog bite stories and big fish stories and getting hit by lightning stories. Whatever it was, she had something to say."

Miss Welty, however, did not extend her friendship willy-nilly. She was kind and generous, but did not suffer fools gladly (though, almost always, she did suffer them politely). As Price observed, "She had a very clear sense of every single thing she did and a powerful sense that she was a great writer. She knew what her friendship meant to us."

Clyde Edgerton's experience with Miss Welty was both typical and extraordinary. It began, he said, on "14 May, 1978. Eudora Welty was reading her short story 'Why I Live at the P.O.' on the television, channel four. Her voice. Her words. It seemed like the room filled up with a kind of spirit. I realized the power that writing could have. I wanted that power, the power to create that spirit for other people. The next day, I began my writing career in earnest."

Several years later, as he was achieving those dreams, Edgerton was invited to a dinner. In a pinch-me moment, Willie Morris suggested that he escort another guest, Miss Welty. "I think writers do other writers a disservice when they glorify and adore them," Edgerton said. "But as I was walking up the sidewalk to get her, I truly felt like I was going to meet God. She was in the pantheon of writers whom I admired most— Twain, Crane, Hemingway, O'Connor and Welty—and I was going to meet her. Can you imagine? Well, she was delightfully gracious as she would remain throughout the years when I had the privilege to visit with her. I always felt lucky and awed."

If there is one quality that makes Southern writers a group, a tribe, distinct and distinguished, it is not just where they come from or what they write about but their connection to each other. Miss Welty did not forge that link alone, but it's an enormous part of her bequest. In one sense, her death marks the end of the great period of Southern literature that began in the 1920s. But in a larger sense, her legacy lives on not only through her works, but also through the Southern writers she inspired, nurtured and befriended. A grande dame indeed.

July 29, 2001

William Faulkner's Literary Legacy

William Faulkner was in crisis when he marked his 50th birthday a half century ago,. He hadn't published a novel in five years. His editor had deemed his latest effort unsalvageable. His best work was behind him, and all but one of his notoriously difficult and seemingly regional novels had fallen out of print because of poor sales.

He told a class of graduate students at the University of Mississippi that year, "I feel I'm written out. I don't think I'll write much more."

Yet, at that very moment America and the world were re-examining his work anew, thanks in no small part to publication of Viking's "Portable Faulkner." Soon the awards and wide acclaim he had failed to receive for his earliest and best works were showered upon him. He was awarded the Nobel Prize for Literature in 1949 and in subsequent years garnered one National Book Award and two Pulitzers.

Today, as we near the centenary of his birth, on Thursday, Faulkner towers as the most exalted American writer of the 20th century. His 20 novels and scores of short stories constitute a body of work with few peers for its depth and invention. This year, writers from around the world have gathered in Ashland, Va.; Oxford, Miss.; New Orleans, Paris, Moscow and Beijing to pay homage to and evaluate his legacy.

During the past 25 years, the outpouring of scholarship on Faulkner's work has been immense. One bibliography of works about him runs more than 600 pages. No writer in English, save Shakespeare, is analyzed and debated so thoroughly.

As Robert Penn Warren once said, "For range of effect, philosophical weight, originality of style, variety of characterization, humor, and tragic intensity, [Faulkner's works] are without equal in our time and country."

Faulkner, who died in 1962, is often described as the quintessential Southern writer because his greatest works all centered in his postage stamp of native soil—which he reimagined as the mythical Yoknapatawpha County. It was there that he traced the dissolution of the Compson family in "The Sound and the Fury"; the poignant struggle of the Bundrens to bury their dead matriarch in "As I Lay Dying"; and Joe

Christmas's tragic struggle for his own soul in "Light in August." And it was here that Thomas Sutpen mercilessly tried to bring honor to his family in "Absalom, Absalom!" and where the Snopeses clawed their way from obscurity to attain everything and nothing in "The Hamlet," "The Town" and "The Mansion."

Faulkner derived many of his central themes from the region's anguished past—race, gender, repression, myth and heroism. At root, his work was fueled by a seething hostility, fierce individualism and a fiery subversiveness. He challenged convention, suggesting that society and culture not only shape, but misshape people, preventing them from discovering their true nature and happiness.

Faulkner had the rare ability to create characters and a milieu specifically anchored in time and place and yet absolutely unbounded: "For all his concern with the South, Faulkner was actually seeking out the nature of man," Ralph Ellison once commented. "Thus we must turn to him for that continuity of moral purpose which made for the greatness of classics."

It was not simply what Faulkner said, but how he said it, that set his work apart. He developed dazzling techniques—stream of consciousness, multiple perspectives, the use of unreliable narrators and a disdain for the conventions of grammar and language. Along with writers such as Marcel Proust, James Joyce and Virginia Woolf, his literary daring helped usher in modernism while laying the groundwork for postmodernists such as Thomas Pynchon, John Barth and Donald Barthelme.

The key to Faulkner's accomplishment is simple: He was a genius, born with rare abilities. And yet, by looking at the environment he was reared in, the issues and emotions he was confronted with, we can find clues to why his talent took the form it did.

A PROUD FAMILY IN DECLINE

William Cuthbert Faulkner was born in New Albany, Miss., on Sept. 25, 1897. He was reared in the Jim Crow South, where sentimental stories, romantic myths and pregnant silences were used to mask uncomfortable truths. It was a world informed by the Great Lost Cause, a place where blacks and whites lived alongside one another, their conduct dictated in the smallest particular by unspoken codes.

The first of Murry and Maud Falkner's four sons (we'll get to the missing "u" later), William entered a proud, economically comfortable but declining family.

His great-grandfather, Col. William C. Falkner had moved to the Mississippi Delta from Tennessee in 1841. Vain and ambitious, equally desperate for wealth and honor, he married the daughter of a rich planter and padded his holdings during the Civil War, probably by providing contraband to Union soldiers. After the war, he built a lucrative railroad line and won political office. He was also a writer who enjoyed commercial if not literary success, through works such as "The White Rose of Memphis" and "The Little Brick Church," which blamed Northerners for the slave trade while arguing that Southerners "treat their Negroes with the tenderest humanity."

Difficult, brash and confrontational—all Falkner family traits—he had shot two men dead in duels and was killed himself by a rival on Oxford's main square in broad daylight in 1889. He was buried next to an 8-foot marble statue of himself that still stands on a 14-foot high pedestal in the town cemetery.

Though William Faulkner had never met this figure who dominated family lore, his great-grandfather was a powerful influence. When his third-grade teacher asked about his future, young William replied: "I want to be a writer like my great-granddaddy." But Faulkner would later learn other lessons from the Colonel's life, that behind the genteel veneer lay rougher truths he would explore in his fiction.

Faulkner's grandfather, the heavy-drinking and brusque J. W. T. Falkner, was one of Oxford's civic and social leaders who operated a bank and the family railroad. That enterprise was the true love of William's father, Murry. A withdrawn and disengaged man and a parent with little wit or flair, Murry was crushed when J. W. T. sold the railroad in 1902; Murry passed the rest of his life in nondescript jobs and alcoholism. Upon Murry's death in 1932, it fell to William to support his family.

In his exhaustive 1974 biography, "Faulkner," Joseph Blotner captures the hostility that undergirded the relationship between father and son. Blotner quotes a childhood friend who recalled playing golf with William and his brother Jack: "As we approached the sixth green, having already played our drives, here came Bill's father in a rage. Jack and

I picked up our balls and turned tail. Not Bill. He carefully selected an iron, cried 'fore' and addressed the ball directly toward his father."

That strained relation reflects one of the many paradoxes of Faulkner's character. Though much of his work aimed at deflating the South's heroic myths, he seemed to blame his father for not maintaining the family's name and position. As soon as he could afford his own home, he bought a crumbling mansion in Oxford, christening it Rowan Oak. Years later, he would buy a plantation. Faulkner's desire in ordinary life to be a *pater familias* and a Southern gentleman was as strong as his need to show the hollowness and danger of those notions and traditions in his fiction.

Through his mother's family, Faulkner found more constructive ways to express himself. Like the Falkners, the Butlers had seen their best days when William was born. One of the first families to settle near Oxford, in the 1830s, they supported themselves through property ownership and government work and by running Oxford's leading hotel. They were nearly ruined when Union soldiers burned down much of Oxford. The Butlers were more educated than the Falkners—many of their men attended college. Maud's mother, Leila, had training as a painter and sculptor. Her father, Charlie, was the town marshal. Charlie also brought disgrace to the family in 1887 when he absconded with the town's money—and, perhaps, his African American lover.

Faulkner's doting mother, whom he adored, sparked his love of art and literature, which provided a window on the larger world and a way to express his swirling emotions. As Joel Williamson, professor of humanities at UNC-Chapel Hill wrote in "William Faulkner and Southern History": "No other individual influenced him so profoundly. Faulkner outlived his mother by only two years, he lived in her home during a large portion of his adult life, and even after his marriage he dropped by her house for a visit almost every day when he was in Oxford. Maud's faith in 'Billy' as she always called him, was absolutely unshakable. When so many others easily and confidently pronounced him a failure, she insisted that he was a genius and that the world would come to recognize that fact."

Maud was a strong independent woman who hung a board in her kitchen that read, "Don't Complain, Don't Explain."

PRECOCIOUS, PARADOXICAL CHILD

Exhibiting the paradoxical characteristics that would mark his mature personality, Faulkner was a quiet but mischievous child, polite and rude, loving and withdrawn. He was precocious, excelling at painting and drawing. He was also a born storyteller who delighted in blurring the lines between fantasy and fact. His grandmother said, "It got so that when Billy told you something, you never knew if it was the truth or just something he'd made up."

For Faulkner these flights of fancy rose in part from being a gifted person consigned to a provincial habitat. He began writing poetry at an early age, he said, "to complete a youthful gesture I was then making of being 'different' in a small town."

He was a top student in grade school but was a truant in adolescence who scored poor marks and quit school altogether after the sixth grade. He was willful, convinced that others had little to teach him. "The good artist believes that nobody is good enough to give him advice," he said years later. ". . . He has supreme vanity."

Yet, like so many of Faulkner's autobiographical statements, this was only partially true. He ravenously learned from others, devouring the Bible, the works of Tolstoy, Dostoyevsky, Shakespeare, Cervantes and mountains of other books. In his teens he was taken under the wing of a Yale-educated townsman, Phil Stone, who recognized Faulkner's budding talent and continued the boy's informal education. (When Faulkner was in his 20s, the writer Sherwood Anderson would fill a similar mentoring role.)

Thanks in part to his grandfather and perhaps in frustration at being a small man—he stood 5-foot-5 as an adult, with a high-pitched, somewhat effeminate voice in a culture with rigid ideals of masculinity—Faulkner's mind was filled with dreams of heroism. When World War I broke out, the United States decided he was too small to serve in the armed forces, so he claimed British citizenship and enlisted in the Canadian Royal Air Force.

On his application to the RAF he added a "u" to his last name, for obscure reasons that nevertheless signaled his desire to forge a new identity, though one not too far removed from his old self.

Faulkner never saw combat duty but returned to Oxford in 1918 wearing his officer's uniform and carrying a swagger stick. Years after he had established his reputation as a writer, he was still telling people he had been a flying ace, severely wounded so that he had a silver plate in his head.

In the decade that followed, Faulkner donned a host of other identities, alternately an aristocrat, a bohemian or a derelict. As Daniel J. Singal notes in his compelling intellectual biography "William Faulkner: The Making of a Modernist" (1997), "By the late 1920s a pattern of two central selves—old-fashioned country gentleman and contemporary writer —became reasonably well established."

TWO SELVES IN CONFLICT

Yet, Singal writes, Faulkner never fully integrated these two selves: "All his life Faulkner would struggle to reconcile these two divergent approaches to self-hood—the Victorian urge toward unity and stability he had inherited as a child of the Southern rural gentry, and the modernist drive for multiplicity and change that he absorbed very early in his career as a self-identifying member of the international artistic avant-garde."

Faulkner put it this way: "I think a writer is a perfect case of split personality. He is one thing when he is a writer and he is something else while he is a denizen of the world."

Ultimately it was the fact that he never could, or never wanted to, resolve these conflicts that gave his writing such force. It allowed him to use racial epithets in casual conversation and to write books that contained a profound indictment of the South's racial system; to publicly turn and walk away when people told obscene stories or used foul language but to create tales decried as "repulsive" by many contemporary critics for their frank handling of rape, abortion, impotence, incest, prostitution and miscegenation; and to treat his wife and only daughter abysmally while creating some of the strongest and most resilient female characters in the literary canon.

During the 1920s he lived in New York City, Paris and New Orleans for short spells, but while many American writers of his generation thought they must live abroad for their writing to mature, Faulkner settled in Oxford. As Williamson wrote, "The power of the artist sprang from the terrific tension that lay at the base of his psyche: always he was an outsider observing critically the social universe to which he was born, which he knew marvelously well, and which, paradoxically, gave him both sustenance and pain."

This rich and troubled family life, the anguished history and vibrant mythology of the Old South and Faulkner's relentless invention and self-invention became hallmarks of his work.

The vast majority of even first-rate writers struggle to find their voices and, once they do, continue to explore yet operate within them. Faulkner, while putting his distinctive trademark on every book, was relentlessly experimental, giving each book a distinctive identity. "Faulkner wrote 20 novels and used 20 different narrative strategies to write each," says M. Thomas Inge, Blackwell Professor of Humanities at Randolph-Macon College in Virginia and the author and editor of numerous works on the writer including "William Faulkner: The Contemporary Reviews" (1995). "He was never satisfied simply to do what he had done before, but, sometimes almost in spite of himself, redefined his style with each book."

But narrative structure was not the only way he experimented. Faulkner excelled in traditional ways that a writer must. He possessed great knowledge, a vast vocabulary and a gift for metaphor and simile—as in this description of the gangster Popeye in "Sanctuary": "His face had a queer, bloodless color as though seen by electric light; against the sunny silence, in his slanted straw hat and his slightly akimbo arms, he had that vicious, depthless quality of stamped tin."

But when the English language did not seem to offer the *mot juste,* Faulkner crafted his own neologisms, like "dimatchment" and "succembence." Likewise, he thought of grammar as a tool to be employed when useful and discarded for something better when the need arose—though some of his 300-word sentences are more successful than others.

NOT TRUTH, BUT PERCEPTION

Just as Faulkner fashioned differing personae for himself, his work is marked by the use of multiple perspectives, which present differing versions of the story being told. "As I Lay Dying," which follows the journey—through fire, flood and other catastrophes—of the Bundren family as they endeavor to bring the body of their dead matriarch to her chosen resting place, is told by 15 characters through 59 monologues. The voices are joined in a single purpose, and experience the same events, but this chorus often sounds cacophonous, as they contradict one another, choosing to include and withhold information in presenting their very personal interpretations of the trip.

This technique underscores Faulkner's larger theme—that there is no single fixed historical truth but only stories about those truths. We are guided not so much by indisputable facts but by mutable and morphing points of view.

It is easy to see the personal appeal of such a view for Faulkner, a writer who bristled at the conventions of his society. For if those shackles had no fundamental basis—if they were merely versions of reality—then their hold might be loosened.

Yet, Faulkner was at heart deeply pessimistic, or tragically realistic, believing that society's grip and the weight of history could only be overcome through enormous struggle. In "Light in August" he examined the very core of this search for identity through the character Joe Christmas. Christmas's dilemma plumbs the core of Southern identity. He has been told he might have some black blood, a "taint" that, in that color-obsessed society, hurls him into a profound crisis of self.

At the book's end, when Christmas finally resolves his problem by rejecting society's rigid categories and accepting himself, he also commits an act of virtual suicide, allowing himself to be murdered in retribution for a crime he did not commit. And there's the rub. Faulkner believed that the individual who doesn't try to discover his identity doesn't truly live in the world but that self-knowledge comes at a heavy price.

Faulkner's literary experimentation is not just dazzling but powerful because he blurred the line between style and substance. How he told the story was part of the story itself. Consider his use of time. Before the 20th century, most novelists told linear, chronological tales that marched along from beginning, to middle to end. Following James Joyce's lead, Faulkner discarded this convention, often jumbling events, much as the human mind does not recall occurrences in precise order of time, but in a sequence determined by the emotional resonance of events, a prime example being Benjy's opening narrative in "The Sound and the Fury."

But this was not experimentation for its own sake. It fit into the novel's larger theme of the way time and history shape, trap, torture, bedevil and define us.

Though we can point to major themes in Faulkner's work—he valued nature over man-made things, thought the institution of marriage unnatural and believed the roles assigned to the genders were criminally limiting—the strength of his vision came from its mass of seeming contradictions. Find Faulkner staking out a position in one passage, and he is almost certain to confound it in the next.

In another writer, these inconsistencies might seem like weakness. They were Faulkner's greatest strength. Though he was intent on exposing the falseness and hypocrisy of Southern history/mythology, he refused to fall into the same trap of dogmatism and didacticism.

Instead, as in "Absalom, Absalom!," he told the tale of Thomas Sutpen through several, largely unreliable, narrators. Each has his own self-interest, his own version of what happened, and Faulkner never tells us what the real truth of the matter is. Instead he forces readers to do what his characters must: decide whom to trust about what, to piece together the story from disparate fragments of evidence, to create your own version of events. In doing so he forces readers to confront the very nature of storytelling and truth.

This approach has led some writers/critics, including Reynolds Price —who says Faulkner is a "great" but overrated novelist—to consider Faulkner a "willfully difficult writer." And yet it was at the very core of Faulkner's ethic of radical individualism: Just as he didn't want society to tell him who he should be, as a writer he resisted telling his readers what they should think.

In a telling comment to the Paris Review in 1956, Faulkner said: "I myself am too busy to care about the public. I have no time to wonder who is reading me. I don't care about John Doe's opinion of my own or anyone else's work. Mine is the standard which has to be met."

And so, not merely this week, but every day of the year, whenever his books are opened, the world celebrates that achievement. If there is a key beyond his sheer genius that explains Faulkner, it can be found in his Nobel Prize acceptance speech in 1950 in which he said that the thing alone that makes good writing is "the human heart in conflict with itself."

It also made a life.

Sept 21, 1997

Fellowship of Southern Writers
Seeks Future As Bright As Its Past

William Faulkner had been gone for a quarter-century when the brightest stars in Southern letters first convened to celebrate the joys of life and literature. Called the Fellowship of Southern Writers, they've met every two years since 1989 to kindle a sense of kinship and try to unravel the enigmatic question Faulkner posed in "Absalom, Absalom!":

> "Tell me about the South. What's it like there? What do they do there? Why do they live there? Why do they live at all?"

But the story of the South has never been just moonlight and magnolias, and the Fellowship, despite the festivity of its gatherings, has always been haunted by death. That fact is much on the mind of one of its founding members, Louis D. Rubin Jr.

In the cluttered study of his North Carolina home, Rubin, 83, describes the vintage photograph of literary giants who helped him start the fellowship. His voice fills with rueful playfulness as he moves across the bottom row:

> "Cleanth Brooks, he's dead. Blyden Jackson, he's dead. Elizabeth Spencer. Andrew Lytle, he's dead." Moving to the back row of standing figures, Rubin continues: "Lewis P. Simpson, he's dead. George Core, George Garrett. Fred Chappell. Shelby Foote, he's dead. C. Van Woodward, he's dead. Walter Sullivan, he's dead. Myself, going fast, and Sally Robinson."

Rubin, the author of more than 50 books and an editorial genius who helped launch the careers of Lee Smith, Clyde Edgerton, Kaye Gibbons,

Jill McCorkle and John Barth among others, is now focusing his boundless energies on ensuring that the Fellowship does not go the way of its founders.

"I believe the original reasons we had for starting this group, to recognize that there is a thing called Southern literature, to honor those who have defined it and to recognize those who are redefining its purpose and legacy every day, are still valid," he says. "To continue and expand those efforts, we have to get our house in order."

Throughout its history, the Fellowship has concentrated on three main tasks, starting with organizing its biennial conference at its home base in Chattanooga, Tenn. The group also awards eight prizes each year, mostly to younger writers who are placing their stamp on Southern poetry, drama and fiction. The other task is maintaining the elite membership, which is capped at 50. This has kept the all-volunteer group plenty busy.

"Writers live complicated lives," Rubin said with a laugh. "Most have teaching duties and their own work to attend to as well as the occasional divorce, health scare and other personal problems that seem to go with the territory."

But he's no longer satisfied with relying on the initiative of a few members. Last month, the Fellowship elected its first board of directors to help transform the group from one that bestows honors to an active outfit that spreads the good news about Southern literature. The board appointed the fellowship's first executive director, Susan Robinson, to coordinate and publicize the group's work.

"We want to raise the visibility of the awards and widen the net of recognition for good writing," said the novelist Richard Bausch, who is a member of the board. The 10-year plan seeks to ramp up the Fellowship's writers-in-schools efforts, launch a program of readings/conferences around the country, publish a newsletter about its activities and organize fund-raising campaigns to pay for it all.

While the Fellowship is responding to its own aims and concerns, its push reflects a larger movement among arts groups across the country. As funding sources have dried up and mainstream media outlets have curtailed coverage, many organizations have discovered the empowerment of self-reliance.

"There is a new type of aggressiveness on the part of arts organizations as they realize that if they don't market themselves, if they don't do outreach, no one will do it for them," said Felicia Knight, director of communications for the National Endowment for the Arts.

One example: For much of its 33-year history, the National Book Critics Circle, like the Fellowship, focused its efforts on awards. Four years ago, with newspaper space for reviews shrinking, it began sending members to book conferences, sponsoring literary panels and maintaining a Web site, Critical Mass, as a source for news and views about good writing. The result: Paid membership has more than doubled, to 716.

The NEA's Knight observed: "After years of despair, arts groups are taking up the challenge and telling the public why their work matters, why it's worth supporting."

FINDING A VOICE

The landscape of Southern literature is ever-changing, but Rubin says the forces that necessitated the Fellowship have not abated. For one thing, a narrow focus on Northeastern writers persists in New York's powerhouse book world.

"Last year, when the New York Times named the best novels of the last 25 years, they asked very few Southerners to vote, and consequently, very few works by Southerners made the list," he said. "We have tried to provide a forum, especially for young writers, so their work wouldn't be judged by people who thought everyday life in the South was freakish or unimportant."

Hillsborough, N.C. essayist Hal Crowther underscored this point in a phone interview: "About 10 years ago I asked this really well educated editor, a good friend, a New Yorker, 'Which Southern writers do you like?' He couldn't come up with anybody."

Such disregard helped fuel the Fellowship, which Rubin said was the brainchild of the literary critic Cleanth Brooks (1906–94), who had spent his life trumpeting the work of others.

"He talked about it for years, but I resisted it because I knew it was going to be a lot of work," said Rubin, who founded Algonquin Books in Chapel Hill. "After Cleanth's wife died, he brought it up again, and I figured it was the right thing to do."

Its logical home was one of the region's two main literary hubs, Vanderbilt University or UNC-Chapel Hill. Both were rejected, Rubin said, "because they were associated with particular groups of writers, and we didn't want to appear to be associated with any cult or writing center."

Impressed by the Southern Conference on Literature, organized by the Arts & Education Council of Tennessee, Rubin contacted the group. It leapt at the chance to host the Fellowship and establish a symbiotic relationship. Since 1989, the council has hosted the group at its biennial Southern Conference on Literature in Chattanooga. In turn, the Fellowship's literary firepower has added a major draw to the event.

The conference has enabled Southern writers to meet their readers and their heroes. Tar Heel novelist Clyde Edgerton remembers walking into a small room two decades ago when he was just starting out.

"There were Eudora Welty, Walker Percy and James Dickey," he said. "I just stood there looking at the backs of the heads of these people, my literary gods."

Doris Betts, the Chatham County writer, recalls eating breakfast with Mississippi writer Ellen Douglas. "I'd read her for years but had never met her," Betts said. "It was such a privilege to spend time with her."

Another board member, retired UNC-CH professor John Shelton Reed, remembers drinking bourbon with poet Andrew Lytle. So does Edgerton: "He loved talking about bourbon almost as much he loved drinking it."

Edgerton, who plays a mean banjo, also remembers the jam sessions with various artists/musicians, including Rubin on harmonica.

SENSE OF COMMUNITY

It's more accurate to say that the Fellowship tapped into, rather than created, a strong sense of community among Southern writers. But it is hard to overstate its role in maintaining that camaraderie.

At a time when the idea of the South, not to mention Southern literature, can seem archaic, when the arrival of newcomers and the rise of global economy are transforming traditional culture, the Fellowship's gatherings offer stark reminders of kinship.

"You get in the same room with all these folks, and you realize how much you have in common," Reed said. "There's no question that the humor is similar and different from what it is in the rest of the country. There are shared assumptions, things that go without saying, the joke ahead of the joke."

Edgerton adds: "The Fellowship meetings have become like a family reunion, where you run into people you don't see but once every two years but still feel close to them. You end up talking about history and names and funny family stories and food, always food, because that's what Southerners do."

The organization hopes to spread those feelings of regional identity and pride, that sense of fellowship its members feel with writers and readers across the South. Rubin believes its reorganization will allow it to better fulfill its core mission: to celebrate and encourage literary greatness.

"When we started the Fellowship of Southern Writers, we wanted to create a group that would outlive us all," Rubin said. "I do believe we are well on our way."

November 4, 2007

JUST THE FACTS?

NONFICTION REVIEWS

They Had Their Troubles;
We Have Ours

On July 4 we will gather once again to pay homage to our American gods. Not burgers, beer and fireworks, but Washington, Jefferson, Franklin and the other Founding Fathers.

We are a blessed nation. The Greeks had to consult mystic oracles to glean the teachings of Zeus, Apollo and Poseidon. Our Olympian ancestors left us clear instructions through their shimmering prose on politics, especially the Constitution. We ask, they answer:

- What is the proper status of women? Second-class citizens who should not vote.
- How should we treat African Americans? States should have the right to enslave them.
- Does the death penalty constitute cruel and unusual punishment? Not at all, neither does castration or a long spell in the pillory.

That can't be right—sounds more like a mullah than Madison. Yet that's just some of Founding Fatherly wisdom Richard Brookhiser details in his breezy new book, "What Would the Founders Do? Our Questions, Their Answers." Through dozens of short essays Brookhiser, a libertarian columnist who has written four previous books on the Founders, scours their writings to suggest how they might have handled today's pressing issues.

Here's a sample:

- Would they favor gay rights? (No.)
- Would they support stem-cell research? (They would have respected science but bowed to popular will.)

- How would they fight the war on drugs? (With taxes, not guns.)
- What would they think about partisanship? (They invented it.)
- Would they fight pre-emptive wars? (Only if another nation seemed poised to attack us.)
- Would they accuse one another of being chicken hawks? (They judged people by their Republican ideals, not their battlefield experience.)

Of course, the Founders weren't a choir; there was as much discord as harmony in the rooms their voices filled. They did not chisel their words into stone tablets but wrote instead on a magic mirror that reflects the words liberals, conservatives and Americans of other stripes want to see. Even socialists quote the Founders.

Brookhiser is a thoughtful writer, and he's no fool. He knows that today's airport book buyers—who have turned Founder tomes into a mansion industry—prefer the David McCullough treatment: gentle, respectful with just a whiff of idolatry.

Brookhiser delivers. As his smart, entertaining pages fly by, it's hard not to conclude that the Founders are the last people we should turn to for concrete answers to contemporary conundrums. Rather than confront this fact, and thereby diminish his saintly subjects, Brookhiser skips along, reverently invoking their anachronistic wisdom.

Yet how could they provide us with sound counsel, when their world was so different from our own? Brookhiser writes: "The founders lived in a small country—in 1776, America had about 2.5 million people. Philadelphia, the largest American city, had 35,000 people. . . . Americans were Protestant Christians. . . . In 1785, there were only 24,500 Catholics in the United States—less than 1 percent of the population. There was also a handful of Jews, less than one-tenth of one percent."

Most of the Founders could handle a gun and knew the back end of a plow—Franklin believed that schools should teach gardening, mechanics, drawing and swimming. They knew nothing of Marx, Freud, Einstein, Edison or Jobs.

Transported through time, most Founders would be mortified by the superpower they had midwifed. They were a conservative crew, extremely suspicious of corrupting power. They favored states' rights and a weak federal government. Most shared Washington's fears about foreign entanglements. When a group of Revolutionary War veterans wanted to start a nationwide club, "the plan caused intense alarm," Brookhiser writes. "American life was so local and scattered that there were no other private organizations that spanned the nation."

And yet, these wealthy conservatives were also wild-eyed revolutionaries who took to the barricades against their government. In his famous defense of popular uprisings, Jefferson wrote, "The tree of liberty must be refreshed from time to time with the blood of patriots and tyrants. It is its natural manure." Timothy McVeigh was wearing a tree of liberty T-shirt when he was arrested for the Oklahoma City bombing; it's hard to imagine that many other contemporary Americans share Jefferson's sentiment.

When Brookhiser asks "What Would the Founders Do?" the best answer is: "Who cares?"

As each year passes and our world diverges a little more from theirs, the Founders become less useful as history's answer to Dear Abby.

Though the sands of time often bury the past, they also wear away softer material that surrounds the hardest rocks, revealing that polished core. So it is with the Founders, whose legacy is not a set of timeless answers, but a shining example. Their noble schemes show us what we might dare to dream; their failures remind us that even the mighty stumble. Above all, these revolutionary men, who ushered democracy into the modern world, challenge us to confront our own problems and find our own solutions.

July 2, 2006

Quick, Fast, in a Hurry

Ambivalence seems so yesterday in our 24/7 world. Who has the time to be torn?

As the Dow soars and unemployment plummets, our sense of distraction, disquiet and discombobulation deepens. But who has time to think?

It is to James Gleick's credit that he tackles this paradox in "Faster."

Through 37 zippy chapters, the popular science writer and author of the bestseller "Chaos," shows how speed has overtaken, and largely overwhelmed, our lives: from the sound bites that constitute our news to quick-cut images that try to entertain our overstimulated minds, from fax machines, cell phones and e-mail to "instant coffee, instant intimacy, instant replay and instant gratification."

"We are in a rush," Gleick writes. "We are making haste. A compression of time characterizes the life of the century now closing. We live in the buzz. We wish to live intensely."

We race through yellow lights turning red, apply makeup while barreling down the interstate, lean on the elevator's "close door" button—as if that makes any difference—and feel a coronary coming on when that sweet computer operator tells us "your wait time will exceed . . . three minutes."

Slam.

I could go on detailing Gleick's documentation of this trend, just as I could provide exhaustive proof that the Earth is round. But life's too short. We don't need a book to tell us that hectored, hurried, frazzled and fried have become our reality as we dream of having just a little more time to . . . get more done.

Of greater interest are Gleick's thoughts on how we got here. He argues convincingly that the machines we have made have remade us. He notes that when the Lilliputians first saw Gulliver, they assumed his wristwatch was his God because "he seldom did anything without consulting it."

In the 19th century, Thoreau noted: "Have not men improved somewhat in punctuality since the railroad was invented? Do they not talk and think somewhat faster in the depot than they did in the stage office? There is something electrifying in the atmosphere of the former place."

Gleick then quotes a modern man who admits: "Ten years ago, I was delighted and enthralled that I could get a telegram-like e-mail from Philadelphia to London in only 15 minutes. Now I drum my fingers on the desk when a hundred-kilobyte file takes more than 20 seconds to arrive" from New Zealand.

How many overnight packages do we send because we feel they absolutely, positively have to be there?

But has technology made us quick and dead? Gleick expresses quali-fied ambivalence. He notes that attention deficit disorder has become the new order among Americans who are bored easily—where's that remote? Existing at warp speed, we crave what's new, hot and trendy. Movies, records and books now have the shelf life of, as Calvin Trillin put it, "somewhere between milk and yogurt."

At work, the desktop lunch is de rigueur. "At mid-century," Gleick writes, "a typical business would keep on a few over-the-hill workers in harmless nonjobs, would overlook an occasional late-afternoon card game in the office, would tolerate the routine two- or three-martini lunch. Not anymore. All these inefficiencies represented slack" to be economized away. We sleep 20 percent less than we did a century ago.

The result is a meaner, crabbier world. Yet, Gleick maintains, there is "a disparity between how we feel and how we act. Unless we are mas-ochists and lemmings, we must know something that we aren't telling ourselves. We like the E-mail. We like the connectedness. We do not seem interested in an about-face toward the simpler lives we recall with that rosy nostalgic glow."

Technology is a dream factory amping up the human machine. Phones allow us to hear people beyond shouting distance. But a life spent with disembodied voices is alienating. "We make choices. But we have a sense that our choosing is not entirely free."

Technological change is dictated by the imagination of scientists and entrepreneurs, not by popular votes to determine the kind of world we wish to inhabit.

Change has been so relentless this century that it is impossible to say whether our ambivalence stems from a fundamental disconnection from human scale: Is the world too fast and too full for the human mind? Can we square technology with contentment?

Or perhaps we have not had the time to adapt: Maybe we'll be happy someday.

In a world in which technological change is viewed as inexorable, do these questions really matter? Could we change society's high-tech direc-tion even if we wanted to? And, who has time to imagine how we might?

September 19, 1999

Our Machines, Our Selves

Americans greet every technological advance as if it had been delivered by the stork. We coo over each bundle of perfection, foreseeing only a brilliant future.

Then reality strikes. We recognize that along with all their blessings, these little darlings have transformed our lives in less beneficial ways. The airplane has delivered on its early promise of once-unimaginable mobility, but it is also a merciless engine of war. TV delivers important information, but it's also a colossal waste of time. Cars provide great freedom, but they have spawned a sprawling, disconnected nation with a crushing dependence on foreign oil.

So it is with the great innovation of our time, the Internet, whose birth and early childhood have been hailed in rapturous terms. Much of this praise is on target: It is a revolutionary tool that puts the world at our fingertips, giving voice to far-flung folks who do not own a printing press or movie studio.

But it's not all peaches and cream, as Lee Siegel argues in "Against the Machine: Being Human in the Age of the Electronic Mob." While recognizing the Internet's many splendors, the National Magazine Award-winning critic deploys a cold eye and sharp wit to illuminate the troubling ways that it is "reshaping our thoughts and ourselves, other people and the world around us."

Technology is not a one-way street. Like planes, cars and televisions, the Internet doesn't just cater to our needs, it also changes how we think and feel. It expands our capabilities but also messes with our minds and culture.

No technology works with a blank canvas; its impact is shaped by the pre-existing habits and desires of its users. Siegel persuasively argues that the Internet has intensified trends brewing at least since the 1960s: our rampant narcissism, the blurring lines between reality and fantasy, the free market's push to commodify human experiences, and the devaluation of expertise in a culture that conflates knowledge and opinion.

Siegel begins by noting how the Internet homogenizes human experience. In the past, shopping, writing letters, reading political commentary, watching TV and even procuring pornography were distinct acts. We had to get up and go to different places, see different people, use various parts of our brain to accomplish them. Now we can do all that and more seated before our monitors, seamlessly shifting from one activity to the next. "Everything," he writes, "taboo and familiar, occurs on the same screen."

Because things look the same, they tend to feel the same. We see pictures of our child's birthday party on the same screen as photos of Girls Gone Wild. Similarly, the line between truth, truthiness and outright falsehood blurs as authoritative reports in Scientific American or the Encyclopedia Britannica appear in the same context as the rantings of anonymous bloggers and the often-inaccurate entries on Wikipedia.

We can still exercise judgment, skepticism and discretion. But these skills are being eroded by the paradoxical nature of Web culture. Even as it flattens life, it trumpets the loudest, most outrageous utterances, allowing "the strongest assertions to edge out the most conscientious talent."

Siegel explores this techno-dumbing down by challenging the widespread belief that the Internet is solely a force of creative freedom. At times, it is. But it is also a powerful engine of conformity. Cyberspace is not ruled by the artist's credo articulated by the philosopher Baruch Spinoza "all things excellent are both difficult and rare." Quality still counts, but not as much as popularity, "which is the sole criterion" of cybersuccess. A novel or poem that few people read can still be hailed as a masterpiece. Like soda pop or packaged cookies, a blog posting or YouTube video rises or falls based on the number of views it receives.

This bottom-line mentality discourages people from developing their own ideas and identities. It prods them to find ways to please others, rather than to be themselves. This helps explain why precious little Internet content is truly illuminating. It is hard to challenge and enlighten people when your chief goal is to satisfy them in a world where "the greatest success is often the result of following conventions more diligently than anyone else."

Brilliantly, Siegel shows how this popularity imperative is transforming our very sense of self. Social networks such as MySpace and Match.com, he argues, are making us see ourselves, and sell ourselves, like products. In trying to cast ourselves in the best light, we end up sounding like everybody else. On the Web, everyone is an attractive, successful, fun-loving nonsmoker who enjoys movies and walks on the beach.

"Against the Machine" is a polemic in the best sense. At a time when the rare Internet critic is routinely dismissed as a Luddite who fears all change, Siegel's book raises profound and disturbing questions. Above all, it reminds us that technology is not just a tool, it's also a way of being.

June 23, 2008

How to Idle in the Fast Lane

> One by one . . .
> Take a nap!
> Have a smoke!
> Gaze at the stars!
> . . . they don't sound . . .
> Have sex!
> Drink tea!
> Go to the pub!
> . . . like revolutionary slogans.

But in Tom Hodgkinson's sly manifesto, "How to Be Idle" they become a stirring call to minds. Hodgkinson, the editor of the British magazine the Idler, advances a simple yet spot-on thesis: that our communities, businesses and governments want us to be good citizens, shoulders to the wheel, rather than satisfied human beings alive to simple, satisfying pleasures.

Drawing on sources as diverse as the Bible, the writings of Dr. Samuel Johnson, John Keats and Walt Whitman, and films such as "Ferris Bueller's Day Off," Hodgkinson reveals how the powers that be demonize and dismiss activities like thinking, dreaming and talking that don't serve the state but the soul. "As with all aspects of idleness," he writes, "we should resist the pressure to reject the elements of our lives which do not fit into the productive, rational, busy paradigm that society and our own selves impose upon us."

Hodgkinson makes his case in this wise and playful book, which opens up wondrous possibilities by questioning our basic assumptions. In 24 chapters, one for each hour of the day, he extols the virtues of "Smoking," "The First Drink of the Day" and "The Art of Conversation" while lamenting "The Death of Lunch" and "Toil and Trouble."

Hodgkinson reminds us how 19th century we still are. Back then the industrial revolution was transforming cottage industries into factories, providing employers with great wealth but less control over their swelling ranks of workers. While manufacturers controlled the workplace through regimentation and the clock's tick-tock, civil authorities and scolds used moral condemnation to rein in private lives, warning against Gluttony, Sloth, Fornication and other threats to the well-oiled machine. Today we laugh at that effort, without noticing how effectively our culture has recast those edicts.

Our Viagra culture, he writes, has caught up sex "in the striving ethic. It has become hard work; something we have to 'perform' at; a competitive sport." Starbucks has transformed the cafe—that traditional "loafing zone" of quiet reflection and spirited conversation—into "pit stops for working machines, petrol stations for human beings." "Patronizing self-help books," he writes, "regale us with various bullet-pointed strategies to become more productive, less drunk and more hard-working."

We pride ourselves on never taking a sick day and having lunch at our desks. We envy those who sleep only four hours a night. "Sleep," he writes, "is a powerful seducer, hence the terrifying machinery we have developed to fight it. I mean, the alarm clock. Heavens! What evil genius brought together those two enemies of the idle—clocks and alarms—into one unit? . . . The alarm clock is the first stage in the ungodly transformation we force ourselves to endure in the morning, from blissed-out, carefree dreamer to anxiety-ridden toiler, weighted by responsibility and duty."

"How to Be Idle," however, is no ode to slackerdom or laziness. As Robert Louis Stevenson wrote, "Idleness . . . does not consist in doing nothing, but in doing a great deal not recognized in the dogmatic formularies of the ruling class."

It bids us to take a nap when we are tired so that we might be more efficient while we're awake; to gaze at the stars so that we might contemplate our place in the universe and think more deeply about our lives and the world; to visit the pub or take a leisurely lunch so that we might engage in pleasant conversation with one another. Have a cup of tea at 4 because it "injects idleness into the working day. It provides a stop, a moment of calm." Take a casual walk each day so your mind can roam free. Don't snap-to at the alarm's ring, but lie awake in bed, mapping your day or just enjoying the pleasures of semi-consciousness.

"So much," Hodgkinson writes, "can be accomplished by doing nothing."

"How to Be Idle" is compelling because it suggests easy ways to remain human in a mechanized world. It does not ask us to throw over our cars and computers, or suggest that Walden Pond offers the only path to salvation. Even if, like me, you do not completely accept his Orwellian view of culture—if you believe that being a good, productive citizen can be healthy and satisfying—his central advice is compelling.

Stop. Look Around. Think. That's the pause that refreshes.

June 19, 2005

Our Children, Ourselves

Sometimes I look at my children and think, "You little ingrates, after all I've done, you're going to up and leave one day." On other occasions I add enough years to my youngest kid's age to get her to 18, apply the same number to my own total and fantasize about the wonderful new life that will begin when I'm, egad, 56!

According to the writer Jane Adams, my kids may be less ungrateful than I suspect and I may be a lot older than I imagine before my happy nest becomes an empty home. Her new book, "When Our Grown Kids Disappoint Us," argues that baby boomers have raised a generation of Evergreens firmly planted in their parents' back yard. For example:

- "Fifty-eight percent of 21- to 24-year-olds live at home or have boomeranged back in the last two years; for 25- to 34-year-olds, the figure is 34 percent."

- "Over half the parents of 21- to 32-year-olds contribute a quarter or more to the income of their grown children, in money, goods and services."
- "Independent adulthood is achieved five to seven years later by young adults than it was in 1960."

Adams, a Seattle journalist who has trained as a psychotherapist, cites studies suggesting that these Evergreens have root rot. She notes that people 21 to 32 are the biggest consumers of antidepressants, and that heroin and amphetamine use has quadrupled among young adults in the last five years. "Suicide, alcoholism, eating disorders and depression among young adults over 21 have tripled in the last two decades," she writes.

These findings are not surprising. When I told a group of mature women about Adams's book, they responded with nodding heads.

What is new, and alarming, is the radical advice Adams offers parents of struggling adults: Reject your nurturing instincts and start looking out for No. 1. Instead of offering tips on how to help struggling Evergreens thrive, Adams urges parents to seek "emotional detachment" so they can "take charge of their destinies." Her book's subtitle says it all: "Letting Go of Their Problems, Loving Them Anyway, and Getting on with Our Lives."

Adams's book is filled with anecdotes about folks whose grown children can't hold jobs, who have ended up on drugs or in prison, borne children out of wedlock or been married as often as Drew Barrymore. The reader feels for parents forced to put their lives and dreams on hold as they ceaselessly bail out their troubled progeny.

Adams admits that baby boomers share the blame. Where earlier generations hoped their kids would lead productive lives, she writes, boomers encouraged their children to consider themselves special, prodding them to seek the far trickier goal of personal fulfillment. This reinforced "the sense of entitlement believed by many to be at the root of our kids' problems."

Some of Adams's advice is sensible. "We cannot make our grown kids happy," she writes. "As long as we expect that we can, they will, too. And we will both be disappointed."

Unfortunately, Adams couches such suggestions in language that is chillingly narcissistic. Her book is not a genuine grappling with difficult circumstances, but a manifesto of radical selfishness. It is all well and good to applaud a mother who says, "It was either pay for his third rehab or my first face-lift. I decided it was time to do something for myself." What the author doesn't address is how this mother might feel if her son died of an overdose while her bandages were being removed.

For Adams, emotional detachment has only an upside: the opportunity for a generation "very used to the limelight" to devote their time, energy and financial resources to themselves. Parents may be overly involved in their adult children's lives, but viewing troubled progeny as a hurdle to be jumped and left behind is heartless and simplistic.

Adams's book is dangerous because it is so in sync with our times. During the past 50 years, the rise of radical individualism has frayed the bonds and responsibilities many Americans feel to their nation and their neighbors—the "bowling alone" phenomenon Robert D. Putnam and other scholars have detailed in the vast literature on the breakdown of community life. In this context, the family can be seen as the last great frontier of human connection to be severed in pursuit of "personal fulfillment."

Of course, many of life's deepest satisfactions are achieved with other people. In some respects, Adams's book can be seen as a healthy sign for suggesting that many parents are deeply engaged in their troubled children's lives, despite the emotional and financial costs. The danger is that "When Our Grown Children Disappoint Us" may signal the emergence of a new ethos that promises instant gratification but delivers a lifetime of loneliness.

July 13, 2003

Adventures in Literature's Gray Area

Jane Juska is a revolutionary. Her weapon of choice is not the Molotov cocktail but the personal ad. It goes like this:

"Before I turn 67—next March—I would like to have a lot of sex with a man I like. If you want to talk first, Trollope works for me."

Juska, a semiretired schoolteacher from Berkeley, Calif., received 63 responses to the ad, which she placed in the New York Review of Books—from men much older than she and from a few young enough to be her son. They gave her what she wanted and then some, as she explains in her wonderfully written, often graphic memoir, "A Round-Heeled Woman: My Late Life Adventures in Sex and Romance."

A cross between "Bridget Jones's Diary" and "Sex and the City" informed by seven decades of life experience, Juska's book is the vanguard of a literary revolution: Works by and about senior citizens moving forward, looking ahead.

Older people aren't newcomers to literature—the finest book I've read on late life is the Nobel Prize-winning author Knut Hamsun's memoir, "On Overgrown Paths" (1949). But older characters have tended to spend their time recalling their youths or coming to terms with their mortality. Now we are seeing the rise of books about sexto-, septo- and octogenarians who are seizing the here and now.

Philip Roth has allowed us to watch recurring characters such as Nathan Zuckerman ("American Pastoral") and David Kepesh ("The Dying Animal") go every way but gentle into their good nights while John Updike has produced several colorful books with gray protagonists, including "Toward the End of Time." In recent weeks Anita Brookner has published a novel about a 73-year-old man trying to find new meaning in his life, "Making Things Better"; Gail Godwin has written a heart-rending, semiautobiographical novel about a woman in her late 50s coming to grips with her husband's death, "Evenings at Five"; and Annette Sanford has penned a splendid story of a 69-year-old woman and a 70-year-old man who discover passionate, gently erotic love for the first time, "Eleanor & Abel."

Why are we seeing these books now? Certainly medicine has played a part, enabling more people to enjoy longer, healthier lives. As young people show less interest in books, older readers are becoming a vital market for publishers. Above all, we are witnessing the last great sea change of the 1960s.

On the highest plane, members of the "silent generation" and baby boomers who fought for gay rights, civil rights, women's lib and other causes that removed societal constraints are now battling the barriers imposed on the aged. On a lower plane, the most self-absorbed people in U.S. history are sticking by their narcissism till the bitter end—their favorite subject has been and always will be themselves. Americans who once vowed to never trust anyone over 30, who spent their lives fashioning a youth-obsessed culture, are refusing to act their age, with powerful results.

Jane Juska tracks this history in "A Round-Heeled Woman"—a vintage term for a loose gal. In alternating chapters she vividly details her recent encounters with sexually charged men and recounts her sexually repressed youth in Ohio. (Did I mention there is a lot of sex in this book?) Her mother called menstruation "the Curse," and Juska was embarrassed by her large breasts, which she usually covered in extra-large sweat shirts.

Nevertheless, she liked drinking and smoking and loved the touch, feel and look of men—especially their legs and buttocks. In 1955, fresh out of college, she had sex, got pregnant and married an unhappy alcoholic. They separated four years later. She bundled her kid in the car and began a new life in Berkeley.

The next 30 years involved little sex but plenty of alcohol and unhappiness. Finally, after years of therapy, she righted her ship and began to wonder: "What if I never have sex with a man again?"

Hence the ad in the New York Review, which led to a series of stimulating dalliances in person and on the phone with a series of, er, interesting men. They included "Danny the Priest, Jonah the Thief, Robert the Liar, Sidney the Peculiar and Graham the Younger," a 33-year-old Yale grad and aspiring novelist, who is "six feet, slim as a reed" and loves to discuss Kant's categorical imperative and quote "The Canterbury Tales" in perfect Middle English.

Juska is a smart, clever and provocative writer. "My heels are very round," she writes. "I'm an easy lay. An easy sixty-seven-year-old lay. 'Twas not always so. As these pages will show."

Clearly she is not your grandmother's grandmother. Instead, Juska is giving us a first hint of how a generation that redefined youth and middle age plans on gilding the golden years. As they take the wisdom of their poet laureate, Bob Dylan, to heart—"he not busy being born is busy dying"—senior moments of passion will become the norm, and not just between the covers of books. So long as my parents never read Juska's book, I say, hurrah.

May 18, 2003

Self-Service Happiness

The high-brow self-help book only sounds like an oxymoron. The inestimable Leo Tolstoy devoted his final years to fashioning the Chopraesque volume "A Calendar of Wisdom: Daily Thoughts to Nourish the Soul Written and Selected From the World's Sacred Texts."

The modern master of the form is the British writer Alain de Botton, whose works include "How Proust Can Change Your Life," "The Consolations of Philosophy" and the current best seller, "The Art of Travel." Like Tolstoy, de Botton taps the wisdom of the ages to enable us to become better travelers and, thereby, better people. Where more mainstream self-help writers channel long-dead Egyptian pharaohs, de Botton draws on the lives and writings of William Wordsworth and Gustave Flaubert, Vincent van Gogh, Edward Hopper and Charles Baudelaire.

De Botton's reliance on other people's ideas, which he describes in lucid, engaging prose, is wise. His own insights are so precious and banal—"Few seconds in life are more releasing than those in which a plane ascends to the sky" or "Journeys are the midwives of thought"— that an age-old question emerges: "If you're so well-read, why aren't you smarter?"

As de Botton plumbed the urge to travel and showed how to apply what we learn abroad at home, another question popped into my mind: "If self-help books really work, why are there so many of them?" On the surface it makes sense that if an author has truly unlocked the key to happiness and/or success (Message to America: They are not one and the same) then we should all read his book and be done with it. But, to paraphrase the Bard, the fault lies not with self-help books but with ourselves.

I, for one, felt like a changed man after reading "How Proust Can Change Your Life," which used the French writer's work to argue that we could extract more enjoyment from life by paying greater attention to it. For a few weeks, I was a stonecutter and humanity was my diamond. Each facet of word and deed sparked my curiosity. It was enthralling. Then, I guess, it became exhausting. I stopped paying close attention—a failing I only became aware of while reading "The Art of Travel," in which de Botton recycles his earlier argument.

Once again I was fired by his advice. De Botton argues that travel, like life, is made dull by passivity. Tourists dutifully visit the attractions highlighted by guide books, swallowing information such as "erected in 1608" and "a fine example of Baroque period" without allowing their curiosity to flourish. "Unfortunately," he writes, "most objects don't come affixed with the question that will generate the excitement they deserve."

To help us develop the art of active observation, de Botton quotes the philosopher Friedrich Nietzsche, who urged us to see magnificent buildings or works of art as anchors against lonely despair—"the happiness of knowing that [we are] not wholly accidental and arbitrary but grown out of the past as its heir, flower and fruit"—and as examples of sublime possibility. If our forebears created great things, why can't we?

William Wordsworth believed that pastoral retreats can refresh our city-weary souls. Don't just drink in beauty, the poet argued, but make its memory a sustaining well: "There are in our existence spots of time / That with distinct pre-eminence retain / A renovating virtue . . . / That penetrates, enables us to mount / When high, more high, and lifts us up when fallen."

De Botton says we can apply these lessons at home, becoming happier, more engaged people by remembering to think like artists. Painters such as van Gogh, he asserts, did not reimagine life but "enable[d] viewers to see certain aspects of the world more clearly." The English critic John Ruskin taught working people to draw because, de Botton writes, "If drawing had value even when practiced by those with no talent, it was, Ruskin believes, because it could teach us to see—that is, to notice rather than merely look. . . . In the process of re-creating with our own hands what lies before our eyes, we seem naturally to evolve from observing beauty in a loose way to possessing a deep understanding of its constituent parts and hence more secure memories of it."

Possessing zero talent for drawing, I find these ideas inspiring. I went so far as to think about purchasing a sketch pad. I recalled my spots of time with nature—I see two squirrels scampering up a tree in my back yard. I tried to remember Nietzsche's advice, but couldn't.

I did come to understand why so many people read so many self-help books. Just one won't do. Our natural state is an unimproved one. And nature is a tough mother, incessantly urging us to chill out, choose the path of least resistance, don't worry, be happy. How often do we correctly identify a problem, determine exactly what we should do to correct it, and then find ourselves unable to act?

Only through constant vigilance, and nudging, can we remember how we'd like to be. The historian Edmund S. Morgan makes this point in his new biography of America's greatest self-helper, "Benjamin Franklin": "Eventually his self-control became a great political asset, but by the time Franklin had entered politics it had become second nature to him, no longer something he had to keep reminding himself of in the maxims of Poor Richard."

Like the sayings of Poor Richard, "The Art of Travel" doesn't tell us anything we don't already know. Truth is not obscure, just hard to realize. In urging us to pay attention, de Botton reminds us that self-help is the easiest thing in the world, and the hardest.

September 1, 2002

A Feminist in Bold Relief

I thought I knew everything I wanted or needed to know about Andrea Dworkin. She was the foul-mouthed, fat feminist who favored overalls and supposedly claimed that sex between men and women is rape.

I opened her new memoir, "Heartbreak: The Political Memoir of a Feminist Militant," with a red marker in my hand and one question in my mind: How nutty can nutty be?

But Dworkin pulled a fast one. Instead of launching into a tirade against the follicly challenged half of humanity, she described her youthful love of classical music: Mozart, Czerny and Bach. Turns out the fire-breathing radical might have become a professional pianist if only she could have mastered Tchaikovsky's notoriously difficult Piano Concerto No. 1. "That failure," she writes, "told me that I could not be a musician."

Her tale of dashed hopes, of a young woman able to admit a hard truth to herself, captures the spirit of Dworkin's memoir. The woman who has been caricatured so cruelly—she has never asserted, for example, that heterosexual sex is rape—comes across as a confrontational and courageous person whose motto might be "to thine own self be true."

"Heartbreak" does contain strident attacks on the patriarchy. The bomb-throwing author of "Woman Hating" and "Pornography: Men Possessing Women" displays a gift for invective, a searing self-righteousness and a rare ability to hold grudges. She settles many old scores here, with everyone from Allen Ginsberg and the National Organization for Women to her ninth-grade English teacher. But above all she comes across as an admirable figure with rare commitment to speak the truth, as she sees it.

"Heartbreak" is also a portrait of a provocative mind formed by three powerful forces: her radical family, leftist literature and American history. Born in New Jersey in 1946, Dworkin was reared in a progressive home. Her mother "supported legal birth control and legal abortion long before these were respectable beliefs." Her father told her to read books with varying points of views because "sometimes writers lie." She continues: "My mother's real failure was in telling me not to lie. . . . Whether the issue was segregation or abortion, I, the sixth-grader, was going to deal with it, and my vehicle was going to be truth: not a global, self-deluded truth, not a truth that only I knew and that I wanted other people to follow, but the truth that came from not lying."

Dworkin devoured texts that challenged convention. She devoured the works of Marx, Freud, Eugene V. Debs and Norman Thomas. Holden Caulfield, from "The Catcher in the Rye," was her hero. This fiery young woman imbued with anti-authority ideology and a take-no-prisoners attitude found plenty to rail against as America segued from McCarythism to the bitter battles of the 1960s.

As a Jewish child, she refused to sing "Silent Night" with her classmates at Christmas. "I knew I wasn't a Christian and I didn't worship Jesus," she writes. "I even knew that Christians had made something of a habit of killing Jews, which sealed the deal for me."

When her teachers drilled students in hiding under their desks in case of nuclear attack, she felt that this was more about "saturation propaganda" aimed at instilling fear than mounting a defense. She challenged her teachers, then refused to submit, telling them, "I'd rather take a walk if I'm about to die now."

She disrupted a lecture on sex education by demanding—"I couldn't let it go, as usual"—that the speaker discuss contraception and abortion, which were still illegal in the United States.

"What I learned was simple and eventually evolved into my own pedagogy: listen to what adults refuse to say; find the answers they won't give; note the manipulative ways they have of using authority to cut the child or student or teenager off at the knees; notice their immoral, sneaky reliance on peer pressure to shut up a questioner."

During the 1960s, Dworkin fought segregation with the Black Panthers, housed Vietnam draft deserters in Sweden and worked for prisoner rights. In finely etched recollections, she describes the thoroughly traditional male values that informed most progressive movements. Equal rights, they seemed to believe, applied to only half the world.

Dworkin increasingly focused on the women's movement, especially the plight of battered and abused women who too often were forgotten by the mainstream women's movement. "The women I've met are very often first raped, then pimped inside their own families while they are still children. Their bodies have borders. Middle-class women, including middle-class feminists, cannot imagine such marginality. It's as if their story is too weird, too ugly, too unsightly for an educated woman to believe." Dworkin's impressionistic self-portrait provides few details of her controversial views on sex and the First Amendment (she is an ardent opponent of pornography). Unfamiliar with her arguments, I cannot say to what extent I would endorse or challenge them.

But "Heartbreak" has given me a deep respect for their author. Like the autobiography of the great labor leader Mother Jones, it is the story of a deeply committed human being willing to challenge injustice where she sees it. Like Benjamin Franklin's autobiography, it is as much the story of a singular life as it is a manifesto on how to be a good person. In our deeply conformist age, Dworkin provides a model of conscience in action that should inspire everyone of any stripe to look, to listen, to think.

Finally, she reminded me to resist the urge to stereotype and marginalize strong women.

March 10, 2002

A Poor Excuse for Compassion

Remember when impassioned muckrakers such as Jack London and George Orwell cast comfort aside and lived among the working classes to craft conscience-pricking exposes about the plight of the poor?

I don't. And neither does anyone else, considering the success of Barbara Ehrenreich's book "Nickel and Dimed: On (Not) Getting By in America." This dismal book, which chronicles a social critic's toe-dipping forays into the world of low-wage work, has become a national best seller while garnering admiring reviews. Liberal standard-bearers including Studs Terkel, Molly Ivins and the Nation magazine have offered particularly fulsome praise.

The response is as shocking as it is revealing of a certain strain of liberal thought. London ("People of the Abyss," 1902) and Orwell ("Down and Out in Paris and London," 1933) were fueled by courage, compassion and commitment. Ehrenreich seems driven by contempt—for the facts she uncovers, the hardworking people she is supposedly lionizing and just about everyone else she encounters. Instead of bringing us closer to the difficulties faced by the working poor, Ehrenreich's 12th book exposes the yawning divide separating poor people from many of the progressives who deign to speak for them.

"Nickel and Dimed" is disappointing because its premise is so promising. The great prosperity America has enjoyed since the Reagan years and the nation's simultaneous move to the right has made specters of the nation's poor. They have fallen off the radar of a culture obsessed with success. So, on the heels of President Clinton's welfare reform efforts, Ehrenreich set out to remind us of these invisible Americans.

Specifically, she wanted to see whether anybody could actually make it in America on $7 or $8 an hour. Between 1998 and 2000 she took a variety of low-paying jobs in three states: as a waitress in Florida, a rent-a-maid and a nursing home aide in Maine, and as a Wal-Mart clerk in Minnesota. Such "immersion journalism" succeeds when the reporter surrenders to her subject. Ehrenreich, evidently, couldn't be bothered. She spent little more than a month in each location. This is tantamount to visiting Paris, Rome and Madrid and then passing yourself off as an expert on Europe.

Ehrenreich's "helicopter journalism" dooms her project. It makes her own failed efforts to make ends meet unilluminating while preventing her from entering the lives of her co-workers. Her reporting is so thin that we never learn about the working poor's long-term survival strategies, the networks of family members and social agencies they rely on, the ingenious coping mechanisms they have devised. Her lack of curiosity about them is staggering. None are rendered as complex human beings. They are merely props in her immorality play.

Ehrenreich may be unwilling to live among or communicate with the poor, but she is eager to be their champion. Less a reporter than an ideologue, her brief sojourns become an excuse for railing against corporate America. She describes the modern workplace as a "dictatorship" and a "POW camp." She is particularly enraged by strategies employers use to control their workers, including pre-employment drug and personality tests, the rigid use of time clocks and the insistence that employees stay busy. "When you enter the low-wage workplace . . . you check your civil liberties at the door."

The circumstances she describes sound troubling. However, she never tries to reconcile her employers' posture with the conduct of some of her co-workers. Most of her colleagues seem diligent. But in her brief stints she encountered a co-worker who came to work drunk, a thieving dishwasher and a manager who raided the cash register to buy crack. Ehrenreich quit one job by walking away in the middle of a shift and another by simply failing to show up. It is impossible to draw larger lessons from these anecdotes, but they do suggest why some employers feel the need to corral their staff.

The most interesting sections of the book reveal her co-workers' lack of class consciousness. Most cling to the notion of a day's work for a day's pay. They do not resent the success of others. "It motivates me," a fellow maid explains. "It's my goal to get where they are." Rather than explore this mindset, Ehrenreich dismisses it as the brainwashed mindset of deluded chumps.

Her book is also marred by gross generalizations that border on bigotry. She tells us "visible Christians" are the worst tippers. She describes the owner of the rent-a-maid outfit she works for—whom the other employees seem to like—as a "pimp." Working at Wal-Mart, she says, "I even start hating the customers for extraneous reasons, such as, in the case of native Caucasians, their size. I don't mean just their bellies and butts, but huge bulges in completely exotic locations, like the backs of the necks and the knees."

"Nickel and Dimed" is a betrayal of the people and ideals it pretends to champion. Liberalism's power stems not so much from the defensible political positions Ehrenreich espouses—increased unionization and a higher minimum wage—but from a liberal spirit toward our fellow citizens. Righteous anger is most useful when it is a tool of compassion. You don't have to be of the people to be for people, but you must care about them as people. In "Nickel and Dimed" Barbara Ehrenreich seems more attracted to the idea of the working poor than their reality.

June 24, 2001

Thinking Outside the Penalty Box

I never really thought about the death penalty until I started reading about it. Although most Americans say they support capital punishment, the vast majority of books and articles on the subject are written by its opponents: indignant true believers who dismiss their fellow countrymen as vengeful Neanderthals. Books such as "Who Owns Death?" by Robert Jay Lifton and Greg Mitchell, "Proximity to Death" by William S. McFeely and "A Handbook on Hanging" by Charles Duff constitute a literature of contempt. The authors' passion is admirable and understandable, but their moral conviction is so fierce that it renders them incapable of accepting that good people can have good reasons for supporting a practice as old as civilization.

The result, too often, is foaming condemnation in which highly charged terms such as "barbarism" "blood lust" and "blind retribution" stand for reasoned discourse. For example, in "Proximity to Death," McFeely notes that the death penalty has been abolished in every developed nation except the United States. Scornfully, he asks: "Why has the United States, with its claims of moral leadership, gone precisely in the opposite direction? Why are we Americans so enamored of the death penalty? Shouldn't it have gone the way of witch trials and slavery?"

They are powerful sentences, filled with conviction. But as a Pulitzer Prize-winning historian, McFeely must recognize the naked weakness of his analogy: The victims of witch trials and slavery were innocents; most targets of capital punishment victimize the innocent.

Every inmate on death row has been found guilty of a heinous crime. We don't execute people for stealing bread—we impose the ultimate penalty on a tiny percentage of our worst offenders. Timothy McVeigh, for example, is awaiting execution because he blew up 168 strangers in Oklahoma City.

Death penalty opponents often argue that taking the life of people like McVeigh degrades us all, makes us no better than the criminals we punish. But this is a matter of opinion, perception and faith—as is the proposition that "life is sacred," another splendid notion with little appeal in a nation that supports legalized abortion and enjoys sports such as NASCAR that inevitably take lives. Its proponents offer no more evidence to support this conclusion than their adversaries can for the equally spurious idea that the death penalty deters crime.

History makes a far more compelling case that Americans embrace capital punishment because we are a violent nation than vice-versa. And, while I can appreciate the real difference between executing prisoners and locking them in cages until they expire, I don't see how either option edifies us.

But now, some death penalty opponents, recognizing the ineffectiveness of their moral arguments, are taking a new tack. Austin Sarat, a teacher at Amherst College and author of "When the State Kills: Capital Punishment and the American Condition," recently advised his fellow "abolitionists" not to try to derail McVeigh's desire to have his sentence carried out.

"Even if that battle could be won," Sarat wrote in the Los Angeles Times, "it would come at the cost of associating the campaign against the death penalty with one of America's most heinous killers. Though it might be right to help McVeigh if he wished to live, it is also true that concentrating efforts on the case of one famous criminal would divert attention from the daily realities of capital punishment."

In essence, Sarat is saying let's tone it down, stop preaching to the converted and start looking for new ways to change our opponents' minds. By focusing on the contradictions, inequalities and injustices inherent not in the idea of capital punishment but in its application, they believe they can win converts.

Their three main arguments are: The death penalty is ineffective because is does not deter crime. It is unfair because it is disproportionately imposed on African Americans and other minorities. It is nonsensical because it represents too final a judgment in a fallible world.

Jim Dwyer, Barry Scheck and Peter Neufeld took this approach with powerful results in their book "Actual Innocence." Drawing from 67 cases in which convicted felons (not all of them on death row) were exonerated, they showed how racism, often-faulty procedures and the tendency of some prosecutors to seek convictions rather than justice should make us all wary of irrevocable sentences.

Books like "Actual Innocence" have made me re-examine my support for the death penalty because they forced me to think about the issue. I'm still not convinced that capital punishment is morally indefensible, but my immersion in the subject has helped me to see that it is a deeply problematic practice that offers society no real advantages.

This final point was brought home in the conclusion of Robert Jay Lifton and Greg Mitchell's "Who Owns Death?" The authors cite polls showing that majorities in France and England favored capital punishment when the practice was abolished. Their governments' unpopular" acts brought not a hue, cry or whimper. At day's end, the people didn't really care whether their monsters were removed from society through execution or life imprisonment.

My guess is that most Americans would respond in the same way. And if we are not willing to fight for the death penalty, why should we oppose its abolition?

March 25, 2001

The Heartbreak Behind the Buzz

Dave Eggers's memoir, "A Heartbreaking Work of Staggering Genius" is so of the moment that it is hard not to read deep significance into it.

For starters, the author is 29, a Gen-Xer, a member of the wired posse seizing the reins of our youth-obsessed culture.

And Eggers talks the walk. He has founded two surpassingly hip and influential magazines, Might, and McSweeney's Quarterly Concern, which he runs from his Brooklyn brownstone. His writing is smart, ironic, self-conscious and very funny, *au courant* to the max.

Finally, in this tell-all age, Eggers describes a life full of sadness and dysfunction. His father was a distant, alcoholic lawyer; his beloved mother was prone to violence. When he was 21, both his parents died of cancer within 32 days of each other. Though aided by his older siblings, Eggers became the prime guardian for his 8-year-old brother, Toph. Characteristically, the author acknowledges that he is "not the only person ever to lose his parents and inherit a youngster. But . . . he is currently the only such person with a book contract."

It is not surprising that "A Heartbreaking Work of Staggering Genius" is the book of the moment. Maybe you've heard Eggers on "Charlie Rose" or National Public Radio's "Fresh Air." His book is a bestseller whose reviews, most glowing, some deliciously snarky, have been marked by a rare, passionate intensity.

I join the chorus: Dave Eggers has written a superb memoir. But his book is not a manifesto. Though told in the hip voice of his generation, the work soars because it is, simply and tremendously, an honest and moving account of one man's life. In the process, he reminds that while the language and style of literature are always changing, it is forever about coming to terms with the timeless conflicts of the human heart.

The book's key passage is its title. "A Heartbreaking Work of Staggering Genius." It couldn't be more ironic. The schmaltzy hyperbole tells the reader: Don't take this too seriously. Open the book and Eggers starts pushing you away. Like a scientist detailing the actions of tear ducts to explain a person beside himself with grief, Eggers defuses his story's rich emotional content through 32 pages of introductory material that outlines the book's main themes—e.g. "the part where the author either exploits or exults his parents, depending on your point of view"—and provides "An Incomplete Guide to Symbols and Metaphors."

And yet, the title couldn't be more sincere. As he confesses his grandiose plans for himself and his magazines—"[we] are taking a formless and mute mass of human potential and are attempting to make it speak, sing, scream, to mold it into a political force . . . All we really want is for no one to have a boring life"—the reader has no doubt that Eggers believes himself a staggering genius.

The tale of his cursed life—which also details the death of one friend, the suicidal tendencies of another, the freak accident that renders a third comatose and the way these tragedies have made fear, anger and guilt Eggers's constant companions—is indeed heartbreaking.

Stunningly, he transforms postmodern irony, the studied detachment that insulates people from commitment and feeling, into a pathway toward sincere emotion. In a section dealing with his concerns about his parenting skills, Eggers writes, "I feel horrible and guilty much of the time." He quickly adds, "Because I do not make him [Toph] breakfast and drive him to school, he will grow up to skin rabbits and re-create with crossbows and paint guns."

Eggers peppers every wrenching scene with disarming humor; just when you expect soul-searching, he cracks a joke. In the best comic tradition, he makes us laugh to keep away his own tears. His deflection is aimed not at us, but himself. As Eggers reveals himself, we see a man still trying to come to grips with his life and his feelings. As he shows us that irony, self-mockery and wit are the clever mechanisms he uses to avoid a complete surrender to despair, his distancing appears unutterably poignant.

"A Heartbreaking Work of Staggering Genius" is not about redemption but struggle. The writer addresses this directly toward the book's end when he agonizes about revealing the secrets of family and friends in order to deal with his pain. He likens himself to a Nazi and a cannibal, "Look at what I'm doing, with my tape recorder and notebook . . . calculating, manipulative, cold, exploitive."

Dave Eggers is all of those things, and none of them. Like all of us, he uses his life and imagination to make sense of the world. Like the very best writers, he does not try to manufacture cheap answers. We never learn how Eggers overcame this guilt of exposure. And, we believe this is because he hasn't, either.

March 12, 2000

Ink-Stained History

Fifteen years ago, enraptured by the glistening prose of Russell Baker and the tenacious truth-telling of Woodward and Bernstein, I became a journalist. I thought it was a noble profession.

We didn't just report the news, we made it through a vitally nebulous process called editorial judgment. Mixing hard facts and supple imaginations, we sifted the current conversation to edify the national dialogue. We identified the issues people ought to care about and used lively, engaging storytelling to make them care.

Sure, that vision sounds arrogant and elitist, but it doesn't discredit my claim. Ask most Americans why Paula Jones, Monica Lewinsky and the state of the Clintons' marriage have dominated our news, and they'll blame the national media's obsession with scandal. "They won't shut up about it," is the common refrain.

Unfortunately, that proof of the press' power also exposes my initial impulse as rose-colored and naively romantic. The proud citadel of my mind's-eye now seems more like an asylum run by barbarians from the hostile regions of Tabloidiana, Cablevania and Internetia.

Stuck in a nasty paradigm shift, I asked: What is journalism? What do we journalists do?

As I read and thought on the matter, I realized that the mindless, salacious puffery that now dominates the national media is not a corruption, aberration or mutation. It is business as usual, albeit in extremis.

Journalism has always been sublime and rambunctious, a hydra-headed beauty and beast. On the one hand, New York University's recent list of the 20th century's best American journalism will convince you that reportage is popular art with teeth: Ernie Pyle's poetic dispatches from the front lines of World War II; Ida Tarbell's muckraking classic, "The History of the Standard Oil Company" (1902–04); Edward R. Murrow's and Fred Friendly's televised investigation of Sen. Joseph McCarthy (1954); and Pauline Kael's seminal work of cinematic criticism, "Trash, Art, and the Movies" (1969).

Yet, it is equally true that the seamy, the tawdry, the impolitic and the impolite have long been our bread and butter. Patricia Cline Cohen's "The Murder of Helen Jewett" describes how Jacksonian America became obsessed with the trial of a 19th-century yuppie accused of murdering a fetching prostitute. In his absorbing new memoir, "The Times of My Life and My Life with the Times," Max Frankel, the former executive editor of the New York Times, explains that the journalistic creed of "objectivity" is a relatively new ideal, born out of "a reaction against the fevered fulminations of partisan editor-owners like Horace Greeley, James Gordon Bennett, William Randolph Hearst and Joseph Pulitzer."

Journalism has always been a balancing act between the tabloid and the tutu, covering the stories that rubbernecking humanity is naturally drawn to—sex, fluff, mayhem, more sex—with thoughtful renderings of gnarly issues. Its tradition is embodied as much by Liz Smith as Mary McGrory.

Plenty of tough-minded work is being done these days, but the age-old seesaw has most certainly teetered Liz's way. Paradoxically, this recent dip has come about because of lofty intentions.

A legacy of the 1960s was the breaking down of the wall between the public and private. From sexual mores to the relevant private conduct of public figures, formerly shrouded issues were suddenly on the table. As Frankel notes, the news business widened its palette beyond "the Congress yesterday" to include more of life's colors. Social issues once scoffed at as "soft" news—changing hemlines, family issues, stories about what we are eating and what we're buying—took their proper place on page one.

Exactly when this healthy interest in personal issues transmogrified into our sickening obsession with private lives is impossible to pinpoint. But the advent of 24-hour cable news channels, the sale of innumerable news organizations to massive corporations whose closest brush with idealism is the worship of profits, and the effort by newspapers to stanch declining circulation by becoming more "reader-friendly" have exacerbated the trend.

But at heart, it is a failure of the imagination. We tell the easy stories because they are easier to tell. Getting spun by one side and then the other—becoming a fax machine for the establishment—is cheaper, safer and simpler than illuminating opaque policies and untangling serpentine boondoggles. The most egregious hack can titillate a flea with rumored peccadilloes, but it takes time, effort and talent to make overstimulated readers care about defense spending.

What journalists—and readers—need is more uninformed nostalgia, more rose-colored glasses and more romantic yearning.

The soaring work of Murrow, Pyle and Tarbell may be the exception, but they should rule our expectations. For good, or ill, we frame, as Frankel put it, "the intellectual and emotional agenda of serious Americans." This is a great gift, and an even greater responsibility.

March 21, 1999

Crunching Numbers, Finding Us

Crime was out of control during the early 1990s. As the crack boom raged, experts warned of "blood baths" fueled by "superpredators" beyond the reach of law or reason.

Then, without warning, the crime rate began to plummet. The same prophets who had been blowing dark smoke rushed to explain this fortunate turn. Some of their analysis was spot-on, noting the benefits of more cops on the streets, longer sentences for criminals and changes in crack-dealer culture. But, according to Steven D. Levitt, a prize-winning economist at the University of Chicago, they ignored the single greatest cause of the drop in crime: legalized abortion.

In his captivating though flawed new book, "Freakonomics," Levitt observes that the Supreme Court's 1973 decision in Roe v. Wade led to an upsurge in abortions. About 750,000 such procedures were performed in the year after the ruling. That number climbed to about 1.6 million abortions a year, where it leveled off.

Levitt and his co-writer, the journalist Stephen J. Dubner, note that wealthier women always had access to abortions. The prime beneficiaries of Roe were poorer, less-educated women, who, statistics show, are more likely to have children who turn to crime. Legalized abortion dramatically reduced the numbers of such offspring, who would have hit their late teens, their prime crime years, during the 1990s.

Levitt caps his argument with three persuasive pieces of evidence: First, the crime wave initially declined in the four states that had legalized abortion a few years before Roe: Alaska, Hawaii, Washington and New York. Second, states with the highest abortion rates enjoyed the sharpest drops in crime. Third, studies in Australia and Canada have found a similar link between abortion and crime.

The unexpected consequence of Roe is the one truly stunning piece of analysis Levitt offers in this vastly entertaining book, which challenges the notion that "figures lie, and liars figure" by scrutinizing raw data to yield insight into human nature.

Levitt has a supple, playful mind. This enables him to ask unexpected question: Does Christmas make "honest" people turn to crime? (Yes.) Can bald men achieve more success in the online dating scene than rich and handsome fellas? (Yes, when they post a photo and the other guys don't.) Does money determine the outcome of American elections? (No.)

Answering these and other questions, Levitt digs up plenty of interesting trivia: Cheating is rampant among Japanese sumo wrestlers, many crack dealers live with their mothers, the Ku Klux Klan invented a "secret" language by affixing "Kl" to many words (they'd hold "klonversations" in the local "klavern"—how clever!).

"Freakonomics" is part of a wave of semi-intellectual books that have sprung up on the best-seller list in recent years. Like Malcolm Gladwell's hugely successful works, "The Tipping Point" and "Blink," Levitt's book dazzles at first with its promise of secret knowledge. Page by page, you think, Aha!

Yet, like Gladwell's books, "Freakonomics" pales upon reflection; the more you think about it, the less satisfying it is (except for the chapter on Roe). The book's major flaw is hubris. Levitt and Dubner position their work as an assault on lazy thinking. "The conventional wisdom," they proclaim, "is often wrong."

"Freakonomics," however, suggests the opposite. Much of its analysis is fascinating . . . and unsurprising. Are you shocked to learn that real-estate agents squeeze out more money for their own houses than they do for their clients'? Is it hard to believe that bottom-level crack dealers don't make much money? Or that swimming pools claim far more children's lives than guns? Or that 90 percent of white men and 97 percent of white women who said race didn't matter to them in their online dating profiles sent e-mails to white people?

Consider his long chapter on parenting. Combing mounds of data, Levitt reports that many factors assumed to affect children's school performance have little impact. These include the amount of TV they watch, whether their families are intact, whether a parent stayed home with them until kindergarten or whether they were read to every day. His message to parents—what you do makes little difference—seems revolutionary. Until, that is, you read its corollary—who you are makes all the difference. That is, children with wealthy, highly educated, intellectually curious parents tend to do better in school than kids whose parents do not possess those qualities.

Surprise!

Of course, there is a big difference between thinking something is true and knowing it is. The wonder of "Freakonomics" is not that it upends conventional wisdom but that it supports it. It's a fast-paced engaging work that unintentionally carries a welcome message: You're smarter than you think.

May 22, 2005

Paradox and Poetry of Chernobyl

'What's it like, radiation? Maybe they show it in the movies? Have you seen it? Is it white, or what? What color is it? . . . If it's colorless, then it's like God. God is everywhere, but you can't see Him."—Anna Petrovna Badaeva, resettler

"We didn't understand then that the peaceful atom could kill, that man is helpless before the laws of physics."—Nadezhda Petrovna Vygovskaya, evacuee.

Here are the facts: At 1:23 a.m. on Saturday, April 26, 1986, a series of human and mechanical errors caused thunderous explosions in the Soviet nuclear power plant at Chernobyl. As the reactor's core smoldered for nine days, it released radioactive fallout about 350 times greater than that from the bomb dropped on Hiroshima. So far, 56 fatalities have been attributed to the disaster. About 2.1 million people still live on land contaminated by the accident.

But dates and death tolls do not begin to suggest the disaster's enormity, how it cut the lives of millions into two distinct periods: before and after Chernobyl.

"There you are: a normal person. A little person. You're just like everyone else. . . . And then one day you're suddenly turned into a Chernobyl person. Into an animal, something that everyone's interested in, and that no one knows anything about."—Nikolai Fomich Kalugin, evacuee

"I got home, I'd go dancing. I'd meet a girl I liked and say, 'Let's get to know one another.' 'What for? You're a Chernobylite now. I'd be scared to have your kids.'"—Viktor Sanko, soldier

The gifted Russian journalist Svetlana Alexievich documents the disaster's human fallout in her superlative book, "Voice from Chernobyl: The Oral History of a Nuclear Disaster" (translated from the Russian by

Keith Gessen). In 1996, she interviewed hundreds of people transformed by the meltdown: the firefighters and soldiers sent to quell the reactor; the "liquidators" who shoveled away contaminated topsoil and killed diseased animals; the men, women and children whose genes and minds were scarred forever by the radioactive elements such as cesium that filled the air they breathed and the food they ate.

"We see a woman on a bench near her house, breastfeeding her child—her milk has cesium in it—she's the Chernobyl Madonna."—Marat Filippovich Kokhanov, nuclear engineer

"Even if it's poisoned with radiation, it's still my home. There's no place else they need us."—Unidentified resident

A gifted writer, Alexievich turned her interviews into intimate and powerful monologues. Most are short, a paragraph or two, that, like the very best literature, relate worlds of experience in an image or phrase.

"My daughter was six years old. I'm putting her to bed, and she whispers in my ear: 'Daddy, I want to live, I'm still little.'"—Nikolai Fomich Kalugin, father

"We came home. I took off all the clothes that I'd worn there and threw them down the trash chute. I gave my cap to my little son. He really wanted it. And he wore it all the time. Two years later they gave him a diagnosis: a tumor in his brain."—Valentin Kmkov, soldier

The longer monologues that open and close the book, narrated by women who watched their husbands' bodies slowly eaten away by radiation poisoning, read like the finely observed work of Anton Chekhov.

"The person I loved more than anything, loved him so much I couldn't possibly have loved him more if I'd given birth to him myself—turned—before my eyes—into a monster. . . . Something black grew on him. His chin went somewhere, his neck disappeared, his tongue fell out. . . . He wrote in his notebook in large letters with three exclamation points: 'Bring the mirror!!!' . . . I brought him the mirror, the smallest one . . . pleading with him, 'As soon as you get a little better, we'll go off to a village together, an abandoned village. We'll buy a house and we'll live there . . . We'll live by ourselves.'"— Valentina Timofeevna Panasevich, wife of a liquidator

Alexievich does not provide a comprehensive history of the disaster, no tick-tock of doom or quotes from political leaders or historians. Yet her book tells us far more about "what happened" than timelines and learned analysis ever could. We like simple measures of our disasters—number killed, people displaced, reductions in productivity. Alexievich reminds us that the true impact is revealed through specific effects on myriad individuals.

Like poetry, "Voices from Chernobyl," is so rich, it's best read in small doses. Each monologue encompasses its own tragedy—its own universe—that readers can inhabit upon reflection. It lets us enter its subjects, suffusing us with a range of thoughts and emotions that comes together as the often paradoxical wisdom of experience.

"Death is the fairest thing in the world. No one's ever gotten out of it. The earth takes everyone—the kind, the cruel, the sinners. Aside from that, there's no fairness on earth."—Zinaida Yevdokimovna Kovalenko, resettler

"We played soccer. We went swimming. Ha. We believed in fate, at bottom we're all fatalists, not pharmacists."—Alexsandr Kudryagin, liquidator

January 15, 2006

Only an Empty Memory?

The second greatest crime of the 20th century is the way we remember the Holocaust, how we have turned a symbol of human degradation into a feel-good cause for optimism.

Every year millions of people visit the Holocaust Memorial Museum in Washington, donning its gift shop buttons that promise "Remember" and "Never Again," while touring the place President Clinton called "an investment in a secure future against whatever insanity lurks ahead."

And yet, as the New Yorker staff writer Philip Gourevitch reminds us in his powerful new book, "We Wish to Inform You That Tomorrow We Will Be Killed With Our Families," a year after the museum was opened in 1993, the United States and the rest of the world stood by as Rwanda's Hutus perpetrated a genocidal war upon the nation's minority ethnic group, the Tutsis.

The slaughter erupted on April 6, 1994, when the African nation's president, a Hutu, was assassinated—probably, Gourevitch writes, by extremists in his own entourage.

Under the rallying cry, "Do your work," the Hutus murdered 75 percent of Rwanda's Tutsis within a month. "Take the best estimate: eight hundred thousand killed in a hundred days," Gourevitch writes. "That's three hundred thirty-three and a third murders an hour—or five and a half lives terminated every minute. Consider also that most of these killings actually occurred in the first three or four weeks, and add to the death toll the uncounted legions who were maimed but did not die of their wounds, and the systematic and serial rape of Tutsi women."

Most fell from the blows of spiked machetes. But, as a survivor told Gourevitch, " 'One hopes not to die cruelly. Not death by machete, one hopes, but with a bullet. If you were willing to pay for it, you could often ask for a bullet.'"

Though Daniel Goldhagen's 1996 book, "Hitler's Willing Executioners" stirred angry debate by arguing that most Germans were complicit in the Holocaust, there is no dispute that the vast majority of Rwandan Hutus were directly involved in the slaughter. "These dead and their killers had been neighbors, schoolmates, colleagues, sometimes friends, even in-laws. . . . Neighbors hacked neighbors to death in their homes, and colleagues hacked colleagues to death in their workplaces. Doctors killed their patients, and schoolteachers killed their pupils."

Gourevitch traces the genocide to the racial caste system enforced by Germany and then Belgium when they held Rwanda as a colony. They anointed the minority Tutsis—whose features they considered "nobler" and more "aristocratic" than the "bestial" Hutus—as their puppet leaders. When independence came in 1961, the Hutus took control. In this poor and corrupt land, they perversely used violence against the Tutsis—in 1959, '61, '63 and so on through '94—to forge a fragile and fleeting unity that could only be maintained by another round of terror. "Killing Tutsis was a political tradition in postcolonial Rwanda; it brought people together."

Though the causes of this genocide are specific to Rwanda's history, the world's reaction, we might hope, would have echoed the universal pledges, "Remember," and "Never Again." Heartbreakingly, Gourevitch reports, the United Nations commander in Rwanda said he could stop the bloodshed with "5,000 well-equipped soldiers and a free hand." Instead, he got the cold shoulder. "The desertion of Rwanda by the UN force," Gourevitch writes, " . . . can be credited almost single-handedly to the United States," which was wary of UN peacekeeping missions after suffering televised casualties in Somalia.

Meanwhile, the pro-Hutu French forces who were dispatched "supported and preserved the same local political leaders who had presided over the genocide permit[ting] the slaughter of Tutsis to continue for an extra month."

Indignation is the natural—and necessary—reaction to Gourevitch's book; to abandon our revulsion is to abandon hope. And yet, the false comfort our emotion provides should not blind us to the darker truths that Rwanda (and Cambodia and Bosnia) reveal about how we have responded to genocide since the Holocaust.

I can think of no better distillation of this wrenching abyss between our empty resolve and deadly inaction than the two quotes from Holocaust survivor Primo Levi which Gourevitch uses as epigraphs.

In 1958, Levi wrote: "If there is one thing sure in this world, it is certainly this: that it will not happen to us a second time."

But by 1986 Levi had realized: "It happened, therefore it can happen again: this is the core of what we have to say. It can happen, and it can happen everywhere."

What Gourevitch—and Rwanda—show us is that memory only has meaning as a prelude to action.

September 27, 1998

TAKING COVER

THE ASSAULT ON THE BOOK BUSINESS

A Room with a Low Ceiling

Peck. Peck. Peck. Our tweedy Chicken Littles squawk: Literature is falling (and it can't get up). They say the only thing declining faster than the quality of serious literature is its audience. Peck.

Technology is creating a warp-speed world that is anathema to reading's leisurely pace. Peck.

Literature is too demanding to compete with TV, movies, the Internet and other easy diversions. Peck.

The situation can appear so dire that America's most prestigious book section, the New York Times Book Review, recently ran an essay titled, "Remember When Books Mattered?" In it, hotshot critic Walter Kirn offered a Boschian vision of modern literature through a critique of contemporary book reviewing.

The "truth about reviewing," Kirn writes, is what he calls "Oswald's law: No one who has any stake in the issue will ever believe that a negative review was the work of a lone gunman. No, there must be a plot. A web of evil. Those who think of themselves as publishing 'insiders'— agents, editors, authors' spouses . . . hold especially to this notion. . . . According to the insiders, if a critic went to extremes in a review, something besides the prose must have provoked him."

Negative reviews arouse suspicion, Kirn argues, because they are so rare. In our literary snake pit, harsh opinions are seen as vendettas; reviewers hold their tongues for fear of retribution. They "subdue all passion, don gloves and a muzzle and fill [their] mouths with pebbles" because no idea is worth risking one's career over. Their lifeless, "forgettable" reviews tell readers that books are lifeless and forgettable. "No wonder," Kirn writes, that the public has "given up" on "serious literature."

No wonder the question on most people's lips is not "what do you think of Don DeLillo's latest?" but "Is 'Survivor II' on tonight?"

The Chicken Little inside us urges Kirn on.

I say grab his beak and squeeze TIGHT.

Yes, contemporary reviewing is flawed. But a fairer conclusion is that it always has been and always will be. Read "Books of the Century," an anthology of 20th-century reviews from the Times, and you'll probably agree that the writing and thinking have improved over time.

Instead of surveying this history, Kirn opts for languid nostalgia. The "remember when" part of his essay is based on a long-ago moment when Norman Mailer and Gore Vidal almost came to blows. This is his proof that once upon a time the literary set cared only about ideas, that their smallest concern was truth itself.

This is nonsense. Ambition and careerism, cowardice and compromise, are fat dull threads on history's loom. That's a hard truth, but *c'est la vie*. Kirn shrinks from this. Like all Chicken Littles, his pessimism is informed by a paradoxical optimism: The suggestion that there was once a Golden Age when our better angels ruled gives oomph to the damnation while making redemption seem possible. (Thirty years from now, the critic who will inevitably reiterate Kirn's essay will surely point to the ongoing feud between Tom Wolfe and three titans who panned his last novel—John Updike, John Irving and Norman Mailer (of course)—to upbraid his contemporaries.)

Kirn's piece is less interesting for its take on contemporary reviewing than the rampant gloom it reflects. Rather than wondering "why has literature run afoul?" it is more useful to ask "why are literate people so fearful?" The main reason is unrealistic expectations.

To begin, let's recognize that literature provides the reference point for most writers and deep readers. They believe it represents the highest form of human expression. Open yourself to literature and art and you enter a magic kingdom of depth and possibility. Proust captured this mind-set when he wrote: "The great quality of true art is that it rediscovers, grasps, and reveals to us that reality far from . . . the conventional knowledge we substitute for it . . . which is simply our life, real life, life finally discovered and clarified, consequently the only life that has really been lived."

Until recently, most people were functionally illiterate. Literature and art were beyond their reach or grasp, the domain of a tiny elite.

In one sense all that has changed. Higher education is practically a birthright in modern America. The rise of mass media has allowed culture to reach every nook and cranny of our land. Television, in particular, is a dizzyingly powerful medium that is profoundly democratic: The networks may shape our taste but they also give us what we want.

Turn it on and see the people's choice. I don't have to tell ya, it ain't Shakespeare.

It is this cathode-ray truth that so dispirits learned folks. Here they are producing a quality product that promises a rich life. Can you blame them for thinking they should have lines around the block?

And yet most people still have little interest in literature or art. Though Kirn says the public has given up on serious literature (or ballet, or opera, jazz and the fine arts), the truth is they have never held it close.

The truth is there is no "remember when" when it comes to high culture. It seems destined to be a micro-minority taste (Updike, for example, can only sell about 75,000 hardcover copies of his novels to a nation of 281 million people).

But unlike their artistic forbears, today's writers and artists can believe that a mass audience is within their reach. They can almost touch the brass ring.

Don't get me wrong. I don't think I'm a Pollyanna. I don't believe that all is right with the world. We need Chicken Littles not to bring us down but to raise our sights. Literature should always want more; it should always strive to be more. Books, and book reviews, can always be better and bolder.

But the sky isn't falling. Our salon just has a low ceiling.

February 18, 2001

America the Literate

Bean counters, numbers crunchers, the green eyeshade brigade—these devotees of the almighty dollar have seized control of the publishing industry during the last quarter-century, making the art of the bottom line the literary world's guiding aesthetic.

Funny thing is, their reign has been marked by the kind of explosive growth in America's book culture that their tweedy forebears could have imagined only after their third martini at the Four Seasons. Go figure.

This surprising news is detailed in a new report, "Best and Worst of Times: The Changing Business of Trade Books, 1975–2002," which journalist Gayle Feldman prepared as a fellow at Columbia University's National Arts Journalism Program. Among her findings:

> The number of new books published annually in the United States increased about 300 percent between 1975 and 2000, to 122,000 from 39,000.
>
> Sales of best-selling books during the last quarter-century have grown more than 1,000 percent: The leading title in 1975, "Ragtime" by E. L. Doctorow, sold 230,000 copies; in 2000, "The Brethren" by John Grisham topped out at 2.8 million copies.
>
> Name-brand writers such as Grisham, Danielle Steel and Stephen King have been the greatest beneficiaries of these increased sales, but literary authors such as Jonathan Franzen ("The Corrections" sold 720,000 copies in 2001) are sharing in this bonanza.
>
> Works of fiction that earn some of literature's highest honors, the National Book Award, the Pulitzer Prize or selection as a New York Times "editor choice," were far more likely to appear on Publishers Weekly's best-seller lists during 2000 than they were in 1975.

The publishing boom Feldman documents is a welcome rejoinder to the doom-and-gloom mentality that informs so much discussion of American culture: More people are buying better books than ever before—they're also purchasing more books of questionable merit, but hey.

Driving this surge is the rise of a better educated, more literate public that seeks to balance its swelling consumption of trash culture with bigger doses of high art (think of books as Metamucil for the soul). Ironically, it is the commercial forces which so many bibliophiles bemoan that have enabled publishers to exploit this literary desire.

Like it or not, we live in a mass culture; books are one of many options people have to fill their leisure time. To thrive in this environment, books must vie for attention against many popular and well-heeled competitors including television, movies, video games, sporting events, etc. Thus the consolidation of publishing—five major houses published 84 percent of the best sellers in 2000—was necessary for books to have the financial muscle to thrive in a crowded and expensive marketplace. Similarly, for all their drawbacks, the rise of chain stores such as Barnes & Noble and Internet retailers such as Amazon.com have afforded books a large-scale presence far beyond the capacities of the independent, and indispensable, local bookshops. Size matters in modern America.

Where books once rose or fell on their own steam, aided perhaps by a small ad in the New York Times, they are now propelled by sophisticated multimedia advertising programs concocted by marketing whizzes who call the shots at the major houses. Writers are coiffed and sheened, their pearly whites scrubbed to blinding perfection so they can dazzle morning show hosts. This year, for example, aggressive publishers generated huge sales for an array of first novels, including "The Lovely Bones" by Alice Sebold and "The Dive From Clausen's Pier" by Ann Packer. Cynics might charge that publishers have become as adept at manipulation as their brethren in the detergent business. But, as always, the consumer is the final power broker: Folks are no more likely to purchase books they don't enjoy than they are to purchase soap that doesn't get their whites white.

Most writers, however, aren't on easy street. Feldman's most astounding finding may be that the vast majority receive almost no promotion. Even the biggest publishers engage in massive triage, anointing a handful of titles for mega-support while ignoring the rest. Earlier this year two authors told me that their New York publishers not only failed to promote their books but discouraged them from arranging their own publicity. As a book critic I am constantly amazed at how little effort publicists expend to bring even works of strong local interest to my attention.

Feldman also notes that the major houses are no longer interested in publishing "books with a limited potential readership (5,000 copies and under)." Those authors are increasingly turning to university and other small presses that have little marketing clout. Renowned FSG editor Elizabeth Sifton told her, "by the 1990s it was clear that editors were valued for the deals they could do, not for work well done or talent nurtured."

That is not happy news, but it is mitigated by two factors. First, despite their concentrated marketing strategies, publishers continue to print boatloads of books. Second, there is no evidence that small books are experiencing declining sales. Authors destined to sell only 5,000 to 15,000 copies may be better served by university and boutique presses, which may lack promotional power but will answer their calls.

Readers can take heart from Feldman's report. Good books have a firm footing in America's mass entertainment culture—though a network television show that draws the same size audience as a mega-selling book is taken off the air quicker than you can say "For Whom the Bell Tolls."

Aggressive marketing has made it far easier to learn about the books "everyone is talking about." But many good books are off the radar. Nowadays, savvy readers must think like good detectives, who always consider the usual suspects but never fail to develop less obvious clues that can lead them to their desired quarry.

December 15, 2002

If You're Hip Say Golly Gee Whillikers

Sucker! Chump! Nerd!

The putdowns that strike fear in the high schooler's heart are following us into adulthood. In our fast-change culture, rampant insecurity seems the only constant. Our cultural coping mechanism is a never ending string of trends, buzz and hype. If we embrace the voguish curve we achieve the nirvana of modern personhood (and adolescent dreams): we're considered hip, cool, with-it. Unfortunately, all that acceptance leaves little time for reflection; we celebrate the next new thing, no questions asked—if you have to ask, you just don't get it.

A recent example of this unquestioning acceptance is Malcolm Gladwell's recent New Yorker article on the future of the book business. "The Science of the Sleeper: How the Information Age could blow away the blockbuster" is a doe-eyed appreciation of how technology will "re-shape the book market."

Gladwell begins his story at an independent bookshop in Blytheville, Ark., run by Mary Gay Shipley. A hand-seller extraordinaire, Shipley is not just a bookseller but a tastemaker: Most readers frequent her shop "to find out what Mary Gay thinks they ought to be reading." With conviction and taste, Shipley has used her forum to help turn sleepers such as Rebecca Wells's "Divine Secrets of the Ya-Ya Sisterhood" into best sellers.

The decline of independent bookstores, Gladwell notes, means "the number of Shipleys out there creating sleeper hits has declined as well."

The megastores that now dominate the industry offer so many books, and so little guidance, that readers are nonplussed. In response, they tend to stick with the name brands, authors such as John Grisham, Danielle Steel and Tom Clancy.

But lo and behold, Gladwell proclaims, technology may offer us a way out of this blockbuster mentality by creating computerized versions of Mary Gay Shipley. The process he touts is called "collaborative filtering," which he elegantly describes as "a kind of doppelganger search engine." Collaborative filtering assumes that the best way to determine what you will want is by knowing what you have wanted. So you tell a computer which books you've loved and which you've hated. It aligns your preferences with those of others who share your tastes (they are your doppelgangers) and spits out recommendations that will almost certainly please you.

Pretty cool, huh? So what's my beef?

Collaborative filtering does sound nifty and efficient. I'd love to give it a spin. Still I have concerns. My first—which extends to the golly gee whillikers attitude that informs so much reportage of technology—is Gladwell's failure to explore the troubling implications of this technology. (Maybe they don't bother him. Fair enough. Trouble is, he doesn't say.)

For example, when Kenneth Starr subpoenaed Monica Lewinsky's receipts from a Washington bookshop, many Americans were outraged. Collaborative filtering will only work if we turn over that same information. But isn't there a difference between willingly handing over personal information and being forced to surrender it? I'd say that line blurs to nothing when it becomes society's modus operandi. Gladwell paraphrases an e-commerce consultant who says we will soon see "the rise of what they call 'informediaries,' which are essentially brokers who will handle our preference information. Imagine, for example, that I had set up a company that collected and analyzed all your credit-card transactions. That information could be run through a collaborative filter, and the recommendations could be sold to retailers in exchange for discounts."

Will we swap our Social Security numbers for bar codes?

I also dispute Gladwell's idea that collaborative filtering will favor sleepers over blockbusters. A computer's output is only as good as its input. A machine cannot read a book. It cannot decide, like Mary Gay Shipley, to trumpet an obscure book like "Ya-Ya Sisterhood." In an automated world, who will get the book rolling?

The deepest problem Gladwell fails to address is the creeping alienation that mechanization is stamping onto modern life. Technology is like booze. It can make life smoother, easier and more agreeable, but is also leaves us cranky, impatient and disagreeable. The more time we spend buying books—and doing everything else—in our solitary cubicles, the less connected we feel to one another. This separation from real people and real things begets a disquieting life. Is it any wonder our prosperous nation feels so cold and distant?

A machine may be more efficient at determining my tastes than a bookseller. But hooking up with my virtual doppelgangers can never replace the fundamental and necessary human experience of interacting with a fallible, flesh-and-blood person. As we embrace change, we must never stop asking: Is this really progress? Only suckers, chumps and nerds would fail to ask such a basic question.

October 24, 1999

Ban the Book! Really!

Book lovers are a passionate and grouchy lot. If they aren't extolling the virtues of literature, they're complaining that too few Americans share their love of reading.

Me? I'm as surly as they come. Give me some Sunday space and I'll moan as loudly and vociferously as any tweedy professor about the dumbing down of America and the problems faced by a culture that extols bad movies, ranting Internet sites and silly television shows. This is the last season of "Friends"? Good riddance, you enemies of genuine thought and feeling.

Nevertheless, it is high time that we bibliophiles stop whining about these cultural bogeymen and start confronting the single biggest obstacle to reading in America. The culprit cannot be found in Hollywood, Madison Avenue or cyberspace. It resides in every Barnes & Noble, independent bookshop and library across our great land, where it holds court in brazen triumph. It is a cagey and dire enemy precisely because it seems so benign and friendly. It challenges us because it has made us love it.

I speak, of course, of the book. Laugh if you will, resist all you might, but hear me now or listen to me later: It is the book that is holding back publishing and limiting literature. It is the book that is preventing so many of our brethren from discovering and embracing the writers we love. The only way we can build new readers is by destroying the book.

"But I love the book," you say. I do too. It has served us well during the past 500 years. Pleasing pages so easy to read; bound in a sturdy cover that can withstand rain, snow, gloom and heat of night at least as well as your average mail carrier; light enough to carry up the highest mountains, across endless deserts or frigid arctic plains—try doing that with your iMac!

The book is, in fact, one of the few perfect inventions. Like the wheel and the french fry, it cannot be improved. Therein lies the problem. Though modern people crave constancy, they are attracted to change. We abhor chaos, but it's the next new thing that gets our juices flowing. We are a people of progress, and imperfection is the lifeblood of advancement.

Consider recent history. The music industry got a shot in the arm in the 1980s with the introduction of CDs, which led music lovers to replace their scratchy old vinyl records with shiny digital discs. Today, DVDs—which don't break or jam as readily as fragile VCR tapes—have injected life into movies. The new technology has turned millions of

Americans into cineastes who possess the kind of film libraries only a few universities could have matched a decade ago.

Does anyone doubt that the CD and DVD, which marketers assure us are perfect in every way, will be shown to have a fatal flaw? Does anyone doubt that the improved new formats will not just lighten our wallets but heighten our interest in music and films?

Publishers tried to tap into this high-tech magic in the 1990s by trumpeting electronic books. Problem was, they were trying to get us to replace the perfect with the imperfect. And quite frankly, we are nowhere near producing a fancy new product that can compete with Gutenberg's invention.

What should publishers do? Two things. First, they must keep trying to improve e-book technology. Second, they should do everything they can to manufacture shoddy books.

Durable hardcovers, for example, are a big problem. From now on, print only paperbacks. Instead of sewing or gluing the pages to the binding, use Scotch tape. Acid-free paper has to go—replace it with stock that burns at the touch. Use ink that smears easily but never washes off hands or clothes. Use small print that gets teenier and weenier with each passing page.

Invert some pages and leave whole paragraphs off others—with an apologetic note describing the difficulties inherent in such an archaic medium and directing fussbudgets who insist on seeing every darn word to visit a Web site.

Before long, even bibliophiles will start souring on the book. They'll want something better. Digital books will look like an upgrade. Book excitement, perhaps even bibliomania, will grip the land.

In that brave new world our now illiterate friends will stop talking trash and start discussing Trollope.

And when, years hence, their fervor starts to wane, publishers can re-re-stimulate their interest in reading with a novel format: the book.

October 12, 2003

The Words That Sell the Words

In today's cutthroat market, selling books is a tricky business. With some 60,000 new titles printed each year, publishers try to set their titles apart through a combination of brawn and brains. By brawn I mean the high-priced publicity campaigns, payoffs to large booksellers and extensive author tours—"If it's Tuesday, it must be Topeka"—that are now *de rigueur.* Though less heralded, the brains are just as important: A perfectly crafted blurb and a finely honed book catalog description can spell the difference between ka-ching and kerplunk.

The best blurbs practice the politics of inclusion, encompassing every possibility in a few brief words. A classic of the genre graces the cover of Stephen J. Pyne's "How the Canyon Became Grand": "No one," Tony Hillerman enthuses, "who has stared in awe at the Grand Canyon should miss this great book. And those who haven't should read this immediately."

Niche marketing can be equally effective, using taglines that establish the author's expertise. Kelly Lange's new novel from Simon & Schuster proclaims, "Gossip by the author of Trophy Wife." Likewise, Doubleday informs potential readers that Mame Davis Kellogg delivers the goods in "Nothing But Gossip" because she also wrote "Tramp."

Publishing may have dipped a bit down-market of late, but make no mistake, quality still sells. The jacket on "Marking the Sparrow's Fall" trumpets it as "Wallace Stegner's biggest collection and the first since his death in 1993." Peter Fromm may not be as famous or industrious as Stegner, but his short story collection "Blood Knot" tells readers that the Montana writer is "the Chekhov of Great Falls."

A work's success or failure is often decided before it even arrives at the bookstores. Sparking that first make-or-break wave of interest is the job of creative editors and publicists who write the catchy copy for the house catalogs that booksellers and reviewers rely on. The work is nothing less than daunting. Imagine for a moment that you work at the University of South Carolina Press and you've been handed Andrew F. Smith's study,

"Popped Culture: The Social History of Popcorn in America." Could you have produced this? "While debunking many myths [Smith] discovers a flavorful story of the curious kernel's introduction and ever increasing consumption in America. . . . His familiarity with the history of the snack allows him to form expectations about popcorn's future in the United States and abroad."

Impressed as I was with that sweet rhapsody, I must say it pales in comparison to the effort of the anonymous scribe at Chronicle Books who imagined this mise-en-scène for Burton Silver and Heather Busch's forthcoming book, "Betty and Rita Go To Paris": "They were free dogs in Paris, unfettered and alive . . . Two travelling Labradors tour the City of Light in this charming portrait of Paris and irresistible celebration of canine joie de vivre. Lingering in front of the Louvre, pondering Jim Morrison's grave, befriending a poodle at Les Halles, or enjoying a baguette at the Eiffel Tower, Betty and Rita take in all the sights . . . ."

Is it too much to suggest that the author may well be the Chekhov of catalogs?

Not all descriptions hit the mark. Sometimes they assume too much knowledge on the reader's part. Soho Press sees big things for "Getting it On: A Condom Reader" edited by Mitch Roberson and Julia Dubner because "Everybody has an anecdote about buying condoms, finding used condoms, fumbling for condoms in the dark. So why not a book?"

Other times, they tell us more than we want to know. This June Harmony Books will publish "In the Spirit: Conversations With the Spirit of Jerry Garcia" by Wendy Weir, sister of Garcia's Grateful Dead band mate Bob Weir. The catalog reports that hours after Jerry died, Wendy tried to contact the dead guitarist. "At first she cannot talk to Jerry's spirit because he is too happy to be free. Only with the telepathic help of her brother is she able to break through Jerry's barriers and remind him that he can't leave, he still needs to fulfill his mission on earth." With friends like that . . .

Finally, the best way to sell a book is with a catchy title, one that lets readers know that this one's for them. "Food and Drink in Medieval Poland" by Maria Dembinska says it all. And if you see someone buying Robert Young Pelton's "Come Back Alive: The Ultimate Guide to Surviving Disasters, Kidnappings, Animal Attacks, and Other Nasty Perils of Modern Travel" give them a little advice from me: STAY HOME!

February 14, 1999

Oprah's Little Golden Books

Twenty million.

Plop.

That's the number of books Oprah Winfrey has helped publishers sell since she started her book club in 1996.

One hundred-seventy-five million dollars. That's how much those sales have generated for the industry.

Plop. Plop.

Winfrey's love of literature has also helped to spark a renaissance in reading groups, whose numbers have doubled, to roughly 500,000, since 1994.

Plop. Plop. Plop.

Winfrey is the book industry's golden goose. It is so grateful that she has taken it under her wing that the National Book Foundation, which sponsors the National Book Awards, honored her in November.

Despite her contributions and acclaim, Winfrey has drawn criticism from some in the book world. Their charge: She has been a boon to commerce but a bane to art. Specifically, they take issue with the types of books she picks, her touchy-feely approach to literature, and her power as a taste-maker. Though I agree with some of their arguments, ultimately, her detractors are off the mark.

Let's start with her book choices. In many ways her latest pick, "Gap Creek," by North Carolina native Robert Morgan, is a typical Oprah selection. Beautifully written and delicately textured, it is unquestionably literary. Winfrey may not favor experimental or complicated works, but she never picks trash. Like many Oprah selections, "Gap Creek" concerns a woman who perseveres through hardship. Julie is a teenage bride who lives in the mountains of Western North Carolina around the turn of the last century. Her cupboards are nearly bare and she has a plate full of sorrows: She is taken by a con man, causes a kitchen fire that leads to a death and is abused by her husband. Despite these troubles, her dignity, perseverance and sexuality are undiminished. In Oprah's literary world, characters are damaged and scarred, yet they always endure.

In a Dec. 26 article in the New York Times Magazine, the journalist D. T. Max wrote: "Part of [Oprah's] strategy is to make the book-club episodes resemble all her other shows. She chooses books that focus on issues, like schizophrenia, cheating husbands or foster children . . . [Then she and her audience] talk about what they thought of the book and—especially and extensively—its relevance to their own lives."

Winfrey told Max, "Reading is like everything else. You're drawn to people who are like yourself."

Echoing other commentators, Max found this "therapeutic approach" to literature troubling. "There's something odd about Winfrey's insistence on treating novels as springboards for self-reflection. Aren't novels about stepping outside one's experience?"

I, too, shudder at Winfrey's penchant for turning novels into self-help manuals. Yet, I also reject Max's assertion that novels are about any single experience. Literature is an inside-outside game: It slides us into other people's worlds as it pushes us to probe our own feelings. It forces us to reach out as we dig down, introducing us to others as we try to find ourselves. On one level we have nothing in common with the characters of Austen, Dickens and Joyce; on another, we feel they are us.

Ideally, Winfrey would highlight this complex interaction, selecting a broader range of books to explore how empathy is both a private and a public act. That she does not is a lost opportunity. But her me-centered approach to literature is hardly beyond the pale. And, at a time when many people feel too busy to read, showing them how literature applies directly to their lives makes sense. Given a choice between the soul-sapping literary theory that holds sway in many college classrooms and Oprah's empowering navel-gazing, it's the Big O by a KO.

Much of the consternation about Winfrey derives from her alleged power. Max dubs her "the most successful pitch woman in the history of publishing." That is true but misleading. She is a taste-maker, but only among her fans, who, Max notes, are not hard-core readers. Most pick up a book because Oprah tells them to. If that were not the case, viewers who fell in love with Jacquelyn Mitchard's "Deep End of the Ocean" or Chris Bohjalian's "Midwives" would have rushed to buy those writers' next works. None of the authors Winfrey has rocketed to stardom has realized wide success with their non-Oprahized follow-ups.

Besides, I see no evidence that Winfrey is influencing which books newspapers and magazines send out for review or the approaches to literature taken by critics. Nor has her power to move product affected which books get published. She directs perhaps $75 million in sales each year in a multi-billion dollar industry. Considering that hundreds of literary novels are published each year, it would be foolhardy for houses to arrange their business around Oprah's long-shot lottery.

Nevertheless, to paraphrase Whitman, "I celebrate Oprah" because she celebrates literature. In the process she turns a few books into golden eggs. Plop. Plop. Plop. . . . Plop!

January 23, 2000

High Art, High Dudgeon

What would Shakespeare do?

He might have transformed this petty squabble of spurned advances and bruised egos into an epic clash between the hoity-toity and hoi polloi. He might have imagined the novelist Jonathan Franzen as a cosmic symbol of snobbery and pride while rendering Franzen's adversary, Oprah Winfrey, as a generous yet calculating queen who will not suffer those that question her authority or reject her gifts.

We can almost hear Franzen lamenting "the slings and arrows of outrageous fortune" while wondering: "To sell-out or not to sell-out? That is the question." And we can hear Oprah warning: "Better thou hadst been born a dog than turn down my nationally televised largess."

Shakespeare's most devoted audience, the unschooled groundlings, would have loved it.

The events that could spark such drama unfolded Tuesday when Oprah stunned the literary world by reversing course and saying she would not feature Franzen's highly acclaimed new novel, "The Corrections," on her TV show. In a tersely worded statement to Publishers Weekly, she said: "Jonathan Franzen will not be on the Oprah Winfrey show because he is seemingly uncomfortable and conflicted about being chosen as a book club selection. It is not my intention to make anyone uncomfortable or cause anyone conflict."

Imagine! A writer turns his back on millions of dollars and hundreds of thousands of new readers. One of the most powerful people in the book world feels so insulted that she pulls the plug on a mammoth undertaking. If God is in these details, they must be devilishly good.

Franzen is not the first literary heavyweight anointed by Oprah. Toni Morrison, Joyce Carol Oates, Sue Miller, Kaye Gibbons and Ernest Gaines are some of the other top-notch writers who have tapped a vast new audience through her book club. Franzen is the first writer to publicly state his ambivalence about winning Oprah's lottery. In a recent interview with the Oregonian newspaper, he said, "After I heard [about being selected], I considered turning it down."

One reservation, Franzen explained, concerned the practice of emblazoning book club picks with Oprah's label. "I see this as my book, my creation," Franzen told the newspaper, "and I didn't want that logo of corporate ownership on it. . . . The reason I got into this business is because I'm an independent writer, and I didn't want that corporate logo on my book."

Franzen's assertion that he is an "independent writer" who eschews "corporate logos" is a little loopy. After all, "The Corrections," like all books, bears a corporate logo—that of his publisher, Farrar, Straus and Giroux. And his book has achieved great success in no small part because of the massive publicity campaign launched by FSG, which is a subsidiary of a multibillion-dollar global conglomerate. As someone who has championed the long out-of-print novels of Paula Fox, Franzen knows that quality does not guarantee success.

But his larger point is well-taken. He, alone, spent years writing "The Corrections," the story of an American family's efforts to fix the forces that are tearing its members apart. Once Oprah chooses a book, it becomes an Oprah book. Her endorsement confers a type of ownership.

The second source of Franzen's discomfort is more problematic. In an interview with Terry Gross of National Public Radio, he lamented that readers had told him they were "put off by the fact that it is an Oprah pick."

The author elaborated on this idea in his Oregonian interview, saying, "I feel like I'm solidly in the high art literary tradition, but I like to read entertaining books and this maybe helps bridge that gap, but it [Oprah's pick] also heightens these feelings of being misunderstood."

This is claptrap, though of a rather interesting variety, because it reveals the insecurity that underpins all snobbery. If Franzen were truly confident about his "high art," he would scorn the pseudo-intellectual poseurs who hesitate to buy his book because Oprah found it engaging. Instead, he would embrace those readers for whom his book might present a rewarding challenge—imagine if Shakespeare had hesitated to produce "King Lear" because "the groundlings won't understand it."

And if, in her presentation, Oprah misrepresented "The Corrections," Franzen would have been there to set her straight. If anything, his "fears about being misunderstood" might make a better Oprah program than a discussion of his book.

Of Oprah's thinking we know less—all we have is her statement to Publishers Weekly. Most rational people would concede that Franzen's comments were rather tame. Only a person with remarkably thin skin could respond the way she has. Perhaps what galled her was Franzen's assertion that his book would do "as much for her as it does for us." Her message: Thanks, praise me, and shut up!

Fortunately, our story's close seems a happy one. Oprah will continue as the queen of daytime TV and a literary tastemaker. Franzen's bestselling book is favored to win the National Book Award for fiction on Nov. 14.

As they say, "All's well that ends well."

October 28, 2001

Bound by Time

Book dude confesses: I spend a lot more time thinking about Yankee baseball, Ben & Jerry's ice cream and the hazards of Southern sunshine on my Swedish complexion than I do about the brotherhood of man.

However, Stephen King and John Updike recently managed to lift my eyes from my swelling navel—I blame you, Ben, and you too, Jerry. My rather complicated journey to high-mindedness started last week when King began self-publishing his latest thriller, "The Plant," on the Internet. The move seems the latest indication that the traditional bound book may be on its last leaf, a withering redwood being zapped into extinction by the death rays of electronic publishing.

As my mixed-metaphor mind transformed hardbacks into dinosaurs, images of dodo birds and butter churns, hand-cranked ice cream makers and doctors who make house calls flashed before my eyes. Just as the Hanging Gardens of Babylon were coming into view, John Updike appeared—poof!

What's up with that?

Then I recalled Updike's recent paean in the New York Times, in which the prodigious word-charmer avers that books are not merely word packages. Bits and bytes can convey literary thoughts and feelings, but bound books serve so many other purposes, which we forfeit at great risk.

They are, Updike writes, essential furniture in every bibliophile's home—"shelved rows of books warm and brighten the starkest room." He describes the sensual pleasure they provide, "the average book fits into the human hand with a seductive nestling, a kiss of texture." And he reminds us that every book is in a sense a page of its owner's memoir, "one's collection comes to symbolize the content of one's mind . . . books preserve, daintily, the redolence of their first reading—this beach, that apartment, that attack of croup, this flight to Indonesia."

Updike's insights hurried me to my own shelves and Holbrook Jackson's indispensable volume, "The Book About Books: The Anatomy of Bibliomania," which describes scores of ingenious uses for books. They make wonderful footstools, chair cushions and doorstops, reported

Jackson, the late, great English man of letters. Chefs have employed them as pastry parchment, while the English writer Joseph Addison "admitted having lighted his pipe more than once 'with the writings of a prelate.'" Edward Gibbon used books as currency, trading a copy of his "Decline and Fall" for a hogshead of Madeira. "Tolstoy, in his youth," Jackson wrote, "would use Tatishef's 'Dictionaries' as tests of endurance, by holding them in his outstretched hand for five minutes at a time, though the feat caused him 'terrible pain.'"

Jackson added: "Many stories tell how books have stopped bullets in their swift and deadly course, and turned the points of swords . . . the use of books as weapons is recorded by Anthony Trollope, whose father often knocked him down with a 'great Folio Bible' as a punishment for youthful idleness." Try that with a floppy disc.

Yes, yes, I hear you saying, that's all fine and good. I'm convinced that books are more than just words on paper, that the arts of war and peace and home decor will be gravely affected by the death of the bound book. But what has that to do with the brotherhood of man?

To answer that question, let's assume that e-books will carry the day—in reality, of course, the technology is so new, primitive and untested that it will be several years before anyone can speak with authority on the subject. If we entertain the idea that something as dear to us as traditional books might be cast aside, we can begin to appreciate ourselves as people bound by time and place.

In this context, Updike is not a defender manning the barricades but a historian chronicling and bearing witness to how we thought and lived in a time that our progeny may remember as the Age of the Book. Just as some ancients undoubtedly mourned the day that togas went out of style—"but they are so comfortable, and appropriate for both formal and everyday functions"—so we lament the possible passing of bound books.

By imagining traditional books as artifacts of our particular time, we apprehend the much deeper ways that we are united with everyone else sharing this planet for the brief moment of our lives. The brotherhood of man is simply a recognition that all of us alive today are bound together not just by timeless human concerns but by the many passing yet compelling items and issues peculiar to ourselves.

Ages from now, people may stumble across a dusty download hyperlinking King's novel, Updike's essay and Holbrook's book. They'll probably wonder what all the fuss was about. If they figure it out, they might begin to understand what we were about.

July 30, 2000

Nothing to Be Ashamed Of

If contemporary literature were a man, he would be 8-feet tall but worried he is too short.

If contemporary literature were a woman, she would be shockingly smart but unsure of her intelligence.

And, if contemporary literature were an automobile, it would be a Porsche whose driver frets that it cannot keep pace with a Chevy Cavalier.

Complex thoughts of inferiority filled my mind last weekend at the North Carolina Literary Festival at UNC-Chapel Hill. Reynolds Price was there, as were Clyde Edgerton, Allan Gurganus, Doris Betts, Lee Smith, Hal Crowther, Jim Seay and dozens of other rapturously talented writers. Yet, the featured speaker was that modern master of the middlebrow, John Grisham.

As I and hundreds of other serious readers stood under overcast skies listening to Grisham tell us how hard he works (though the pay is pretty good), how tedious (his word) is the process of formulating his stamped tin plots, I was hoping someone whose picture does not run in the newspaper every Sunday would shout: "You have no clothes . . . and you're no emperor."

Because the folks who flocked to Chapel Hill last weekend came not to praise Grisham but to bury the notion that serious, challenging, downright disquieting writing has lost its audience. They filled classrooms and halls to hear Derek Walcott, Rita Dove, Jonathan Williams and Janet Lembke read their poetry; to watch Alice Adams and Daphne Athas delineate the craft of novel writing; and to eavesdrop on John Bentley Mays and Edward Ball as they discussed how the South's rich and complicated past frames, shapes and transmutes its kaleidoscopically protean present.

Yet the festival's organizers—who must be commended for putting on a first-rate event—did not trust the public's taste enough to put all their chips on talent. Instead, they hedged their bets by banking on Grisham's star power.

But it's spring, the birds are singing, so let's chalk up the singular honor the festival bestowed on Grisham as a simple miscalculation born in a moment of first-year jitters. But that is no reason to ignore the dark cloud on the larger literary horizon that Grisham's starring role symbolizes: the blurring of lines between art and the artless in the name of commerce.

In his essay, "Our Absolutely Deplorable Literary Situation—and Some Thoughts on How to Fix It Good," the celebrated man of letters Louis D. Rubin Jr. fingers the two-letter culprit fueling this unhappy development: TV.

The ubiquitous enabler of hyper-mass culture, television has raised the stakes, making über-bigness the be-all and end-all of most every American endeavor. When you can sell a million units of a product—whether it be toothpaste or books—how can you be content selling just 10,000? The goal becomes quantity not quality, market penetration not insight.

In this environment, Rubin writes, "The profit-and-loss performance of literature is being evaluated by people who are chiefly in business to sell mass-market cultural products. It is as if the choice of titles to be issued by the Cuala Press had been up to the publishers of the Guinness Book of Records." The result, he notes, is that "those authors who seem potentially exploitable as celebrities are given essentially the same kind of promotion as Hollywood figures and presidential candidates, and then judged by how well they can conduct themselves in the spotlight—i.e. as public entertainers. A novelist who is unwilling or unable to embark on an extensive author's tour, or who can't be made to perform colorfully on a network talk show, is out of it."

Only those writers lucky enough to be endorsed by Oprah or Imus, shameless enough to peddle their painful pasts or established enough to have their works hawked like any other brand-name product, can expect to thrive in the modern marketplace.

Yet the fact remains, literature will always be a minority taste; a small thing in a big world. To demand that books with an audience of only

10,000 sell a million copies is a recipe for demise, dooming the literary novel to the same fate as poetry.

What's needed is a reality check, a recognition that John Grisham produces books that sell while Elizabeth Spencer creates works that matter. When we confuse and conflate the two in this bottom-line world, when we put them on the same stage, we bolster the notion that Spencer is the less successful writer. What the literary festival reminded us is there is a passionate, albeit small, audience that knows that literature is smoother than any sports car, that it is shockingly smart and eight feet tall. And that's nothing to be ashamed of.

April 12, 1998

BINDING
DEVOTION

BOOK CULTURE

The Book on Wilt Chamberlain

I started receiving condolence calls shortly after Wilt Chamberlain's death was announced Tuesday. Friends from across the country tried to comfort me in my time of real sadness.

You see, to know me, is to know Wilt. During the last 25 years I've probably spent as much time arguing Chamberlain vs. Bill Russell, Michael Jordan and every other pretender to his rightful crown as basketball's greatest player as I have debating Faulkner and Fitzgerald, Hamsun and Hemingway.

I still save every mention of him I see in newspapers and magazines, in a big box labeled "Wilt Stuff" (lame pun intended). His stats roll off my tongue—scored 100 points in a single game, averaged 50.4 per game for an entire season, the all-time leading rebounder (averaging 22.9 per game for his career), the only center to lead the league in assists (1967–68)—as easily as my children's names. My home office has just two framed pictures on its walls, one of Jerry Garcia, the other of Wilt, his graceful 7-foot figure extended to the heavens, snagging a rebound against the New York Knicks. (My wife wouldn't let me hang them in the living room.)

This devotion may sound strange considering I never even saw him play basketball—I was only 11 when he retired from the NBA in 1973.

What gives?

I never read much as a kid; like a lot of Ritalin babies I was too busy bouncing off the walls to concentrate on words, words, words. That changed when I was 12, the same year my father moved from New York to Los Angeles. My school had a book fair and the first work I ever bought on my own was Chamberlain's autobiography, "Wilt: Just Like Any Other 7-Foot Black Millionaire Who Lives Next Door" (1973). I remember rushing home and curling up with my new friend. During the next year I must have read "Wilt" a dozen times; the pages became so loose in the worn binding that I eventually had to keep them in a plastic bag.

On one level my 12-year-old mind found "Wilt" absorbing because it was the story of a superhero. He dominated. From his high school days in West Philadelphia, to his two seasons at the University of Kansas, his years with the Harlem Globetrotters and then his unparalleled career with various NBA teams including the L.A. Lakers, Chamberlain was, simply and appealingly, the best. When he wasn't scoring a gazillion points, snatching a million rebounds or winning a Most Valuable Player Award, Wilt was driving his Bentley across country at 135 miles an hour, making love to gorgeous stewardesses high in the sky and discussing the differences between Rome and Milan. "I get carried away sometimes," he wrote, "and say I can pass a football better than Joe Namath and drive better than Dan Gurney and cook better than Graham Kerr. To be perfectly truthful, probably only two of those three statements are true."

Wilt was gifted, and brash enough to say so. Deep down, we all feel special. I know I did in some unutterable way, and it was liberating to meet someone who made no bones about his ego.

Yet, what also attracted me—a slightly overweight, self-conscious, insecure kid—was his vulnerability. Always tall, he was always different. Everywhere he went, people stared, asked him stupid questions like "how big are you?"—in a good mood, he'd say "7 foot 1," in a bad mood he'd say, "Not nearly as big as your mouth."

He said "Nobody roots for Goliath." I knew I would never be a giant. But I understood, like most adolescents, the feeling that the world is against you.

And despite his accomplishments, Wilt was always called a "loser." He was so much bigger and better than everyone else that it was assumed his teams should win every time. When they didn't, he was blamed. But basketball, like life, is a team sport, and he was rarely supported by a gifted cast. Beginning in 1957, when his Kansas team lost the NCAA championship in a famed triple-overtime game against an unbeaten University of North Carolina team, through his epic battles with Bill Russell, whose dynastic Boston Celtics teams invariably squeaked through to victory, Wilt always seemed to come out on the short end. I raged at the injustice, both the unfairness of other people and of life, which can deny us dreams despite our best efforts. But he never stopped trying.

So you see, Wilt Chamberlain was not just my favorite basketball player, but my first literary hero. "Wilt" was the first book that opened my eyes to the power of literature: a place where misfits can find new worlds and familiar ones. My love for his book led me to other works and other passions. I'll always keep him in my heart, argue his cause and trumpet his greatness as a way of remembering a dear old friend and of paying down a great debt.

October 17, 1999

The Book on the 20th Century

Should we shed a tear or say "Ha" to everyone born too early to witness our times? I know they probably can't hear us, but trust me, I'm going somewhere with this.

They never met Jay Gatsby, Holden Caulfield or Lolita, "light of my life, fire of my loins." The names Joseph Conrad, Marcel Proust and Virginia Woolf would only have puzzled them. The maps of their imaginations had no markings for Winesburg, Ohio, or Yoknapatawpha County. The iceman hadn't yet cometh; they were still waiting for Godot—and Winnie the Pooh, Peter Rabbit and the Cat in the Hat.

To paraphrase Clarence the angel, it really has been a wonderful century. Thank you, Thomas Mann, Willa Cather and Eudora Welty. Here's to you, D. H. Lawrence, Toni Morrison and Franz Kafka. Dare we give a big wet one to T. S. Eliot, W. H. Auden and William Butler Yeats?

Conventional wisdom holds that film is the 20th century's great art form. Others might suggest it is painting, architecture or music. But, you know what, critics would surely make their arguments in a book. Though our century was distinguished by invention and cursed with cruelty, it should also be remembered as the Age of the Book.

The writings of Lenin and Mao liberated humanity only to enslave it. Hitler's "Mein Kampf" (1925) gave words to unspeakable evil.

Yet, for every book that spelled doom, hundreds more created hope. It was through books—including W. E. B. Du Bois's "The Souls of Black Folk" (1903), Ralph Ellison's "Invisible Man" (1952) and "The Autobiography of Malcolm X" (1965)—that African Americans charted their struggle for freedom.

A new dawn for women alighted through Margaret Sanger's "My Fight for Birth Control" (1931), Simon de Beauvoir's "The Second Sex" (1949) and Betty Friedan's "The Feminine Mystique" (1963).

It's hard to imagine what the workplace might be like today if not for "The Jungle" (1906) by Upton Sinclair. In what conditions would the poor still be mired without "The Battle with the Slum" (1902) by Jacob Riis? Would the compassion that long marked our politics have been possible without John Steinbeck's "The Grapes of Wrath" (1939), James Agee and Walker Evans's "Let Us Now Praise Famous Men" (1941) and Alex Kotlowitz's "There Are No Children Here" (1991)? Would the modern environmental movement have taken the shape it has without Rachel Carson's "Silent Spring" (1962)? Whither the counterculture without Jack Kerouac's "On the Road" (1957)?

Dr. Benjamin Spock told us how to raise our children in "The Common Sense Book of Baby and Child Care" (1946). Craig Claiborne showed Americans that life's palette includes more than white bread and red meat in "The New York Times Cook Book" (1961). Dale Carnegie taught American businessmen "How to Win Friends and Influence People" (1936). And Emily Post instructed us on the high art of getting along in "Etiquette in Society, in Business, in Politics and at Home" (1922).

Despite that sound advice, Aldous Huxley warned us of our "Brave New World" (1932) while George Orwell made "1984" (1949) a timeless date of dread.

We haven't even mentioned the writings of Albert Einstein, Sigmund Freud and Jean-Paul Sartre. And then there's . . . well, you get the point.

The tremendous pleasure, pain and insight those works have brought only hint at the power of books during the 20th century. More than any other art form, they made us who we are by imagining who we might be. Knowing them, we know ourselves; ignoring them, we ignore ourselves. At a time when books themselves seem imperiled by digital dreams, when progress and change are so easily confused, we should remember that books remain the best way we have devised to think, to feel and, thereby, to live. One day, perhaps there will be a Web site to rival James Joyce's "Ulysses" (1922). Today, there is still no substitute for books.

Above all, there are the joy, the entertainment and the kinship that have been stoked in each of us by books that would probably make no one's top-10 list but our own. The splendid hours I have spent between the covers with P. G. Wodehouse, Wilt Chamberlain and my father's self-published novel can be measured only by myself.

The magic of reading is that it allows us to dig deep by reaching out. At heart, it is the act of entering someone else's mind by allowing them to enter our own. It is conquest through surrender.

So let us shed a tear for all those impoverished by the accident of fate that brought them life too early. And let's say "Ha" to ourselves, ruefully acknowledging all that lies ahead, and beyond, ourselves.

December 26, 1999

The Real Power of Books

The sun was sitting high in the sky and I was near a shady tree as my kids splashed in the pool. Life was good.

Then I picked up the paper: bombings in Lebanon, massacres in Baghdad, genocide in Darfur.

I looked back at my children, smiled, then marveled at the mind's capacity to take in all the information of the world and then judge our well-being by what's in front of our noses. It's the same thought I have whenever my wife and I discuss our pressing need to add another room to our fairly spacious home, or when I conclude that I really do need a new DVD player or component for my stereo system. I know that there are people in far-flung spots consigned to circumstances so abject they are almost beyond imagining. And yet my desires don't fade—and still I feel good about myself, still consider myself a good person.

This dynamic is particularly troubling for us book-lovers. Besides being a great source of pleasure, books are our primary gateway to other lives and cultures. If books serve a larger purpose, it is their power to brake our God-given selfishness. Nature primes us to look out for our-selves; few of us require help in that regard. What most of us need are constant reminders to consider everyone else, to imagine their needs, hopes, desires and circumstances.

Personal experience has convinced me that books are both the great-est tool for empathy we have created and totally inadequate to the task. Some of the best-read people I know are among the nastiest and most selfish individuals I've never wanted to know. For every person I've met whose character was edified by the written word, scores more leave me wondering how someone who has devoured so much wisdom can be so small-minded.

I know this to be true: Books do not make us better people. They may show us the big picture, but they inspire precious few of us to put away our petty personal concerns. Even the best books cannot make us replace selfishness with empathy.

I also know this to be true: All that is dead wrong. Books make our world a far kinder, more just and empathetic place.

To reconcile these conflicting beliefs, consider the Paradox of Read-ing: Though books make none of us better people, they make all of us better—even those who don't read.

Western history makes this strange notion clear. Remember the world into which Johann Gutenberg introduced his printing press around 1453: Slavery was rampant, women were treated as men's property, and stiff class structures stifled almost everyone's aspirations.

Gutenberg's invention changed that. As his press enabled the rela-tively cheap and easy dissemination of ideas, the status quo came under intense scrutiny. Writers began asking lofty questions about how people should interact. The Renaissance flourished, then the Enlightenment. Rights, equality and freedom became topics of discussion.

The writings of philosophers such as John Locke inspired our Found-ing Fathers to imagine a nation in which every citizen would be treated with dignity. Of course, we are painfully aware of how far the founders fell short of that goal. Western history since Gutenberg is filled with bloody wars and vicious ideologies—including colonialism and Na-zism—that have challenged this story of progress, urging us to see others as less than human.

Progress doesn't follow a straight line. Our instinct to look out for ourselves, to only consider our needs, is powerful.

What's striking is not that this selfishness endures, but that we've made such strides in neutralizing it. It is no coincidence that the civil rights movements that have transformed America in the past 60 years occurred at the same time that we expanded access to higher education. When I look at the great strides made by women and African Americans, as I watch gays and lesbians move toward full equality, I am amazed that anyone can long for the past. Our world is a better place, getting better all the time.

And books are a chief cause. This point is overlooked because while our minds act locally, books work globally. Our instinct is to measure books by their power to transform us personally. What can you do for me? But books operate on a wider scale—slowly but surely changing the values of the larger culture. We, in turn, inherit these assumptions, which shape our standards and expectations.

On the whole, I am a better, more caring and empathetic person than my ancestors who lived in the Jim Crow South. This is not because I've paid more attention to my morality. I just happen to live in a more moral world, one that has been shaped and improved by books.

August 6, 2006

Where Books Lead We Follow

You never forget your first. That's why Anne Fadiman holds a special place in my heart.

Her splendid essay collection, "Ex Libris: Confessions of a Common Reader," ignited my powerful passion for books about books. I was so enthralled by her descriptions of her literary life—of the books she has loved, the challenges of merging libraries after matrimony—that I was eager to follow her anywhere.

She laid out our next rendezvous in the section "Recommended Reading." "My favorite book about books," she wrote, "happens to be called "The Book About Books: The Anatomy of Bibliomania." It is a monumental compendium by Holbrook Jackson."

I thought: Who he?

Turns out he was an English man of letters (1874–1948) whose masterpiece contains 200 lively chapters that draw on a wealth of classical and modern sources to describe "Books and Their Most Excellent Qualities," "The Proper Time for Reading," as well as "The Joy of Book Hunting," "Perils of Fire and Water" and "On Choosing a Library for a Desert Island."

After devouring that classic, I consumed the rest of Jackson's oeuvre, including "The Reading of Books," "The Fear of Books" and "Bookman's Pleasure."

Learning that Jackson had modeled "Bibliomania" on "The Anatomy of Melancholy," I hunted down Robert Burton's 1621 classic. It was a revelation. While I was recommending "Ex Libris" to a friend, he told me about a helpful little book by the author's father, Clifton Fadiman, "The New Lifetime Reading Plan." That led me to still more works as my bookshelves began to moan with delight under the weight of booky books: "Why Read the Classics?" by Italo Calvino, "How to Read and Why" by Harold Bloom and "The Most Wonderful Books: Writers on Discovering the Pleasures of Reading," edited by Michael Dorris and Emilie Buchwald.

"Ex Libris" was the best kind of book: a Gateway Book that opened doors to works, and worlds, beyond itself. Like Alice's looking glass, Gateway Books beckon us to take the plunge. Like Russian nesting dolls, they always seem to contain one more surprise. They earn our trust, so we follow their lead. They fire our curiosity, making us greedy for knowledge.

Gateway Books take us on curious excursions—such as a recent journey that began with Alexander the Great and ended with Wilt Chamberlain. A while back I was enjoying John Prevas's superb biography, "Envy of the Gods: Alexander the Great's Ill-fated Journey Across Asia." That book mentioned Plutarch's portrait of the Macedonian conqueror in "Lives of Noble Grecians and Romans." After reading that chapter, I perused the Roman writer's chapter on Cicero. That reminded me of the book by the Roman statesman sitting on my bookshelf, "On Duties," which my dermatologist had suggested two years before. While pulling that down, I noticed the collection of plays by Aristophanes next to it. Soon my mind was stoked by ancient fires. When a new biography,

"Helen of Troy: Goddess, Princess, Whore" by Bettany Hughes, arrived on my desk I made a date with the face that launched a thousand ships.

Thanks to Helen, I looked at my pile of review copies with new eyes. A series of recent works on historic women jumped out, including "The Peabody Sisters: Three Women Who Ignited American Romanticism" by Megan Marshall and "The Solitude of the Self: Thinking about Elizabeth Cady Stanton" by Vivian Gornick. They reminded me of a recent book on another great American, "A Great Improvisation: Franklin, France, and the Birth of America," by Stacy Schiff. Franklin was one of my childhood heroes. So was Wilt Chamberlain. He is featured in John Taylor's new history, "The Rivalry: Bill Russell, Wilt Chamberlain, and the Golden Age of Basketball," which I am reading now, thanks to Alexander.

While Gateway Books may lead to wild adventures, they can also be like serpents that swallow their own tails. My college-era plan to read a book by every single Nobel Prize winner got sidetracked when I came to "The Growth of the Soil" by 1920 laureate Knut Hamsun. What a discovery! Suddenly, it was all-Hamsun all the time as I pleasured my way through "Mysteries," "Pan," "Hunger, "Victoria," "On Overgrown Paths" and many other of the Norwegian's books. When I came up for air I devoured 1968's winner, Japan's Yasunari Kawabata, whose "Beauty and Sadness," led to "The Snow Country," "Thousand Cranes" and "The Sound of the Mountain."

And on it goes in a process of marvelous discovery. Gateway Books remind us that no work is an island; each is a tiny realm connected to ever expanding worlds. We readers are little Columbuses of the mind who know that our journey with a book often begins after we close its covers—and open another.

October 30, 2005

A Simple Plan

A reader writes: "Hi Mr. Zane, I'm a 49-year-old guy in Cary. I love reading, but lead a busy life and always regret not having enough time to indulge in my passion. I'm curious about your reading habits. I know it's your livelihood, but how much time per day do you spend reading?

Do you have other interests? Movies? TV? I've always been jealous of people who tell me they can read a book in a day. It sometimes takes me a month to get through a book—catching a half-hour here and an hour there, at about a 30-page per hour rate. . . . I guess in my case, it all comes down to priorities. I also read a lot of magazines and, of course, the N&O every day. Not to mention the 9–10 hour per day job, exercise time, etc., etc."

I dashed off a note to this reader, which I've polished for publication.

Dear Sir,

Thanks for your letter. Much ink and plenty of tears have been spilled over the decline of reading, though this strikes me as a false argument. In fact, Americans probably read more—e.g., magazines, newspapers, trade journals, e-mails, Web site information—than ever. This is, after all, the Information Age.

Still, not all information is created equally. Unfortunately, America's hype machine makes keeping up with puffery seem essential—every good citizen must know the difference between Regis Philbin and Richard Hatch—while the latest works from Toni Morrison and Zadie Smith, Peter Gay and Stephen Ambrose seem at best tangential, and at worst irrelevant, to the national conversation.

The result is a culture that discourages serious reading. Books seem like just another take-it or leave-it pastime instead of an essential aspect of life. A 1999 Gallup Poll found that only 38 percent of Americans surveyed said they read at least one book a month. In "The Business of Books," legendary publisher Andre Schiffrin notes that in the 1940s an average issue of The New York Times Book Review was 64 pages, "twice the length of the current Sunday section."

I needn't engage here in a long lament about this situation. While it is true that most anyone can get by without reading books, it is equally apparent that living life without the company of the world's greatest minds isn't really living at all. Instead, I'll admit that there was a time in my life when I gave short shrift to literature. Before joining The N&O's book page in 1996 I had been a reporter specializing in popular culture. I devoted a great deal of eye-time to the newspapers and magazines, television programs and movies that seemed central to my work.

But our lives are a zero-sum game. Time given to one pursuit is time stolen from another. My new job at the paper forced me to neglect my former interests to keep up with my book-load. My stack of barely read New Yorkers and People magazines became as tall as my list of unseen movies. I stood in awkward silence when the water-cooler conversation turned to "Sex and the City."

At first I felt I was missing out. But a wonderful change blossomed as my commitment to books intensified. Day by day, month by month, I began to feel a deeper connection to the world around me. The works of literature, history and biography that I was devouring were speaking more deeply about our society than the more directly relevant information sources I had been consuming. Politics and popular culture came alive for me in more meaningful ways. By thinking more profoundly, I began to care more deeply. I also was having more fun. Once you start reading books—I mean really start—it's hard to stop. My former interests seemed like thin gruel compared with the rich world of literature. They didn't do it for me anymore.

But this is something I had to learn for myself. How can you? There is no easy answer, only a pleasurable one: Make a commitment. Set aside one specific, uninterrupted hour each day, four days a week, for reading. Get up early, stay up late or make Jane Smiley your lunch date. If you read two hours one day, still read another hour the next. If you miss a day, don't figure you'll make it up the next—otherwise you might find yourself having to read for 25 hours in a single day.

Stick to this plan and, reading 30 pages an hour, you'll be polishing off an average length novel every two weeks or a daunting work of history each month. In a year's time, you will have conquered 6,240 pages; you will have completed fat biographies of Franklin, Jefferson and Lincoln, completed "War and Peace," "Anna Karenina" and "Crime and Punishment" and delved deeply into the comic genius of P. G. Wodehouse (start with "The Mating Season").

One other observation: Squirming and squinting are the enemy of literary surrender; invest in a chair and a lamp that won't become retirement plans for your chiropractor or optometrist. Before the year is up, I bet your priorities will change; the time pressures that prevent you from reading will take a different cast. You might even parrot the poet and essayist Abraham Cowley, who wrote, "If once we be thoroughly engaged in the Love of Letters, instead of being wearied with the length of any day, we shall only complain of the shortness of our whole life."

Put another way, get busy and good luck.

October 22, 2000

The Best Gift Reveals Yourself

It's four days until Christmas, Kwanzaa is just around the corner, Hanukkah is in full gear—AND YOU STILL HAVEN'T FINISHED YOUR HOLIDAY SHOPPING!

Fear not, dear reader, I'm here to help. The perfect gift may be closer than you think. It's a book, of course, but more than the desperation choice you might make at a big store display.

Allow me to explain, through a brief story.

A few years ago the Canadian novelist Eric Wright told me that he wanted to write an essay about the book he always gives as a gift. It was an obscure work, "Small Talk at Wreyland" by Cecil Torr, published in 1918. Cobbled from diaries and notebooks of the author's father and grandfather as well as his own observations, "Small Talk" focuses on the mores of a rural English community. Like so many works of that period, it is wistful. Torr knows that modernity has doomed this world, and his book is not just a reminiscence but also a record.

Wright's essay included many quotes and descriptions from the book—he seemed intent on conjuring Wreyland so that he might spend more time there. I sensed that his attachment to the work was grounded in something deeper than literary admiration. Knowing that Wright had been born in England but had moved to Canada while still a young man, I was certain that his ardor was connected to his lost past. I pushed him to explore these personal forces of memory and emotion to explain why he had made "Small Talk" the book he wanted others to think of when they thought of him.

My theory was only half right. This became clear after we took leave of the "Small Talk" essay and Wright crafted a brilliant piece about himself, class-consciousness and E. M. Forster's novel "Howard's End." He wrote:

> "Just before my eldest sister got married, there were 10 children, two parents and a pair of books living under our one roof. . . . I don't know where [they] came from. Perhaps my father 'found' [them] in the back of his van after one of the removal jobs he used to do when he wasn't delivering frozen beef from the London docks to the warehouses. [They] certainly [weren't] bought; by the time I was 6 we had risen to join the lower working class, having just escaped from the underclass, the London poor, but no one at our level had the money to buy books."

So the quiet, rural life I had imagined for Wright couldn't have been further from the truth. My nature boy had been, in fact, a street urchin. His life bore no relation to the book he had thrust into so many people's arms with the words, "from me."

Suddenly his love of "Small Talk" made perfect sense because I had had a similar experience. While still in my 20s and living in the crowded city of my youth, New York, I made a pastoral novel celebrating a lost era my gift of choice. I believed that "The Growth of the Soil" (1917) by the Norwegian Nobel laureate Knut Hamsun was one of the finest books I'd read, but my choice also told recipients something about me.

Like Wright's gift, "The Growth of the Soil" did more than confirm what my friends already knew. Instead of offering a book in sync with our smog-choked lives, "Soil" and "Small Talk" offered a vision of the lives we might like to have led. Instead of showing people our realities, we opened the doors to our imaginations, sharing our secret yearnings.

Which brings us back to your holiday problem.

Obviously you're having little luck figuring out what they would love, so why not give them something you love. Gifts become more than an exchange of loot when they have personal meaning, when their value exceeds their price tags in ways that can only be measured by the heart. Instead of the latest best seller, give them a book with history: the one that you loved as a child, that shaped your life, that carried you through a tough period or gives voice to thoughts you only whisper to yourself at night.

Why just give them something when you can give them yourself?

December 21, 2003

Cure for the Blues Is a Click Away

I'm a springy, sprightly sort of fellow. I may not do a jig very often or click my heels at the apex of a bounding leap more than once a month. But I like to think that when my fellow man gazes upon my map he sees, well, maybe not the essence or ecstasy or the embodiment of joie de vivre but, at the very least, someone who does not spend his days reading Sylvia Plath.

Still, my life isn't all peaches and cream. Sometimes I get bored. Sometimes I get blue. Sometimes I feel stuck on a lonely avenue. I don't trace these feelings to childhood traumas—though I still miss my pet gerbil, J., who impaled himself on his water tube when I was 11. Instead I blame them on books. Others may say that theirs is the loneliest passion—badminton enthusiasts, cigarette smokers and people who still admire Martha Stewart can make a case. But none can claim that title so long as readers roam the Earth.

Here's the strange thing: Everything is hunky-dory when I'm deep in an author's grip. The melancholy only arrives after I stop reading. I look around yet fail to see others with the same interests and loves as me. Devotees of Thomas Pynchon, Frederick Busch or Willem Elsschot. I know they're out there. But where?

But hey! I'm not springy and sprightly by chance. When I'm mired in the slough of despond, when I can no longer find joy in my heart I don't wallow at my private pity party. I have ways and means, methods of operation and high-tech solutions to cure my literary lament.

First, I remind myself of that sage advice Bill gave Monica: Not every day can be sunshine. Sizzle, delight and razzle-dazzle don't always come with the morning coffee.

Then I turn to the one place that always, absolutely and without fail provides me with the excitement and human connection I crave: the Internet. It's almost hard to believe that so much thrilling material, guaranteed to lift my mood and raise my spirits, is only a fingertip away, at Amazon.com.

I type in "Hunger" and instantly meet 56 people who share my undying love for Knut Hamsun's classic novel about alienation and are not afraid to say so in customer reviews. Can I explain the pleasure I feel in the company of the person called "lemontrees" who said "Hunger" offers, "Some of the most courageous, liveliest and wittiest comment on social life that has ever been written"?

When I search for Thomas Pynchon's great novel, "Gravity's Rainbow," the room gets pretty crowded—212 customer reviews. And counting! One friendly soul, identified simply as "a reader," writes: "Thomas Pynchon's mind-blowing masterpiece is easily the finest achievement in American literature. Someone referred to this as America's 'Ulysses.' That it is."

Yes, indeed.

In fact, the Pynchon party is so packed, a dissenter or two has filtered in, including "Vincent Vega from Paris, France," who declares: "I can say this: I have not read the book, but I watched the film, and to be blunt, I've seen better film on teeth. Pick up a classic Stephen King novel like "IT" instead of this pretentious crud."

Of course, I'm trolling for companionship, not criticism. I'm not seeking fair-minded assessments or biting insights but stark-raving raves of my favorite books. When I'm bored I can find 30 people who have read Frederick Busch's terrific novel about Herman Melville and a Civil War sniper, "The Night Inspector"—"I am in total awe of this book, and that's a lot coming from a skeptical person like me," writes "byron 72."

When I'm blue, I get revitalized by the five people who have also devoured Willem Elsschot's marvelous satire on capitalism and ambition,

"Cheese." When I need a little pick-me-up, I can turn to the two kindred souls who recognized the genius of Ursule Molinaro's magnificent "Demons & Divas: Three Novels."

So, if you are ever feeling less than your springy, sprightly best, try my "two click" method of happiness: Click your computer's mouse and then listen. Hear it. That's your heels coming together at the apex of a bounding leap.

January 25, 2004

Novels Found in Translation

It should have been the highlight of his year. It's not every day that your work is quoted at length in the New Yorker.

But something got lost in the translation.

The incident began happily enough when Sverre Lyngstad opened the magazine's Dec. 26 issue and found a long article on the Norwegian writer Knut Hamsun (1859–1952), the Nobel laureate whose reputation was damaged by his late-life support for the Nazis. Lyngstad has worked mightily to raise Hamsun's profile as a father of modernism. Since 1994, he has published a critical study of Hamsun's work and translated nine of his best works into English, including the novels "Hunger," "Pan," "Mysteries" and, most recently, "Victoria."

Sure enough, the New Yorker quoted liberally from Lyngstad's translations. But it never credited his work. When Lyngstad contacted the magazine, he was told that editors feared that including his name would "clutter" the piece. After much back and forth, the New Yorker finally agreed to print a shortened version of his letter to the editor.

"The article left the impression that the translations had just dropped from the sky or that Hamsun had done them himself," Lyngstad told me in a telephone interview. "You always like to be recognized for your work. The absence of such recognition raises the whole issue of the translator's very function and status, in seeming to suggest that citations from a translated text can be made without any mention of the person who brought it into existence."

Few people would endorse the magazine's oversight. Yet we must admit that it offered a little wish fulfillment to some readers. Translators play such a central role in our experience of foreign works that we have a natural urge to erase them from the picture.

Picking up "Madame Bovary" or "Crime and Punishment," we seek to surrender ourselves to the towering genius of Flaubert or Dostoevsky. We don't want to be reminded that our ignorance of French or Russian means we can never fully enjoy their works, but only versions of them created by gifted, but obscure, translators.

First-rate translators convey the story and spirit of the works at hand—capturing Bovary's yearning or Raskolnikov's torment. But then we remember Flaubert, who famously labored to find *le seul mot juste* (the one right word). Even a cursory glance of competing translations displays thousands of differing word choices, many of which alter the rhythm, the syntax and, to varying degrees, the meaning of the work.

To take one telling example, here is Lyngstad's translation of the third sentence from Hamsun's novel, "Victoria": "When he grew up he wanted to be a maker of matches." Here's how an earlier translator, Oliver Stallybrass, rendered it: "When he grew up he would work in a match factory."

I cannot say which version is more accurate, but the differences are plain. Lyngstad gives us an ambitious boy determined to set the world on fire. Stallybrass introduces us to a child whose grim fate seems predetermined.

Translators are like priests who mediate our relationship with literary gods. We depend on them even as we wish for direct contact.

Though translators often get the short shrift, they are more important than ever in this global age. Literature from foreign lands is one of the best ways to understand and experience distant cultures. Yet it represents only a tiny fraction of the books published in America.

Of the 195,000 new titles printed in English in 2004, only 891 were works of adult literature in translation, according to the RR Bowker company, which tracks publishing industry figures.

Nevertheless, thanks to the heroic and often poorly paid work of translators, we will be able to enjoy some wonderful works this spring. They include Irene Nemirovsky's novel of life in Nazi-occupied France,

"Suite Francaise" (translated from the French by Sandra Smith); best-selling French author Michel Houllebecq's futuristic tale of the modern world, "The Possibility of an Island" (translated by Gavin Bowd); and the latest novel from Portuguese Nobel laureate Jose Saramago,"Seeing" (translated by Margaret Jull Costa).

Translators also breathe new life into old works. The Nobel prize-winning poet Seamus Heaney resurrected "Beowulf" in 2000 through a version powerful enough to transform the bane of ninth-grade English into a national best seller. Richard Pevear and Larissa Volokhonsky's fresh translation of "Anna Karenina" led Oprah Winfrey to make Tolstoy's masterpiece one of her book club picks. And Anthony Briggs is generating new interest in another Tolstoy classic, "War and Peace" through his new translation of that sprawling epic.

All of which reminds us of the central paradox of the relationship between readers and translators: We can't live with them, and we can't live without them.

March 5, 2006

Know-How for the New Millennium: Fire and the Art of Library Maintenance

It is hot, *n'est ce pas,* Monsieur Proust? Ha. Ha. Ha. Oh! Hi. I didn't hear you coming. Finished with the sports pages already? You're shocked, I can tell, to find me surrounded by books before this roaring blaze.

On the eve of the new millennium, am I consumed with Y2K madness?

Perhaps. But do not judge me until you have heard my story—and please, hand me another volume.

Once, my library was a land of peaceful coexistence. Raymond Chandler and Anton Chekhov stood side by side like bosom buddies. Gentlemanly Ralph Ellison never complained about his boozy shelf-mate Frederick Exley. I heard nary a peep from Henry James when I slipped Tama Janowitz beside him, even though I suspect he found her rather outré.

But that comity combusted as the millennium drew near. A few nights ago that rabble-rouser Nietzsche declared, "If the world should end, everything is permitted."

The others began to rustle.

"You are human, all too human," St. Augustine replied, trying to restore some order. But to no avail, as long-simmering discontents gripped my trusted friends.

Turns out Arundhati Roy had never liked Philip Roth. She said he was a "porcine misogynist." Roth countered that Roy was "confusing the writer and his characters," which tamped things down until he called her a non-euphemism for a female dog.

Suddenly, Gertrude Stein bellowed that Robert Stone was "a man pleasing itself." Then she added, "No head, does that mean soap?"

Stone didn't know what to make of that. And neither did I, except that it couldn't be good.

Annie Proulx shipped some news Thomas Pynchon's way: "You're paranoid." Walker Percy pooh-poohed Edgar Allan Poe as a poetaster. Poe called Percy a poseur. So unpoetic!

The tension was broken when Jack Kerouac, sounding as if he had gotten an early start on New Year's Eve, accused John Irving of "only having written one decent book."

I realized then that the decision to arrange my books alphabetically had been misguided. Perhaps, I thought, ordering them chronologically, by date of publication, would restore tranquility. But would it be wise to place Norman Mailer next to dozens of other writers instead of just two? Only Naguib Mahfouz and Bernard Malamud seemed to think so.

Should I arrange them by country of origin? Americans here, the English there, the French in one corner, the Russians in another. But the thought of placing Günter Grass near Martin Heidegger was downright scary: "You dirty Nazi." "Ya, what of it?"

As I imagined other schemes, the scope of my problem became clear as the situation got really weird.

Rabbit Angstrom began berating John Updike. First, he called him a "murderer"—to which Anna Karenina and Emma Bovary chimed, "Hear, hear." Then he berated Updike for the self-indulgent sin of gorgeous gorgeosity. "Words, words, words," Rabbit shouted. "You're not Shakespeare, you know."

Meanwhile Lolita was castigating Nabokov for being "a dirty old man" while Captain Ahab made a lewd gesture toward Herman Melville, daring him to "call this Ishmael."

Nat Turner quieted the crowd, albeit momentarily, when he confessed that William Styron had "got me just right."

The silence was broken by shrieks behind my office door. I rushed from my living room to find my paperbacks enraged. Though they, too, had serious reservations about their own standing orders, they were speaking as one voice: "You show off the hardcovers in the nicest room of the house, shunting us off in this hole. Do we embarrass you?"

"Not guilty," I proclaimed. Then I looked at their tattered covers and added, "But look at yourselves. You don't even have dust jackets."

Big mistake.

I felt a sharp blow and crumpled to the floor. I'm sure it was that madman Quixote.

I awoke to a scene too horrible for words. Some paperbacks were dog-earing one another, while others were cracking the hardcovers' spines. Wallace Stevens was showing William Butler Yeats at least 13 ways to loose "mere anarchy upon the world." Homer and Plato were leading a posse of dead white males exercising a little authority over the postmodern literary critics. My biographies were pure bedlam: "Ali" pummeled "Woody Allen" while "T. R." wielded a really big stick against "Titan: The Life of John D. Rockefeller Sr." My six-volume history of the French Revolution was in flames.

All the while the collected writing of Abraham Lincoln despaired about "a shelf divided." It was then I knew it was time for radical deconstruction.

So I lit this fire. But rest assured, it is not fueled by literature—just old newspapers. It's a little warning. I'll douse it soon. But, it's the fire next time. Remember that, Monsieur Proust.

January 2, 2000

Critics Need More Than a Thumb

Every so often an author will write me to say thanks after we run a glowing review.

Usually I reply, "You're very welcome," when what I want to say is, "Don't thank me; you wrote a good book. Fail next time and we'll give you daggers instead of laurels."

Less frequently, I'll hear from a writer whose book was not praised. My usual reply is, "I understand how you feel," when I really want to say, "Write a better book, and you'll get a better review."

But as I end my first year as the News & Observer's book review editor, I must admit that those responses miss the point of our work here. It might appear that we are in the thumbs-up, thumbs-down business, but offering summary judgments on books is the least important and most questionable service we provide.

Let me explain by starting with one of the great conundrums of our business: Why is it that the reviews of some books are all over the map—praised by some, damned by others, yawned at by others still?

Reviewing John Updike's newest novel, "Toward the End of Time," Michiko Kakutani of the New York Times said it "prompts the same question raised by Joyce Carol Oates's last novel: How can such a gifted writer produce such a lousy book?"

Yet in the Times's Sunday Book Review a few weeks later, the novelist Margaret Atwood called Updike's novel "deplorably good. If only he would write a flagrant bomb. That would be news. But another excellently written novel by an excellent novelist—what can be said?"

How about: How can two such highly respected, knowledgeable and literate people have such polar views of the same book?

No doubt politics plays a part in these matters. Some book review editors want to support or debunk certain writers and will go out of their way to find critics who will deliver the goods. And, generally speaking, novelists are gentler than full-time reviewers, perhaps out of empathy or fear of retribution.

But more important than these compromised instances is the fact that reviewing occupies that middle ground between science and art. It relies on a range of learnable, almost objective skills—knowledge, experience and technique—that comes together as personal taste. A score of honest and accomplished critics conducting the same experiment (reading the same book) should reach some general agreement. Just as important, that group should have a few outliers.

All opinions are not equal, which is why not everybody is asked to write reviews. Qualified reviewers have spent years reading and thinking about books. They have read the author's work and know enough to consider it.

They can ask and answer this question: What problems did the author pose and how well were they resolved? Then move on to this: How complicated and nuanced were those problems and how elegant and insightful were the solutions? That question, which can only be answered through the deep knowledge of taste, is crucial. If we only judged books on their own terms, we could not express the qualitative difference between Shakespeare's "King Lear" and Grisham's "The Partner."

This subjectivity of informed taste makes book reviewing tricky because the answers—as Kakutani and Atwood demonstrated—are rarely cut and dried. It means that the least interesting thing about a review is the critics' opinion; the most important thing is how the reviewer arrived at and explains that assessment. There are no right or wrong answers, only compelling ones.

Book reviews are not a literary form of consumer reports aimed at identifying works worthy of our attention. Their purpose is to offer an informed response. The praise or pan is secondary to the act of honestly engaging books because books matter.

This might be navel-gazing crit-speak if we weren't facing a crisis as Sunday book reviews around the country abdicate this intellectual responsibility, becoming quick-hit consumer guides. Some book sections no longer run reviews of more than 500 words, just like People magazine. Others assign letter grades to books, à la Entertainment Weekly.

No doubt some readers like this cut-to-the-chase brevity. But when the least interesting thing we do is raise or lower the thumb, making that the only thing we do is placing book reviewing in critical condition.

December 28, 1997

The New American Dream

Have the American people been misread? Have all those newspaper and magazine stories portraying us as a nation of semi-literate, overworked couch potatoes with barely the time or capacity to choose between a Big Mac and a Quarter Pounder—"with or without cheese???? argh!"—been as on the mark as the headline "Dewey Defeats Truman"?

I struggled mightily with those questions after noticing that Thomas Pynchon's massive new novel, "Mason & Dixon," has been on the New York Times best-seller list for four weeks. That is, one of the most popular books in America is a 773-page novel written in 18th century prose style and filled with recondite concepts, erudite puns and obscure references.

I wondered: Is it possible that we are, in fact, a community of highly intellectual and engaged citizens? Do we actually crave books that are mentally and physically challenging—books so big we cannot read them in bed for fear they'll snap our wrists and crush our chests?

I pondered this for five full nanoseconds before concluding . . . Nah, that's not it.

Then I thought: Maybe people are buying the book, but they aren't actually reading it. And, like any self-respecting journalist, I was not content merely to raise a question,. I wanted answers. So I buttonholed three friends who've bought the book and pressed them relentlessly:

Q: "But have you read it?"
A (1): "Can't wait to get into it."
A (2): "The first 20 pages were INCREDIBLE!!"
A (3): "What's your problem?"

"Mason & Dixon" represents the literary triumph of style over substance. For the moment—the signature time frame in modern America—purchasing this book is as hip as iguanas, expensive cigars and nail polish for men (I kid you not). Around espresso machines across the American landscape, you hear people bantering:

"Got the new Pynchon book yet?"
"You bet. First week it was out."
"Yeah."
"Yeah."
Pause.
"This is Italian Roast, right?"
"No, I think it's French."

Some argue that art is diminished when it becomes a status symbol. I look at it the other way: How much do we elevate our status symbols when we make them works of genius? Besides, it's nothing new. There is a long, cherished tradition of novels regarded not simply as great books—which is, if you think about it, hardly select company—but as rare and rarefied works of incomprehensible perfection known as doorstoppers.

Doorstoppers are those forest-clearingly long, irreducibly complex books that are universally acclaimed despite, or perhaps because of, the fact that almost no one has actually read them—well, maybe, a quarter of the critics who reviewed them and some of the professors who teach them. Everybody who calls himself literate owns a copy of these masterpieces, which, like a Marine drill sergeant, stand ramrod straight upon their bookshelf perch, stiff and pristine, full of haughty, scolding, incessant and inexorable contempt for those not man enough to accept the challenge.

Ahem. Excuse me.

As big, fat and rich as they are, "Moby-Dick," "War and Peace" and "Don Quixote," for example, are merely great books. After all, people who have read them are a dime a dozen.

But Salman Rushdie's "The Satanic Verses," Robert Musil's "The Man without Qualities" and James Joyce's "Ulysses"—now those are doorstoppers. And the granddaddy of them all, of course, the Uber-doorstop, is Marcel Proust's glorious, riveting and sublime—we can all agree on that, can't we?—"Remembrance of Things Past," a three-volume, 3,291-page work that stands as one of the great and true expressions of the human soul. Right?

Admittedly, it is still too early to tell if "Mason & Dixon" is a real doorstopper. It has the potential, but Pynchon will have to hope succeeding generations buy and then do not read his book before it can claim the title.

More importantly, what does the success of "Mason & Dixon" tell us about Americans? It says we are still boundless optimists. We may be stressed out, overworked and glued to the tube, but we still believe that one day, perhaps the better day of tomorrow, we will have the time, energy and inclination to read Proust, Joyce, Musil and still have a little something left for a 773-page novel about two guys who once drew a line.

June 8, 1997

Having a Baby by the Book

My dear wife, Janine, constantly surprises. Like a week ago at Rex Hospital. We were filling out a follow-up form after the birth of our first child, Olivia Catherine—the most beautiful, precious sweet little future heart-breaking, Nobel Prize—winning bundle of pure angelic . . . Ahem.

"How do you learn best?" the form asked, "reading, TV/video, demonstration, listening or doing?" Janine looked at me, her furrowed brow, sloping nose and slightly open mouth winding into a question mark.

I looked back at her—brow even more furrowed, nose more sloped and mouth fly-catchingly agape. "Sweetie," I said, "by way of reminder I'd haul in every baby book you bought during the pregnancy but I don't think they allow forklifts in the maternity ward."

When, already wise beyond her days, Olivia wants to know about her very beginnings, we can show her shelves of books that chronicle the overweening preparations and emotional palpitations of a couple of first-timers trying to do the right thing. It's said that giving something a name makes it real. When Janine and I decided to start a family, she immediately bought "A World of Baby Names."

"Jumping the gun a bit?" I asked.

She shot me a look that could spark many things, but loving union was not one of them.

Nevertheless, conception! And a flood of books—"What To Expect When You're Expecting," "The New Well Pregnancy Book," "Conception, Pregnancy and Birth," "Pregnancy and Childbirth," "The Complete Handbook of Pregnancy." Each detailed and delineated the complex wonders of the human body. Like most self-help books, they basically offered the same advice. And, like most self-help readers, we found each regurgitation endlessly fascinating and bored our friends to tears with each startling detail. "Placenta previa," "amniocentesis" and "sonogram" started tripping off Janine's tongue. I spent hours staring at the diagrams of cell division and the rows of pictures showing a dot turning into a shrimp turning into ET turning, finally, into a huggable little snuggle-bunny.

But we also learned things way beyond the counter-intuitive. We knew that now was not the time to explore the microbrew craze or to make an adult decision about smoking, but "Protecting Your Baby-to-Be" warned that nutritional heavyweights like mushrooms, potatoes, peppers, broccoli, Brussels sprouts, basil and cumin could make Janine or the baby sick. (Janine cut them out with nary a whimper; having to give up chocolate, well, that required a level of sacrifice not seen since the charge of the Light Brigade.)

Things quieted down during the second trimester but in the seventh month capitalism reared its wallet-crunching head. "The Guide To Baby Products" and "Baby Bargains" seemed a cross between consumer activism and corporate shilling, providing invaluable advice on innumerable "indispensable" products, including Diaper Genies and wiper warmers, Baby Bjorns and Pack n' Plays, Exersaucers, 3-D activity gyms and portable baby bouncers "with musical toy bar." And to think I had been satisfied with one GI-Joe and a raggedy blanket.

The eighth month brought fresh loads of baby name books. We bought "The Baby Name Personality Survey," "Beyond Jennifer & Jason," "Unusual & Most Popular Baby Names," and, the mistitled "The Last Word on First Names"—there were scores more we could have purchased (along with dozens suggesting names for dogs, cats and parakeets). Buying a book to find a name is a bit silly. On the other hand, given the endless hours we spent trying to think like a mean-spirited

6 year-old, I was amazed that we could not find one guide that explained how playground bullies can rhyme any lovely and blessed name into a taunting insult.

At this time we started speculating about gender. Our pregnant friend Nancy swore by the Chinese Conception Chart included in a book called "Boy or Girl?" Purportedly divined by a 13th century Chinese scientist, it predicts the baby's sex based on the month of conception and the mother's age. Nancy had tested it on her friends, and reported that it was "almost always right." The test said we were both having girls. Nancy was so convinced, we were convinced.

Then, Nancy had a boy.

When the big day arrived we felt fully prepared, but sometimes knowledge is no substitute for experience. As Olivia slid out I shouted, "It's a boy."

"It's a girl," the doctor shot back. "You're looking at the umbilical cord."

March 23, 1997

ANYTHING GOES

NEW STANDARDS,
SHIFTING BOUNDARIES

Lack of Curiosity Is Curious

Over dinner a few weeks ago, the novelist Lawrence Naumoff told a troubling story. He asked students in his introduction to creative writing course at UNC-Chapel Hill if they had read Jack Kerouac. Nobody raised their hand. Then he asked if anyone had ever heard of Jack Kerouac. More blank expressions.

Naumoff began describing the legend of the literary wild man. One student offered that he had a teacher who was just as crazy. Naumoff asked the professor's name. The student said he didn't know. Naumoff then asked this oblivious scholar, "Do you know my name?"

After a long pause, the young man replied, "No."

"I guess I've always known that many students are just taking my course to get a requirement out of the way," Naumoff said. "But it was disheartening to see that some couldn't even go to the trouble of finding out the name of the person teaching the course."

The floodgates were opened and the other UNC professors at the dinner began sharing their own dispiriting stories about the troubling state of curiosity on campus. Their experiences echoed the complaints voiced by many of my book reviewers who teach at some of the nation's best schools.

All of them have noted that such ignorance isn't new—students have always possessed far less knowledge than they should, or think they have. But in the past, ignorance tended to be a source of shame and motivation. Students were far more likely to be troubled by not-knowing, far more eager to fill such gaps by learning. As one of my reviewers, Stanley Trachtenberg, once said, "It's not that they don't know, it's that they don't care about what they don't know."

This lack of curiosity is especially disturbing because it infects our broader culture. Unfortunately, it seems both inevitable and incurable.

In our increasingly complex world, the amount of information required to master any particular discipline—e.g. computers, life insurance, medicine—has expanded exponentially. We are forced to become specialists, people who know more and more about less and less.

This is occurring at a time when Americans increasingly put work at the center of their lives even as the rise of globalization and other free market approaches have turned job security into an anachronism. In this frightening new world, students do not turn to universities for mind expansion but vocational training. In the parlance of journalism, they want news they can use.

Upon graduation, they must devote ever more energy to mastering the floods of information that might help them keep their wobbly jobs. Crunched, they have little time to learn about far-flung subjects.

The narrowcasting of our lives is writ large in our culture. Faced with a near-infinite range of knowledge, the Internet slices and dices it all into highly specialized niches that provide mountainous details about the slightest molehills. It is no wonder that the last mainstream outlet of general knowledge, the daily newspaper, is suffering declining readership. When people only care about what they care about, their desire to know something more, something new, evaporates like the morning dew.

Here's where it gets really interesting. In comforting response to these exigencies, our culture gives us a pass, downplaying the importance of knowledge, culture, history and tradition. Not too long ago, students might have been embarrassed to admit they'd never heard of Jack Kerouac. Now they're permitted to say "whatever."

When was the last time you met anyone who was ashamed because they didn't know something?

It hasn't always been so. When my father, the son of Italian immigrants, was growing up in the 1930s and 40s, he aspired to be a learned man. Forced to go to work instead of college, he read "the best books," listened to "the best music," learned which fork to use for his salad. He watched Fred Astaire puttin' on his top hat and tyin' up his white tie, and dreamed of entering that world of distinction.

That mind-set seems as dead as my beloved Dad. The notion of an aspirational culture, in which one endeavors to learn what is right, proper and important in order to make something more of himself, is past.

In fairness, the assault on high culture and tradition that has transpired since the 1960s has paid great dividends, bringing long overdue attention to marginalized voices.

Unfortunately, this new freedom has sucker punched the notion of the educated person who is esteemed not because of the size of his bank account or the extent of his fame but the depth of his knowledge. Instead of a mainstream reverence for those who produce or appreciate works that represent the summit of human achievement, we have a corporatized and commodified culture that hypes the latest trend, the next new thing.

People are shaped by the world around them. In our here, now, get-the-job-done environment of modern America, the knowledge for knowledge's sake ethos that is the foundation of a liberal arts education—and of a rich and satisfying life—has been shoved to the margins. Curiously, in a world where everything is worth knowing, nothing is.

November 6, 2005

Reading Loses in This War

I can still hear my old history teacher proclaiming: What's past is prologue; those who do not remember the past are condemned to repeat it.

It was a comforting idea. By mastering the past, we could control the future. Hit the books, boys!

His class offered lessons and analogies galore, and I gleaned something else from that march through time: History is a cavalcade of unintended consequences and uncontrollable forces. It's not so much one darn thing after another, but a string of Pandora's boxes unloosing the unexpected upon the world.

I recalled my teacher's words last weekend while reading about the high-stakes "canon wars" that roiled academia a few decades ago. It was a brutal battle, journalist Rachel Donadio observed in the New York Times Book Review, as great minds argued over the nature of greatness.

What books should students be told to read? What history should they be taught? What standard should be used in establishing the canon, that unofficial list of great books and ideas that we should consider the summit of human achievement?

Reading Donadio's essay, I marveled not just at the high purpose of the combatants but also their hubris. Looking back at these wars, it's clear how their efforts to control ideas were thwarted by unintended consequences and swamped by forces far mightier than they. In retrospect, they seemed like a gaggle of Neros, fiddling while their literary house was burning.

Donadio's piece begins 20 years ago, when the late Allan Bloom published his best-selling assault on academia, "The Closing of the American Mind." Bloom, then a professor of political philosophy at the University of Chicago, decried efforts to replace works by literary icons that had long defined the intellectual gold standard (Plato, Chaucer, Shakespeare) with works by women, African Americans and members of other marginalized groups. The result, Bloom argued, was not a flowering of knowledge, but a dumbing down of universities that had forsaken eternal truths for political correctness.

Bloom's opponents granted that dead white males had much to say. But, they argued, students were more likely to connect with newer works that depicted a broader range of ideas and experiences.

"It's generally agreed that the multiculturalists won the canon wars," Donadio reports. "Reading lists were broadened to include more works by women and minority writers. . . . there has been a decided shift towards works of the present and recent past."

The canon wars were, at bottom, a battle over authority: Which writers would we trust to help us understand the world? The conflict was part of the broader effort that took flight during the 1960s to re-evaluate almost every societal value.

Just as Americans pushed to make more room in our political and cultural life for African Americans, women, gays and lesbians and other excluded groups, many scholars worked to make their fields more inclusive. By expanding the range of voices their students encountered, scholars believed they would help them think more critically about society.

Unfortunately, these vigorous debates shifted attention from a metastasizing cancer. As scholars battled over which voices would have authority, larger forces were working to diminish its force in the culture.

The U.S. Department of Education reports that 1.6 percent of America's undergraduates majored in English during the 2003–2004 school year, while 20 percent majored in business. Broader studies have documented sharp drops in the number of Americans who read. A 2004 survey by the National Endowment of the Arts reported that only about half of Americans read any type of fiction, whether by Danielle Steel or Margaret Atwood. An Associated Press-Ipso poll released last month found that one in four American adults said they had not read a single book during the previous year.

In modern America, it is shameful to be poor but not to be poorly read. There is no stigma attached to cultural ignorance in our money culture. Recognizing this new dynamic, our institutions of higher learning are less interested in preparing their graduates for life than for the workplace.

"In a shift of historic importance, America's colleges and universities have largely abandoned the idea that life's most important question . . . the meaning of life, of what one should care about and why . . . is an appropriate subject for the classroom," Anthony Kronman, a professor of law at Yale University, observed in the Sept. 16 Boston Globe. "In doing so, they have betrayed their students by depriving them of the chance to explore it in an organized way, before they are caught up in their careers and preoccupied with the urgent business of living itself."

Such questions are, of course, the business of literature. Great books are one of the most effective vehicles we have for putting us inside the mind and shoes of another human being. Every true work of literature whether it's Chaucer's old classic, "Canterbury Tales," or Chinua Achebe's modern one, "Things Fall Apart" is subversive because it challenges the authority of "I," urging us toward seeing the world through someone else's eyes.

The multicultural forces that won the canon wars cannot necessarily be blamed for the decline of literary interest that attended their victory. That involved mighty historical forces beyond their control.

And yet, seen another way, their tradition-busting efforts were almost too successful. Instead of questioning the authority of specific writers, Americans increasingly dismiss the relevance of any writer. This in turn reinforces the status quo. The less people read, the less equipped they become to understand and challenge the ideas shaping their world. By hunkering down and focusing on the work in front them, they may create a rich economy but a poor culture.

Perhaps it is time for a new war, one in which scholars and book lovers join forces not to promote specific books, but literature itself. There's no guarantee that reading will make us better people. But it will empower us to understand the world, especially the forces beyond our control.

September 23, 2007

So Long Moby, Hello Aquaman

One day high school students will not be assigned Alexandre Dumas's "The Three Musketeers" but Stan Lee's "The Fantastic Four." Instead of "Moby-Dick" they'll read "Aquaman." Rather than study the careers of Richard the Lion-Heart and George Washington, they'll ponder "The Lion King" and "Curious George."

Sounds far-fetched? It might be unless you consider who is proposing the idea: the editorial page of the New York Times.

In an article last Sunday headlined "Why Comics Are as Important as Shakespeare," Timesman Brent Staples argued that American educators need to rethink their ideas about what is fit to read. His focus was the recent effort of the San Francisco board of education to require that 70 percent of the books read by students—in a district that is about 90 percent minority—be by authors of color. Besieged by critics who argued that shelving the works of dead white males such as Chaucer and Mark Twain amounted to cultural suicide, the board ultimately passed a squishy resolution instructing teachers to assign works that "reflect the diversity of culture, race and class" of the student body.

Staples said that debate is beside the point. Noting the poor performance of San Francisco's students, he agreed that changes are necessary to make reading lists more relevant to students' lives. But rather than increase the number of books by African American, Hispanic or gay authors, he urged educators to ask students what they want to read and start assigning those texts.

Suggesting that there is a strong resemblance between the "bloody and fantastical" Homer and modern action figures, Staples asserted, "Purists argue that children need to read the great books in the original. But from a pedagogical standpoint, what matters most is that they engage whatever they read early and deeply enough to make reading, thinking and writing second nature. Whether it is 'literature' or 'trash' makes little difference."

To his credit, Staples saw that the real question is not whether children should be made to read James Baldwin or Ernest Hemingway but how to get students who do not read to take up the habit. Isn't it better that they read "The Incredible Hulk" than nothing at all? He concluded: "The debate over the difference between 'trash' and 'literature' is fine for cocktail parties. But where children grow up cut off from books, the only relevant question is how to get them to read, write and think. The answer is to start early and use whatever works."

Though Staples insightfully diagnosed the problem, his solution is a retreat of the worst kind. While he tells us that he devoured comic books as a child, this analysis by anecdote is perilously slim evidence that "Flash Gordon" is a gateway to "Light in August." It also sidesteps the larger question of how "trash" that is inherently pedestrian and unchallenging can help students to write and to think.

Dangerously, Staples is buying into the creeping commercialization of education. As dozens of news stories have reported, grade inflation is a growing problem as teachers try desperately to satisfy their customers, the students.

Even before the most recent debate, San Francisco students had a say in picking six of the 10 books they were required to read each year. On the surface, this might seem a noble experiment in giving children a stake in their own curriculum but at root it is an abdication of responsibility.

The purpose of education—as it has been since time immemorial—is not to give students what they want, but what adults who have thought long and hard on the matter feel they must have.

This hardly seems a daunting task. Anyone who has read Charles Dickens's "Great Expectations" or Toni Morrison's "Beloved" knows how exciting and engaging literature can be. If school children do not feel this joy, if they do not hear how great books speak to them and see how they illuminate their lives, the fault lies not with them or the books but with us.

The problem then is the failure of educators—and parents, and the culture at large, which seems to have forgotten the essentiality of literature—to make children understand not only the necessity, but also the thrill of experiencing the summit of human creativity.

If we cannot get students pumped up by the best we have to offer, how can we keep their interest when we only give them our worst?

April 5, 1998

We're Servants of the Overload

We live in an age of too much.

Too much food is choking our arteries. Too much stuff is clogging our landfills. Our rambling McMansions and tanklike SUVs are deepening our addiction to dangerous fossil fuels. America has come to resemble the P. G. Wodehouse character who looked "as if he'd been poured into his suit and forgotten to say when."

While the perils of our material excess are well known, far less attention has been paid to how this epidemic of too-muchness is diminishing our cultural life.

Most commentators including me make the "too little" argument: We cite studies showing declining participation rates in the arts to argue that Americans don't read and write enough, don't avail themselves of the soul-stirring pleasures of art.

I still accept this diagnosis of cultural malaise. But I'm beginning to rethink its cause. I'm beginning to wonder:

Is too much reading killing reading?
Is too much writing killing writing?
Is too much communication killing communication?

Start with books. Recent surveys show that fewer than half of all Americans read at least one work of fiction for pleasure each year. The decline is especially pronounced among teenagers. Many factors have contributed to the trend, but the rise of the Internet is clearly a chief culprit.

Most Web sites are text based, the moving images of YouTube.com and other sites notwithstanding. Surfers are readers. And now that service jobs have replaced manufacturing as the economy's prime engine, Americans spend much of their working life reading.

My guess is that the average American reads more words in a week than our ancestors read in a month. It's just that we're not reading books.

Americans are also writing more than ever. E-mail, instant messaging and text messaging have turned us into a nation of scribes using high-tech gizmos to practice the centuries-old art of communicating with 26 letters and a host of annoying emoticons :(

Novelists often depict Americans as isolated and alienated, cut off from one another. Which leads me to ask: Don't these people own cell phones? Because of this tinkling technology we're never alone. The demands of family and friendship are so great that Americans must use every available moment strolling down supermarket aisles, dining at restaurants and bars, speeding down the freeway, one hand on the wheel (sorta) to maintain this steady stream of communication.

The problem, then, is that we are reading, writing and communicating too much. We have replaced quality with quantity, ushering in an era of shorthand culture. Web sites, e-mail and cell phones prize speed and efficiency. They are in-and-out technologies: make your point, move on.

Instead of conversing leisurely on the front porch, we communicate through snippets of text and talk. Instead of reading 20,000-word profiles in the New Yorker, we devour 200-word items on Gawker.com.

Shorthand culture is insidious because it looks and feels like the real thing. If we spend all day reading at work, is it any wonder that fewer of us want to tackle "War and Peace" in our free time? If we spend an hour or two a day writing e-mail, do we really want to go home and compose a real letter? If we speak to our loved ones five times a day on the cell, do we still feel the urge to have a meaningful conversation?

The danger here is that we may lose the capacity to recognize what we have lost. It's akin to writer Dana Thomas's warning in "Deluxe: How

Luxury Lost Its Luster": The widespread availability of relatively inexpensive products with designer labels has made us forget what items of real craftsmanship look like.

The surrender of quality for quantity has received attention in the world of music. Thanks to iPods and MP3 technology, we can store thousands of songs on tiny players that make music more accessible than ever. But in compressing music into tiny sound files, sonic detail—the clink of a finger cymbal, a virtuoso guitarist's subtle fretwork—is lost.

Of course, most of us don't even know what a finger cymbal sounds like, so the trade-off is a no-brainer. But you'd expect it to matter to such leading classical music and jazz critics as Anthony Tommasini of the New York Times and Terry Teachout of the Wall Street Journal. Yet in the recent Journal article "The Deaf Audiophile: What's So Good About Bad Sound? Plenty," Teachout wrote: "Why do I settle for inferior sound quality? Partly because of the near-miraculous convenience of MP3s."

Which makes me wonder: If the highbrows have jumped ship, is the battle lost?

As Teachout suggests, convenience is a hallmark of the age of too much. We rely on the Internet, cell phones and MP3s because they seem to make our lives easier. There is no turning back, and I, for one, don't want to. But as we enjoy the benefits of these technologies, we should remember that reading blogs is not the same as reading books, that e-mail and cell phones are not always the best tools of communication.

If the modern age teaches us anything, it's this: It is possible to have too much of a good thing.

January 20, 2008

Daily Nuggets of Wisdom

After completing two towering masterpieces, "Anna Karenina" and "War and Peace," Leo Tolstoy (1828–1910) began working on the book he would consider his most important contribution to humanity. The Russian writer devoted the last eight years of his life to creating three volumes of wisdom, drawn from hundreds of sources and dozens of cultures, that would remind people of their better natures and higher callings.

Translator Peter Sekirin has edited the trilogy into a single volume titled "Wise Thoughts for Every Day: On God, Love, Spirit, and Living a Good Life." Each of its 365 entries offers brief yet profound reflections on 30 topics such as "Love," "Effort," "Truth" and "Soul."

"Temptation" is the theme of the three Feb. 18 passages, which include this pearl from the 19th-century Frenchman Felicite Robert de Lamennais: "Nothing hinders the life of people more than making some others do as they wish by force. The day will come when people will understand that there is a common law, not the law of violence but universal law for each other."

As he does throughout the book, Tolstoy amplifies that thought with his own nugget: "Thieves live by stealing. You cannot believe they are decent people until they stop, and prayer and sacrifices make them good. The same is true of the rich and lazy. If they do not work but rely on the labor of others, they cannot be good either, no matter how much they pray and sacrifice."

Those are not simply ideas, but rich statements that suggest Tolstoy's notions of collective responsibility and edification. More important, the insights are not offered as conclusions but launching pads for our own considerations.

I was reminded of Tolstoy's volume last week when I came across a new book he helped inspire: "The Intellectual Devotional: Revive Your Mind, Complete Your Education, and Roam Confidently With the Cultured Class," edited by David S. Kidder and Noah D. Oppenheim. It also offers "365 daily lessons," but the books are worlds apart. For example, the new book's entry for today's date does not ask us to contemplate temptation but delivers a brief profile of the Roman Emperor Constantine, who "issued the Edict of Milan in 313 AD, legalizing Christianity throughout the empire."

As the year progresses "The Intellectual Devotional" provides other Pringles of information. The entry on "Renaissance Art" begins: "The period known as the Renaissance followed the Middle Ages and led to the modern era." Of "Friction" we learn: "Friction is the force that opposes a moving object when the surface of the object rubs against another." And, of course, old Leo gets his own day: "Though history has produced many great novelists, arguably none is held in higher esteem than Leo

Tolstoy . . . [who] concludes that the great shaping force of history is the unpredictability and irrationality of human behavior."

As a columnist, I am drawn to the contrasts between these works, which reflect key changes in Western culture during the last century. Tolstoy's deep spirituality, his focus on love, temptation and other subjects that contemporary sophisticates pooh-pooh, can seem quaint and anachronistic. Perhaps this genius spent his last years trying to reconnect us to these elemental forces because he saw that our ties to them were fraying.

"The Intellectual Devotional" provides information, not inspiration. This quick-hit knowledge is in sync with our jolt culture, where people feel they are judged by their smarts but are too busy to become learned. Don't get me wrong. It's important to know that the "sun burns at 6,000 degrees Celsius" and that "Pablo Picasso's 'Guernica'—a shocking and powerful image of modern warfare—depicts the chaos wrought by German bombers on a small town during the Spanish Civil War." But one needn't be too tweedy to observe that knowing F. Scott Fitzgerald wrote "The Great Gatsby" (page 79) or that Michelangelo painted the Sistine Chapel (page 115) does not immediately make you Immanuel Kant (page 237).

It takes heroic effort to fight off every here's-what-it-all-means fiber in my columnist's noggin and not read too much into the differences between these books. Even as I assert that mainstream culture is becoming ever more secular, that the desire for data, facts and trivia grows daily, and that shallowness is increasingly pawned off as depth, I must acknowledge countercurrents.

Spirituality remains a potent force in American life. Bookstores and libraries are full of recent works chronicling journeys of faith. Other books raise the alarm that fundamentalism is on the rise, that America is in danger of becoming a theocracy.

I am convinced that modern America is more in line with "The Intellectual Devotional" than "Wise Thoughts for Every Day." But I also know that culture is like a book of tricky illustrations, in which pictures of fish are also portraits of birds and sleeping dogs rest in the faces of men. It all depends on how you look at it.

Besides, this is America. Go get both books and enjoy the rewards of each.

February 18, 2007

Idiot's Delight:
The Age of the Moron

They're on TV. They're in the cineplex. They're even at your local bookstore. Wherever you zip or zap you're bound to smack into our newest cultural icon: morons.

Television shows such as "Fear Factor" feature real live adults doing inexplicably stupid things: covering themselves in 200,000 bees, diving in a tank filled with 1,001 snakes, jumping off moving trucks. MTV enjoyed such success with its "Jackass" stunt fest that we now have "Jackass: The Movie." Its tag line: "Same crew, same cast, same level of incompetence."

Buffoonery has always been a staple of popular culture, but stupidity was usually an unintended consequence. We watched and asked, "Don't these people know how dumb they are?"

Today, idiocy is center stage. It is the attraction, the point. We watch and say: "Look at these stupid people."

Hence the bestselling success of "The Darwin Awards" and "The Darwin Awards II," that "commemorate those who improve our gene pool by removing themselves from it." They depict a cavalcade of dearly departed boneheads, such as the 18-year-old man vacationing in Hawaii who ignored the signs warning "Hazardous Conditions—Do Not Go Beyond This Point" to get a better look at Halona Blowhole, "a rock formation that shoots seawater 20 feet into the air." If you're familiar with Wile E. Coyote, you know how this story ends.

Other literary excursions into the land of the cerebrally challenged include two books by Kathryn and Ross Petras, "The 176 Stupidest Things Ever Done" and "Stupid Sex: The Most Idiotic and Embarrassing Intimate Encounters of All Time." And don't forget "Duh! The Stupid History of the Human Race" by Bob Fenster. Academic presses are also getting into the act: Yale University Press has published "Why Smart People Can Be So Stupid," a series of essays edited by Robert J. Sternberg, and the University of Illinois Press has weighed in with Avita Ronell's cultural history, "Stupidity."

Why the fascination with morons? Ironically, the answers involve intricate forces that have placed intelligence at the center of our culture.

For most of our history, "can-do" and "common sense" were the chief American virtues. People engaged in farming, manufacturing and other blue-collar jobs that relied on skills learned by watching their parents or co-workers. Their abilities were identifiable, the quality of their work apparent. Silver-tongued personalities were admired but distrusted. Book learning was dismissed as impractical, and "eggheads" were disparaged as denizens of the "ivory tower" (see Richard Hofstadter's "Anti-Intellectualism in American Life").

The nation has done an about-face since the 1960s. Higher education has become the key to success in a global economy in which mastering a trade no longer guarantees steady employment. Workers must now be "retrained" so they can toil in service-oriented fields that require general smarts instead of specific skills. Intelligence has become the coin of the realm.

Problem is, intelligence—which involves not just intellect but emotion and personality—is hard to define and even harder to measure. The brilliant mathematician might not be able to write a coherent sentence; the soaring poet may be unemployable because he's so, well, weird. It is easy to know if you can fix a car, plant a crop or sew a shirt; but what does smart really mean—especially when we all know how dumb we can be? And if we have reason to doubt our own brilliance, how can we trust the world to bank on it?

Anxiety and democracy go hand in hand—it's tougher to know your place in a fluid, relatively classless society. But a democracy based on the subjective concept of intelligence is a recipe for extreme anxiety.

So we seize on various mechanisms for assurance. The cult of self-esteem, which holds that everyone is gifted and talented, that all opinions have equal weight, is a national religion. The worship of Mammon is an equally popular faith because dollars and cents seem to provide an objective scorecard of success. And the powerful trumpet the idea of America as a "meritocracy"—the dubious notion that our nation offers a level playing field to all—because it justifies their exalted positions. They tell themselves, "I rose strictly through merit."

In the new economy, merit is based on intelligence. When brainpower rules, those who disagree with us must be stupid. Thus, Michael Moore did not title his hugely popular diatribe against Republicans "People with Whom I Have Honest Differences," but "Stupid White Men." Taking a page from Rush Limbaugh—who casts intellectual differences in moral terms—Anne Coulter titled her mega-best-selling screed against Democrats, "Slander: Liberal Lies About the American Right."

The age of the moron, then, is another coping mechanism for anxious souls in a culture of intelligence. In times when many people worry about their place in the new economy, "Fear Factor," "Jackass" and "The Darwin Awards" allow us to tell the world who we are by who we are not. We glom onto idiots because they insulate us from our own fears.

Put simply, dumb people make us feel smart.

October 27, 2002

REALLY?

TRUTH AND TRUTHINESS

Truth, Facts, and CBS

Journalists have been in a tizzy since CBS released an in-house investigation of its story reporting that President George W. Bush and his family pulled strings to help him avoid combat during the Vietnam War (he served in the National Guard).

Conservatives say Memogate, which revolves around forged documents, proves the liberal bias of the mainstream media (the MSM). Not true, respond MSM honchos, who say the story was the result of incompetence, not malfeasance.

I'll let others debate the provenance of the documents, though it's hard to conclude CBS was shooting straight. More interesting are the fundamental questions Memogate raises about the nature of truth.

A century ago William James made a necessary distinction between facts and truth. Facts, he said, are the indisputable phenomena we can all agree upon. The sun rises in the east; rain is made of water; President Bush served in the National Guard. Truth, James noted, is trickier. It is what the mind does with those facts—the ways it organizes, prioritizes and contextualizes them to give them meaning. Are the sun and the rain just weather, or signs of God's blessing or curse? Is Bush's Guard service an old and irrelevant chapter in the president's life or does it pull back the curtain on his character?

Human nature leads us to ask and try to answer such questions, to assign meaning to experience. Yet our private realms of temperament and experience color this process.

Journalists almost always claim the mantle of Joe Friday—just the facts, ma'am. Journalists, however, are not simply fact collectors. They use their professional judgment, honed by years of training, to sift through and organize facts to provide a meaningful picture of reality.

Still, they argue that journalism is as much a science as an art. Reporters are trained to strive for objectivity, to use rigorous methods of data collection and open-ended methods of analysis rather than gut instinct to see what's really going on. Where a successful scientific experiment is reproducible in any laboratory, 10 reporters covering a single event will usually come up with 10 different stories—and sometimes the differences will be more than slight.

Consider again President Bush's service in the National Guard. Apart from the important issue of whether CBS used forged documents in its "60 Minutes Wednesday" segment is the larger question of whether his service is newsworthy. Many people contend that whether Bush sought a special accommodation three decades ago is irrelevant today. Others believe it is a crucial window into his character. The same dynamic informed debate over the swift boat veterans who challenged John Kerry's service in Vietnam. And it is as easy to argue that the mainstream media's coverage of the Iraq war has been irresponsibly negative as it is that it has not been tough enough.

News organizations confront such judgment calls every day, and their answers will never please everyone. How could they?

In her superb new novel "Gilead," Marilynne Robinson observes that each of us crafts his own version of the truth. A character says, "I do believe there is a secret language in each of us, also a separate aesthetic and a separate jurisprudence. Every single one of us is a little civilization built on the ruins of any number of preceding civilizations, but with our own variant notions of what is beautiful and what is acceptable."

That is, there is no single truth, but versions of the truth, the stories we tell ourselves to make sense of it all. Truth is Hydra-headed because we all want different things from it and because each individual (and news organization, for that matter) is too small to see the big picture.

Our task, as William James observed, is to gather as many facts as we can while discarding the notion of a capital T truth. We must use those facts to forge better truths for ourselves. Learn all we can, test all we learn. Dispense with the truth we held yesterday if a more convincing one emerges today. Listen, sift, revise; listen, sift, revise.

This is probably an impossible task. It sets a standard that few people, or news organizations, will attain. Bias is unavoidable. No individual and no institution sees everything in the clear light; perception is always colored by perspective, by our interests and values. But that is not a reason to embrace bias; it shows the necessity of striving to limit it at every turn.

The saving grace is that no individual or institution gets to define truth. All are just a voice in an often cacophonous choir. None of us is able to deliver the final word. But each of us can reveal a facet of the truth that will bring everyone else closer to a better one.

This process has never been easier, thanks to the democratization of information made possible by the Internet and cable TV. Once silent or obscure voices can now thunder. New media worry the mainstream media—with reason. They represent competition. But they also expose us to ways of looking at the world that can add to the material we sift and shape as we try to assign meaning to experience.

January 23, 2005

New Media:
Too Much of a Good Thing?

George Orwell was right—for all the wrong reasons. In "1984" he prophesied a world of totalitarian doublespeak where up was down, black was white and good was evil. We haven't reached those extremes, but I hear his voice in the incessant charges of rampant censorship and media bias.

His warning is echoed in right-wing attacks on the New York Times and books such as "Bias: A CBS Insider Exposes How the Media Distort the News" by Bernard Goldberg. And it is confirmed by liberal salvos against Fox News and works such as "Stupid White Men" by Michael Moore and "What Liberal Media? The Truth About Bias and the News" by Eric Alterman.

These contradictory sources have a single message: The news is more twisted than Enron's tax returns.

These loud and common complaints are undermined by their very expression. Censorship means the absence of dissent; with each broadside critics proclaim "the truth we're not being told." Media bias is problematic when a small number of sources are shaping coverage; the variety of prominent voices proves that the notion of a lockstep media elite is a fantasy.

The rise of the Internet and other alternative news outlets has put an astounding amount of information and opinion just a fingertip away. A generation ago, one had to work mighty hard to track down Marxist critiques of survivalist rants. Back then, you could spend months trying to find someone to ask: "Psst—know where I can get the latest communique from the John Birch Society?" Even then, the usual response was "not a clue."

Now all you have to do is type www.jbs.org and voila, a cornucopia of articles on "Proofs of a Conspiracy," "Your Job May Be Next" and "Inside the United Nations"—trust me, you don't want to go there. Similarly, I receive an e-mail every day from the Institute for Public Accuracy (www.accuracy.org) offering a long list of experts eager to challenge the Bush administration's description of the war in Iraq.

New media has annihilated the notion of meaningful censorship in America. However, it can seem to support accusations of media bias. On the whole, the writers who dominate new and alternative media see themselves less as journalists who try to present an array of opinions than as attorneys who advocate one side of the issue. Joe Friday reporters, "Just the facts ma'am," are fast being replaced by Clarence Darrows, who offer particular perspectives instead of comprehensive overviews. (Likewise, "mainstream" newspapers and magazines are increasingly weaving analysis into their news report in order to tell readers not just what happened but what it means. Such interpretation necessarily invites speculation that often involves personal or institutional bias.)

The result is both a proliferation of bias and an intellectual bonanza that mitigates its effects. Never before have so many viewpoints been available to so many. But each source is to some degree unreliable and incomplete. And never before has so much conflicting information been so readily available. This requires readers to act like jurors, sifting mountains of evidence to develop their own sense of where the truth lies, and where it doesn't.

This vigorous marketplace of ideas contradicts Orwell's nightmare of a world where the truth is misshaped by a single source. Yet the cacophony of voices suggests a reality that sounds like vintage Orwellian doublespeak: Information overload sparks complaints of censorship and bias.

Modern readers can easily sample such a variety of perspectives that they are far more aware of the holes and the biases, the incompleteness of any single story or news report. It is not doublespeak but dead-on to say that it is the richness of news sources that makes the news seem so suspect and thin. Left-wing voices are so prominent and plentiful that it is easy to see how the right distorts and contorts the news—and vice versa. The New York Times's coverage provides plenty of ammunition to those who wish to critique Fox News—and vice versa.

We know what we aren't being told because we've already been told it. If we hadn't, we couldn't complain with such knowledgeable conviction. The media is doing its job so well that we have all become expert media critics.

In an ideal world, every voice would be objective and comprehensive —and ice cream cones would grow on trees. Instead we have seen the emergence of new sources of information, as provocative as they are accessible, that help us see the world with complexity. Their competing claims can be disorienting and disturbing at times, but nobody said free speech was easy.

And the next time people says "this is what they aren't telling you," please remind them, "you just did."

April 27, 2003

No Lie, We Live in An Age of Truth

Lying is all the rage. Bill Clinton, Gary Condit and the Pulitzer Prize-winning historian Joseph Ellis—who was suspended by Mount Holyoke College last week because of self-aggrandizing stories about his service during the Vietnam War—have made dissembling front-page news. These cases have also given legs to two recent books exploring the phenomenon: "The Liar's Tale: A History of Falsehood," by Jeremy Campbell and "The Concise Book of Lying," by Evelin Sullivan.

Undoubtedly, modern notions of truth—which cast it not as a dia-mond but a chameleon—have sparked our interest in falsity. We won-der: If truth is dead, is every lie permitted? The answer is no: We may quibble over the amount, but Clinton, Condit and Ellis have paid a price for their misconduct.

If lying is still a no-no, why do we feel like, maybe, it isn't? Svetlana Boym provides part of the answer in her erudite new book "The Fu-ture of Nostalgia." People have always longed for the "good old days." But Boym notes that this feeling has intensified during the last century because of the disorienting pace of technological, cultural and demo-graphic changes.

In our rose-colored memory, we believe our forebears were grounded by steady and sturdy tradition. In their day, a person's handshake was his bond; truth and justice prevailed.

This is nonsense. Our idealization of the past shortchanges both then and now, rendering history as a caricature of piety while diminishing our own accomplishments. Considering the great strides made by blacks, women and other marginalized groups in America during the last 50 years, it is we today who are living in an age of justice.

We are also living in an age of truth. Ironically it is the "assault on truth" commentators incessantly lament that we can thank for this. Rather than creating falsity, modernist and postmodernist writers and scholars have alerted us to its presence; deception seems to be on the rise simply because they have cleared the bush where the snake was hiding.

Consider the works of William Faulkner. In one sense, he seemed to upend the truth by employing unreliable narrators in novels such as "Absalom, Absalom!" and the Snopes trilogy. Generally speaking, earlier writers had snared us into a web of trust; we took their words as gospel. Faulkner reminded us that the world only works like that in fiction. In fact, stories—the vehicles through which we forge meaning from raw experience—are told by individuals with limited knowledge and tenden-tious imaginations. They have agendas, axes to grind, spin to twist and twirl.

The paradox is that by introducing falsity and doubt into his work, Faulkner brings us closer to the truth. In the process, he also suggests a discomfiting human condition that underscores the danger of lies: Despite our better judgment the need to believe trumps all. Even as we acknowledge the unreliability of Faulkner's narrators, we buy into their stories because that's the only story we have. Doubt is hard and rare.

In recent years, historians have explored these insights with powerful results. Instead of trying to determine "what really happened," they ask, "how did people remember what happened?" In "Race and Reunion," for example, David W. Blight describes the memory wars that followed the Civil War, which pitted "those who remembered the war as the rebirth of the republic in the name of racial equality" against "the growing number who would remember it as the nation's test of manhood and the South's struggle to sustain white supremacy."

Recounting this struggle, Blight shows us how a war-torn nation settled on an understanding—a story about its recent past—that downplayed the role of slavery and racial equality in favor of a version of events that enabled it to achieve a swift reconciliation. Not until the civil rights movement of the 1960s did America begin to own up to the war's root causes, and broken promises. Even today, few people would argue that we face our past with fearless honesty.

The work of Faulkner and Blight and countless other writers and scholars seems to question "truth" because they reveal the central role that falsity plays in our memory, beliefs and understanding. They pull the rug out from under our certainty. This disturbs us and makes us wary; it kindles our suspicion. It can lead us to see liars, liars everywhere.

In fact, they have given us new eyes with clearer vision, and deeper appreciation for the truth. They have made us more questioning, more skeptical, more alert. The "assault on truth" has made us less likely to swallow perceived wisdom. It is not a license to prevaricate but a challenge to scrutinize the ideas we encounter and the stories we hear. It pushes us to weigh, to judge, to think for ourselves. That is the only way I know to become an honest person.

August 26, 2001

We Know It, but We Can't Prove It

Conventional wisdom says we live in the Age of Information. But increasingly it seems that ours is an Era of Misinformation.

In August the mainstream media debunked most of the charges leveled by the Swift Boats Veterans for Truth against John Kerry's service in Vietnam. The group raised some legitimate questions, especially about Kerry's first Purple Heart and his alleged trip to Cambodia. But now it is clear that the Swifties were better at smearing than illuminating Kerry's military record.

Nevertheless, the book containing their charges, "Unfit for Command," remains No. 1 on the New York Times best-seller list for nonfiction.

During the past two weeks the mainstream media have dissected Kitty Kelley's scurrilous attack on President Bush, "The Family: The Real Story of the Bush Dynasty." They have shown that her poorly sourced book—with its unsubstantiated accusations of drug and alcohol abuse, abortions and stubborn cruelty—is an exercise in character assassination.

Nevertheless, Kelley's book is among the top sellers at Amazon.com (it has not been out long enough to be considered for the Times's list).

Inquiring minds want to know: Why are so many people eager to lay down their hard-earned money for these false and misleading works?

Let's note that "Unfit" and "The Family" are hardly aberrations. From Al Franken ("Lies and the Lying Liars Who Tell Them") and Michael Moore ("Stupid White Men") on the left to Ann Coulter ("Treason: Liberal Treachery From the Cold War to the War on Terrorism") and Sean Hannity ("Deliver Us From Evil: Defeating Terrorism, Despotism, and Liberalism") on the right, the number of mean and unfair best sellers is proliferating faster than North Korea's nuclear program.

They're all shams. They play fast and loose while claiming to be straight-up. But condemning them, as necessary and satisfying as that may be, sheds little light on the forces behind their success. To understand their popularity we must acknowledge this irony: The Era of Misinformation has arisen from a desire for truth.

These books—and many blogs—express the beliefs of many Americans that are rarely voiced in the traditional source of political information, the mainstream media. Despite a creeping decline of standards, our leading newspapers, magazines and television newscasts remain committed to demonstrable facts. Their stock in trade is what can be shown and proved.

However, facts and numbers and informed opinions do not always tell the whole story. Sometimes, the lack of proper documents or trustworthy sources prevents reporters from connecting the dots. Sometimes what can be shown doesn't begin to demonstrate what many people hold to be true.

This is the void filled by the new breed of political books. Readers glom onto them because they express beliefs that are deeply held but hard to articulate responsibly. A detailed criticism of Bush's judicial nominees may be the proper way to attack the president, but the fiery anger proclaimed in the best-selling books against him do a better job of capturing the mood of his opponents. Their hatred stems not simply from specific objections to his policies but also from innumerable loose impressions and shards of factoids that have coalesced into strong emotional convictions. That is how the mind works, through the heart.

Despite its faults, Kelley's book expresses the feelings of many Americans that the Bushes are sleazy, duplicitous hypocrites. The Swift Boat crew's charges may be riddled with inconsistencies, but they suggest a widespread belief that John Kerry is not the unimpeachable war hero his campaign portrays.

For readers of these books, truth, at least initially, is not in the details. The "facts" presented may be suspect, but the gist of these works seems far closer to the reality they perceive than the one portrayed in responsible news stories. Once readers become convinced that these books are telling a larger "truth," they start engaging in dangerous mental gymnastics. Their minds begin to work backward; they start believing the debunked "facts" because they build toward the truth they have embraced—and, of course, because they want them to be true.

This seems to be what happened at CBS, where members of the news division became so sure that Bush had shirked his National Guard duties that they convinced themselves that fraudulent documents exposing the president were authentic. The New York Times captured this dynamic in a headline on the CBS scandal: "Memos on Bush are fake but accurate."

That sounds absurd. And to those of us who wish to be guided by reason, it is. But we must recognize that misinformation is an increasingly powerful tool. Sometimes we can't prove what we know. Most of us don't have the time, energy or critical skills to develop PowerPoint presentations detailing precisely why we feel as we do. When the voice of reason fails to speak to us, we are increasingly turning to those who seem to get it right—even when they are wrong.

September 26, 2004

Psst, I've Got a Secret

Psst. Come here. Closer. I want to tell you something. It's personal and rather embarrassing. Something my dearest friends only suspect. So be warned, it might make you a little uncomfortable.

OK?

You're still reading, aren't you? Of course, you are. Who could resist?

Here it is: I love gossip. Who's doing what to whom. I can't get enough of it. Tell me a really juicy bit and I might tell you I want a bar of soap, but what I'm really hoping is you'll spill some more. Dish, poop and inside scoop are like potato chips to me.

My revelation may seem a tad tame, obscenely obvious, but nowadays it is deliciously taboo. We are a nation of Geraldo Riveras who want everyone to believe we are Edward R. Murrows. We tell pollsters our top concerns are health care, social security and campaign finance reform, but let the networks move from INVESTIGATING THE CRISIS to those more high-minded topics, and we reach for the remote. And, what would the newspapers do without editorial, op-ed and book pages, which allow them to condemn the salacious, invasive material they print in their news sections?

I'm not ashamed to say that I'm part of the crowd that has shot "The Starr Report" onto the bestseller list. And civic virtue had nothing to do with it. I bought it because of . . . do I really have to tell you: The most intimate secrets of the world's most powerful man, the story Bill Clinton tried to hide from the world for eight months. A favorite scene: Clinton told Lewinsky that "he suspected a foreign embassy (he did not specify which one) was tapping his telephones, and he proposed cover stories. If ever questioned, she should say that the two of them were just friends. If anyone ever asked about their phone sex, she should say that they knew their calls were being monitored all along, and the phone sex was just a put-on."

That is a bit much, isn't it? I, mean, he is the president. Had enough? But don't you want to know which famous writer eats frozen peas for breakfast?

That would be J. D. Salinger, of course. If Joyce Maynard is to be believed in her book about the year-long affair she had with the reclusive writer a quarter-century ago, "At Home in the World," Salinger also hates doctors, encouraged Maynard's bulimia and recited dialogue verbatim from "The Andy Griffith Show"!

But wait, there's more:

In "Here but Not Here," Lillian Ross reveals the secret she and the late New Yorker editor William Shawn shared for 40 years: They were lovers. (The fusty Shawn liked rich food, fast cars and was a tiger in the sack!)

Paul Theroux portrays his mentor, V. S. Naipaul, as a bigoted, disloyal genius in his new work, "Sir Vidia's Shadow: A Friendship Across Five Continents." Imagine!!!

Although those tawdry tales have a little extra zip because of the star power involved, plenty of complete strangers are eager to reveal their most intimate details—God bless 'em.

Dani Shapiro tells us how she prostituted herself out to an older man in "Slow Motion"; Laura Slater reveals how she had to trade her sex drive for her sanity in "Prozac Diary"; and Catherine Texier lets her two children and the rest of us see what a creep her adulterous husband was—and how remarkable he was in bed—in her memoir "Breakup: The End of A Love Story."

Like a Peeping Tom who has moved next door to a nudist colony, I have only one regret: so much revelation, so little time.

Of course, I know that there's no such thing as a free double latte. To invade everyone else's privacy, I have to surrender my own. I must accept that my employers can peruse my e-mail and tap into my voice mail; that bank, mall, workplace (etc.) video cameras surveil my every move; Internet companies track me on the Web; the magazines I love sell my name and address to people and causes I despise; credit companies I've never heard of hold thick dossiers on me; my supermarket records every one of my purchases—what do they make of the fact that I crave diet soda as much as coffee almond ice cream with chocolate syrup?

Slap a bar code on me, and let's just get it over with.

Sometimes I wonder, is it all worth it? The poop on them for the scoop on me?

But then, what can I do about it? And besides, who can resist?

October 4, 1998

SENSATIONALISM

NOTHING MORE THAN FEELINGS

News as Spectacle (March 13, 2005)

Every so often what passes for normal, everyday and commonplace proves to be so grotesque that we're forced to step back and consider the world we live in.

Thank you, Martha Stewart, for providing a rare moment of reflection.

The massive coverage of the doily queen's release from prison was, of course, unexceptional and inevitable. Who didn't expect the media to lay it on fast and thick when she emerged from her Camp Cupcake prison cell?

Daniel Boorstin described this phenomenon in 1961 when he coined the term pseudo-event—an occurrence of absolutely no importance that is treated like a pressing affair of state. Much of what passes for news today is an unending string of such pumped-up nonevents: Michael Jackson's trial! Brad and Jen's split! The Oscars! The Grammys! March Madness! Mama Mia!

Here's the beauty of the media machine: The perversity and insanity of our celebrity-saturated culture are so well understood that it is tiresome to mention it. Its excess serves to insulate it from meaningful criticism. How clever.

Nevertheless, the Martha Stewart coverage was so over the top—the loop-de-loop television coverage (roll tape, again), the cover of Newsweek and even the front page of the New York Times, for goodness' sake—that even the most jaded observers were shaken from their knowing stupor. Inquiring minds wonder: Does anybody really care about Stewart (except, of course, for Martha herself)?

Short answer: no. However, it is worth our consideration because it reflects a radical change in human consciousness—one that has been driven in no small part by the movies, which have transformed the way we interact with and understand the world.

This began to dawn on me in 1993 when I saw Steven Spielberg's mega-blockbuster, "Jurassic Park." The filmmakers spent ungodly sums of money producing a riveting flick with a plot that made little sense. I left the theater mystified by its obvious deficiencies. Spielberg is a smart man, and if I saw the problems in the story, he must have as well.

Only later did I realize that he didn't care a whit about the plot. His goal was to keep my heart racing and my eyes glued to the screen. He was appealing to my body, not my mind, purveying emotions, not insights. He wanted to provide a thrilling spectacle, a sensuous experience, that would last for the film's 127-minute run. And he left his audience wanting more—of the same.

In the years since, I have watched hundreds of films with such limited aspirations. I have also seen this "Jurassic Park" mentality infect other aspects of our culture. Which brings us back to Martha Stewart. In the current environment, where our ears demand the loudest voice, our eyes the greatest spectacle and our hearts a story packed with disposable emotions, pseudo-events allow the media to blare their trumpets nearly every day in a desperate quest for attention.

Pseudo-events are like television sitcoms—only a steady diet makes them palatable. Ignore the boob tube for a few weeks and then switch it back on and your only thought is: What was I thinking? Similarly, the media must produce a long procession of pseudo-events to condition us to them. Otherwise, we'd laugh them off saying: What are they thinking?

The "Jurassic Park" mentality is also reconfiguring our politics, with frightening results. No doubt, many Americans have deep and bitter differences of opinion about the nation's direction. Such debate and dissent are necessary and healthy. Unfortunately, we are hashing them out through language that appeals not to the head but the groin.

Figures such as Michael Moore and Ann Coulter, Frank Rich and Rush Limbaugh do not traffic in clarification but castigation. They are performers who do not debate ideas but attack their enemies in spectacularly venomous language that casts every news blip as a constitutional crisis: Bush is shredding the Bill of Rights! The Democrats are treasonous louts! Similarly, Internet bloggers make their bones through the high-pitched politics of personal destruction.

All provide their audiences with the same quivering, mindless emotion that motion pictures have made them love. Yet by working so hard to make the news so EXCITING and IMPORTANT, they trivialize it, packaging it as yet another spectacle to be turned on, and turned off.

This is nasty stuff. But we limit our understanding of it—and grant it undeserved legitimacy—by attributing it simply to fractious times. To some extent it does represent healthy passion. But in the largest sense, it reflects a modern mind-set that demands stimulation, not illumination.

As emotion-rich, content-free material increasingly passes as news and discourse, we must admit the troubling fact that the USA is fast becoming Jurassic Park.

Media Sell the Sizzle of Small-Minded Stories

You'd never guess that the issues at stake are life and death. Instead of generating a thoughtful discussion about security in the age of terror, the big stories coming out of the 9/11 commission were remarkably personal and small-minded: the feud between former counterterrorism chief Richard A. Clarke and the Bush administration, and the ultimately successful demands that Condoleezza Rice testify in public before the commission she has already spoken with privately.

The cover of Newsweek succinctly expressed how the national media have cast this story: "Inside the 9/11 Commission: Will It Affect the Election?"

All these stories are worth covering. But are these blame-game, finger-pointing, ginned-up controversies the proper focus of our attention when legions of fanatics around the globe may be plotting to kill us? Do we have that luxury?

Nevertheless, there is an important story here—not about the 9/11 commission per se, but about media coverage of it during this election year. Why have the national media focused on these secondary issues?

The troubling answer is: That's what they do. The merging of news and entertainment, the muscling aside of fact by opinion, and the preference for controversy over illumination is not new. Stacks of books have explored these phenomena; two of the best are by New Yorker writer George W. S. Trow, "Within the Context of No Context" and "My Pilgrim's Progress: Media Studies."

Despite such probing critiques, reversing these trends seems a pipe dream. Still, changing the world is not the only reason for thinking about it; we derive a greater sense of autonomy by knowing what is going on around us.

To understand the true spirit of the modern media, consider Stanley Kubrick's seminal film "2001: A Space Odyssey." It famously features a computer, named HAL, built to serve a spaceship community. Eventually, HAL takes on a life of his own, serving only his own needs. And now, sad to say, we live in the era of HAL media.

The national media are supposed to serve the broader American community—illuminating the forces shaping our world. Editors proudly proclaim their news outlets are the linchpin of democracy. However, like HAL, they are increasingly serving themselves.

The needs of HAL media are familiar to every reader: They are the needs of story. The most engaging stories—the bedrock of every great novel or play—revolve around two elements: people and conflict. Unfortunately, the news often involves dry facts and complex ideas. The media have tried to resolve this tension by turning almost every issue into a tale of interpersonal conflict.

Hence, every election cycle brings complaints about "horse-race" coverage of the campaign, and the response is more poll-driven, who's-up, who's-down stories. The candidates know they will generate more coverage by attacking their opponents than by spelling out their own programs for change. Is it any wonder that our politics are so mean-spirited?

HAL media prefer opinion to fact. This phenomenon is easy to see in the jaw-flapping worlds of talk radio and cable news. It is also coming to dominate the more responsible world of print journalism.

On Feb. 1, the national edition of the New York Times—the earliest paper the Times prints—carried the unrebutted charge by Democratic

National Committee Chairman Terry McAuliffe that George Bush had been AWOL from the National Guard during the Vietnam War.

To add balance to the story, editors inserted a quote in later editions from Ed Gillespie, the head of the Republican National Committee, who called the accusation "slanderous."

The key point is that the Times was content to make this story a he said/he said affair. It presented readers with two contradictory opinions but not the facts necessary to evaluate them. We might chalk up this mis-step to laziness if the Times and other news outlets didn't engage in this practice on a daily basis. It was not a glitch but part of a strategy pursued by news outlets convinced that hot emotion will snare more readers than cold facts.

Perhaps they are right. Readers demand "exciting" stories built around identifiable people and high-stakes conflict. But this trend is leading to tendentious reporting in which the needs of story too often trump reality. For example, on March 27, Times columnist Dan Barry assured readers that a man trying to get a license plate that read "DUMPBUSH" was not a "knee-jerk liberal" because "he supported the military strikes in Afghani-stan after Sept. 11."

This is nonsense. Every poll shows overwhelming support among Democrats for Bush's actions in Afghanistan. Indeed, some argue that Bush should not get too much credit because any president would have done the same. Barry's point is in conflict with reality, but it fits the storyline of this year's election, which is that angry Democrats seem to oppose everything the president has done. Except, that is, for his action in Afghanistan.

National news outlets still produce quality journalism that owes more to A. J. Liebling than Rush Limbaugh. But such work is increas-ingly overwhelmed by demands of HAL media, which is less interested in holding a mirror up to the world than in developing stories that sizzle. Ironically, the effort to craft stories that matter to people is making it increasingly hard to find stories that matter.

April 4, 2004

Littleton: Madness Magnified

For 12 wrenching days it has felt like we all live in Littleton, Colo.

Since two disturbed teens took 15 lives at Columbine High School, the town's tragedy has become our own. Its loss has been our loss; its grief, our grief; its painful questions—how? why?—have wracked our own bodies and souls.

Despite our heartfelt identification with people we know only as televised images and newsprint faces, the post-shooting picture of America that pundits and politicians have painted is chilling.

They tell us semi-automatic pistols have replaced teddy bears as playthings for Johnny, who prowls the Internet for bomb-making tips. With parents as absent as those in a Peanuts cartoon, our children are receiving life-lessons from violent television shows, movies, video games and rock bands. In desensitized America, where death has become our leading form of entertainment, we are advised to look upon every child with trepidation: Who will crack next?

We live in a "culture of death," the writer Peggy Noonan declared in the Wall Street Journal. "Why should young people take life seriously, when their overworked, aborting, day-care, euthanasia culture does not?" columnist Cal Thomas asked in the Los Angeles Times. And in the New York Times, columnist Bob Herbert described America as "a land where the killing is easy," while the author James Q. Wilson suggested, "We have created a new kind of adolescent culture, one that we may never be able to fix."

I have no quarrel with this anger at our violence-soaked culture—I'd support banning most guns, slapping "X" ratings on violent video games and movies, boycotts of reckless television programs and reasonable parental controls on the Internet. But this analysis is only part of the story. Viewing all of society through the fractured lens of this aberrant tragedy, these commentators falsely suggest that our children share more with Littleton's twisted gunmen than with its victims, whose lives were filled with hope and promise.

We are not rearing a generation of monsters. Even Wilson noted that "violence in society, measured by the murder rate, has dropped sharply, and violence in schools is also down."

Though harried and overextended, most parents today—as they race from soccer matches to ballet lessons—are more involved in their children's lives than their forbears ever were. In "The Beggar and the Professor," the French historian Emmanuel Le Roy Ladurie recounts the life of Thomas Platter, a not atypical 16th century boy who, at about age 10, waved goodbye to his impoverished parents and set off "to beg for his bread" across Europe.

Just 100 years ago, countless children grew up in sweat shops. Pre-Freud and pre-Spock, in times of greater want, parents loved and cherished their children but tended much less to their emotional and material needs. Though we are rightly horrified by the hatred espoused by Dylan Klebold and Eric Harris, American kids reared just 60 years ago—when racism and anti-Semitism were a way of life—were much less tolerant.

And yet, we feel that life is spinning beyond our grasp. At heart, I believe, this problem is one of context. The process seems simple enough. We look around, see what we see, hear what we hear, and use those experiences to understand ourselves and the world.

Until recently, most people only had to process immediate information: the life of their families and communities. As Don DeLillo details in his insightful novel, "White Noise" (1985), we are bombarded hourly with cathode rays of far-flung factoids. Flip the switch and find a tragedy: Genocide in Rwanda, war in Kosovo and schoolyard shootings are beamed into every living room, so that across the globe seems just around the corner.

The result is a truly revolutionary change in consciousness, one with which we are only beginning to grapple. In his smart new collection of essays, "Readings," Sven Birkerts observes that ours "is the first epoch in which all-encompassing shifts in the way life was lived have been recorded—by photograph, by film, by video, by recording machines—and then fed back to us, slowly at first, then as part of such a cataract of data and imagery that the reflection of life can itself be seen to be one of the most pronounced features of life."

In this environment our challenge becomes, how do we make sense of the world? How do we filter the overwhelming volume of information to achieve true vision? The very best part of our humanity prompts us to identify with the people of Littleton, to feel their anguish as our own. And we would be foolish not to use their experience to question our own world. But we should also remember that we do not live in that Colorado town.

May 2, 1999

Secondhand Emotions: When TV Filters Our Feelings, They Become Pale Imitations of Life

Like millions of Americans, I watched Marv Albert "tell his side of the story" the other night on "20/20." Barbara Walters asked all the tough questions: Had he assaulted and sodomized his accuser? Did he like rough sex? Was he wearing a toupee? Looking straight into Barbara's eyes with the bloodshot weariness of Job, Marv denied everything (that's a hair weave planted on his dome).

It was an impressive performance, and, no doubt like millions of Americans, I spent a good bit of time afterward listening to the post-game analysis on radio and television. It was the kind of talk we Americans are fluent in, thanks to numerous discussions—and arguments—about Louise Woodward, the Eappens and other cast members of the Nanny Trial. Opinion was fierce on all sides. But most telling was the fact that the debate centered less on the hard evidence in these cases than their emotional content. Did Marv seem to be telling the truth—his guilty plea notwithstanding? Was Louise daubing herself with that white handkerchief for heartbreaking consolation or calculated effect? How do we feel about how they appeared to feel?

I felt a queasy unease during these public deliberations. I couldn't quite put my finger on it until I read Frederick Barthelme's fine new book, "Bob the Gambler," which tells of a couple so bored by ordinary life that they turn to a casino to experience a little oomph. When his father dies, the protagonist laments, "I wanted to do it right, to feel sad, but I didn't."

In that one powerful sentence I found the perfect expression of my discomfiture. Here was a man who had lost touch with genuine emotion. What remained was the notion of how he ought to be feeling.

We Americans, collectively, as a culture, have become like Barthelme's character. Increasingly, we don't know how to feel. And like Barthelme's gambling man, we fill this void with strong impulses rather than genuine feelings.

A paradox emerges. On the one hand we limit the range of acceptable feelings from those in public life—who, by dint of the celebrity we confer or foist upon them, seem to belong to us. We watch Marv and Louise in the comfort of our living rooms and demand that they "do it right," just as we expected Britain's royal family to after Princess Diana's death.

On the other hand, we crave extreme hyper-emotion, no matter how synthetic. We swallow booze and drugs to stoke our engines. We throw away billions each year playing the lottery, slots, craps and the ponies. And we devour raw memoirs that trade in abuse, incest, rape and other facets of degradation. When the temperature is low, it takes a powerful illness to build a fever.

All of which suggests a deep emotional confusion. Mary Gaitskill captured this phenomenon while expressing frustration with readers of her short story, "The Girl on the Plane," who were nonplussed by its description of a gang rape. "Most of us have not been taught how to be responsible for our thoughts and feelings," Gaitskill wrote. "I see this strongly in the widespread tendency to read books and stories as if they exist to confirm how we are supposed to be, think and feel. I'm not talking about wacky political correctness. I'm talking mainstream. . . . Ladies and gentleman, please. Stop asking, 'What am I supposed to feel?' Why would an adult look to me or any other writer to tell him or her what to feel? You're not supposed to feel anything. You feel what you think."

What's behind this?

Many things, of course, although two developments stand out. The first is the onslaught of naked tragedy that defines our world. In his recent review of "Hotel Sarajevo," a novel set during the war in Bosnia, Fred Chappell wrote: "The horrors of real life . . . are more vivid, more lacerating, than any fiction can make them out to be—and yet so continual are they, so multitudinous, that we grow numb to them." And commentators turn their eyes to the great duplicity in Washington and ask, "Where has all the outrage gone?"

The second factor is television, which we are told, hums about seven hours a day in the average American home. Viewing television is an inherently passive act. It doesn't engage us. We watch it. David Foster Wallace nailed the implications of this in his brilliant essay, "E Unibus Pluram: Television and U.S. Fiction" (which is included in his 1996 collection, "A Supposedly Fun Thing I'll Never Do Again"): "The practice of 'watching' is expansive. Exponential. We spend enough time watching, pretty soon we start watching ourselves watching. Pretty soon we start to 'feel' ourselves feeling, yearn to 'experience' experiences."

Television, of course, is a medium of entertainment. It is scripted, not spontaneous; contrived, not truthful; fake, not real. It does not portray life as it is. It is, simply and dangerously, television. Through its easy and seductive ubiquity, it becomes our life, provides our experiences, while offering no real knowledge about actual living.

The box blurs the lines between reality and itself. Real-life tragedy becomes melodrama, entertainment becomes news, news becomes entertainment, all presented within the limited and safe conventions of television.

Because we have so much invested in television, we accept its blurry lines as clear vision. We believe we can gauge Marv Albert's truthfulness by watching him in a make-or-break interview for which he has had weeks to prepare. We are sure that we can determine whether Louise Woodward killed little Matthew Eappen by studying her giving testimony on which she has been repeatedly coached and drilled. If we didn't feel this confidence, what could we trust?

But, even then, we are not really looking for the truth, but for people to act the way they are supposed to on television. To "do it right" does not mean displaying the wide range of responses people are capable of in any given situation but the safe, appropriate ones Gopher would exhibit during a crucial scene on "The Love Boat."

When Deborah Eappen displayed too much cool on the witness stand, public opinion pilloried her, making her somehow complicit in her child's death. As a result, the Eappens felt compelled to clear their name. I can think of no better evidence of how much our culture has lost its capacity for genuine feeling than the pressure put on the Eappens to explain themselves. Where? In the controlled world of "Larry King Live."

For millennia, philosophers have argued questions of epistemology: How do we know what we know? Nowadays, the answer is a snap: Just flick on the box.

We're just not sure how we feel about it.

November 16, 1997

In Search of Amazement

Been there done that? Seen it all? Find yourself saying "borrrring" more often than "wow"? Ladies and gentlemen, children near legal age, leave your ennui at the door. Step right up and experience the most electrifying, mystifying, stupefying, high-flying, energizing show in American literature.

Behold the woman who didn't eat a scrap of solid food for 12 years ("The Fasting Girl" by Michelle Stacey); the Siamese twins who settled right here in North Carolina and fathered 22 children ("God's Fool" by Mark Slouka); the bank robber who enjoyed post-mortem fame as a side-show corpse ("Elmer McCurdy" by Mark Svenvold). Howard Bone will curl your eyebrows with the true-life stories of Nancy the Seal Girl, the Man Who Couldn't Be Hanged and the Pickled Punks ("Side Show").

You say eyebrows can't be curled? Obviously you've never read Jan Bondeson's "The Two-Headed Boy and Other Medical Marvels" or Robert Youngson's "Medical Curiosities: A Miscellany of Medical Oddities, Horrors and Humors."

My friends, those works merely hint at the colorful literature on freaks and geeks, circuses and side shows published in recent years. I command your attention to this carnival of curiosities because it speaks to a deep longing in our homogenized, Starbuckized, soporifically sophisticated culture: the desire for more zip in our Zeitgeist, more wonder in our weltanschauung.

Let me ask you, when was the last time you marveled? Suspended disbelief to open yourself to the kind of eye-popping, jaw-dropping, mindbending experience that left you sputtering and muttering "huhn?"

Face it, my friends, we are beyond amazement. We're too clever, too hip to believe the unbelievable. We've made intelligence the greatest virtue, gullibility the worst sin. Our biggest fear is being played for a fool. So, we don an ironic mask, commit to nothing, respond to everything with a slouch-lipped "whatever."

And who can blame us? We are so entertained, we are beyond amusement. The big top delighted our forebears by providing high-stepping breaks from the norm. Hoopla is beamed into our living rooms 24/7. Thrills and chills are run-of-the-mill.

The spine-tingling books I'm recommending today are the tonic to revive our weary imaginations. They are magic carpets that will transport us to that bygone era when the world was full of surprises. They promise the possibility of secondhand wonder, letting us become one with characters who couldn't believe what they were seeing but accepted it nonetheless.

What a gift.

Still you doubt me. I can tell. And I grant you: Something more than boredom is fueling our fascination with freaks and geeks. They do allow writers and readers to explore cutting-edge issues of identity and otherness in extremis. No one had to grapple more mightily with what it means to be different than Siamese twins, the skin-deformed Alligator Man or Nancy the Seal Girl, who, Howard Bone explains, was only 3 feet tall "with arms, legs, and feet stubby enough to resemble the flippers of a seal"?

Nevertheless, I guarantee you that these books are chiefly a response to our ho-hum culture. I'll prove my point by citing a related publishing trend—a two-for-the-price-of-one column. Who besides freaks and geeks can make us believe the impossible? The answer, of course, is those bastions of bamboozle, those honchos of humbug, those captains of quackery: con artists.

Grifter tales have become a mini-industry in publishing. They include "Drake's Fortune: The Fabulous True Story of the World's Greatest Confidence Artist" by Richard Rayner, "How to Become a Professional

Con Artist" by Dennis M. Marlock, "The Museum of Hoaxes" by Alex Boese and a collection of stories about flimflammers from the television program "60 Minutes" titled "Con Men." And did I mention the book that inspired Steven Spielberg's new movie, "Catch Me If You Can: The Amazing True Story of the Most Extraordinary Liar in the History of Fun and Profit," by Stan Redding and Frank W. Abagnale?

You say my connection between geeks and grifters seems forced. I ask you: Is it merely a coincidence that Darin Strauss followed up his novel on the Siamese twins "Chang and Eng" with the story of a legendary boxer/con artist, "The Real McCoy"? Does mere happenstance explain why Ricky Jay has given us both a wondrous survey of oddities, "Learned Pigs & Fireproof Women," and "Jay's Journal of Anomalies: Conjurers, Cheats, Hustlers, Hoaxsters, Pranksters, Jokesters, Impostors, Pretenders, Side-Show Showmen, Armless Calligraphers, Mechanical Marvels, Popular Entertainments"?

No, my friends, these writers are responding to the yawning yearning of a people—of you and me—who feel trapped in a culture that provides everything but surprise. Freaks, geeks and con artists allow us to recall a time when Americans could be awestruck. They revive the days when folks were willing to buy into almost anything because it was more fun to say "Gee whiz" than "Give me a break." They enable us to tap into something grand and dear that we have lost through the knowledge and insight we've gained: the wonder of wow.

Step right this way. Prepare to be amazed.

January 12, 2003

LETTING IT ALL HANG OUT

THE RISE OF RAUNCH

Though Our Goodness Grows,
a Culture of Cruelty Thrives

Entertainment news used to be a Camelot of airbrushed perfection. Fan magazines gave us the inside scoop on Elizabeth Taylor's marital bliss, Michael Jackson's charitable work with children and Rock Hudson's lovely new girlfriend.

Nowadays, celebrity coverage is less fantasy than tragedy. It has become a series of bloody accidents on the information superhighway, and we're all rubberneckers.

In recent months the mass media—from obscure Web sites and celebrity rags to CNN and the New York Times—have offered saturation coverage of troubled young women. Britney Spears's apparent nervous breakdown, Lindsay Lohan's drug use and Paris Hilton's troubles with the law have been covered in pitiless detail.

Even lesser figures get the star treatment if their private problems are desperate enough. Reality TV has invited us into the troubled living rooms of Ozzy Osbourne and Paula Abdul, Anna Nicole Smith (who later died of a drug overdose) and Danny Bonaduce (who tried to take his own life during the show's first season).

Their lives have become our modern soap operas, roller-coaster sagas filled with ups—She's finally entered rehab!—but mostly downs—She's relapsed!

But these are not scripted programs heading toward an inevitable happy ending. They're the struggles of real people in real pain who are flushing away their lives through reckless and boorish behavior.

And yet we follow it all with merciless delight, as if Britney, Lindsay, Paris and Anna Nicole were fictional characters. Prestigious outlets such as the New York Times and the Washington Post report it all. The worst of the new media—such as the celebrity Web site Perezhilton.com, which reportedly draws more than 4 million visitors a day—revel in each fateful misstep.

What's missing from this coverage are empathy and compassion, a sense of the terrible sadness of it all.

These star-crossed stars are responsible for their actions; on one level, they are getting what they deserve.

But our fascination with their self-destruction is disturbing. It reflects a mean-spirited and unforgiving nation, disconnected from decency, eager to revel in the misery of others.

Evidence of this hard-edged incivility is not confined to our treatment of celebrities. We see it in the angry talking heads who scream from radios and TVs, the filthy language that courses through our music and movies, the vicious voices that hold court in the blogosphere.

When did we become so nasty? How did our culture become so ungracious and rude?

Paradoxically, the roots of this sad situation can be traced back to happier developments that have also made us a kinder and fairer nation. By most accounts, Americans were far more civil during the 1950s and early '60s. Men wore ties to baseball games; etiquette encompassed a set of rules to live by.

Ugliness, however, percolated throughout polite society. Legal racism infected the nation, condemning blacks to second-class citizenship. Homosexuals were forced to live in the shadows.

Women had few choices. Their plight is evocatively portrayed in the new TV series "Mad Men." Set in the go-go world of Madison Avenue advertising executives in the early 1960s, it brilliantly evokes the misogyny that pervaded American culture.

The articulate men in their handsomely tailored suits treat their female subordinates—who are almost all secretaries, because that was as high as most women could rise—as potential conquests. The men undress the women with their eyes and remind them with their words that they are the second sex.

Watching this series today, it is almost hard to believe that such conduct was normal. The social movements of the 1960s and '70s largely ended that world. But the assault on a status quo that oppressed women, blacks and other marginalized groups also dismantled the traditional codes of propriety that defined polite society.

As equality and freedom spread, so did rude and coarse behavior. Americans became more civilized but less civil. We began treating one another far better, and far worse. While rejecting old behaviors that oppressed certain groups, we embraced a popular culture with a nasty, more personal edge.

We are left with a riddle: If the social movements of the 1960s and '70s led us to treat one another with respect and dignity, how could we succeed so spectacularly and fail so miserably?

It is tempting to see a direct link between these developments.

When the cultural cruelty that oppressed marginalized groups became unacceptable, we sought other forums for the release of our darker impulses.

Such a view regards cruelty as an inescapable human trait. The mean-spiritedness that prompts us to shout and curse at one another, to dehumanize troubled young women such as Britney, Paris and Lindsay, may be rooted somehow in our history.

But if the past six decades have taught us anything, it is that the most deeply ingrained habits and assumptions can be overcome.

August 5, 2007

Paranoids Return!
But Exhibitionists Seize the Day

Literativille, March 16: Shaking off years of self-imposed irrelevance, the Paranoids have hurtled back into the news with a full-scale assault of cranky misanthropy.

Led by those venerable pooh-bahs of seclusion, J. D. Salinger and Thomas Pynchon, the Paranoids have mixed mysterious inscrutability with misdirection and mistrust in a quixotic effort to reinvigorate an arcane value: privacy.

But their battle cry is sounding more like a swan song in the wake of punishing counterattacks from the Exhibitionists who now rule Literati.

With legions of memoirists at their command and the prevailing winds of the Oprahgeist at their backs, the Exhibitionists have penetrated deep into the formerly unassailable regions of individual boundaries and personal space. Novelists Kathryn Harrison and David Leavitt have led the charge, peddling tales of such raw intimacy that they should provide soap-on-a-rope with each hardcover. After this foray, it appears nothing will be off-limits.

"The Paranoids? Who are they?" said one Exhibitionist. "I once had a parakeet. I was 3. It was green and blue with this thick dark tongue and a sharp beak. It bit me once and I . . ."

The beat-infused Paranoids receded from public view during the 1960s as a rejection of mass popular culture and the growing cult of celebrity. They made stealth stylish, refusing to grant interviews, have their pictures taken or, ultimately, to write. In the years that followed, wide-eyed college students piled into cars to locate these exiles. Seeking enlightenment, they more often received anatomically impossible suggestions from their heroes.

The Exhibitionists burst into full bloom during the 1990s. Dominated by a blessed generation that had suffered neither war nor want, they never knew anything larger than themselves. With situation comedies and daytime talk shows as their muse, they skillfully turned navel-gazing shamelessness into million-dollar advances.

Salinger fired the first shot in January by authorizing publication of his first new hardcover in three decades. That the novella in question, "Hapworth 16, 1924," was published in a 1965 issue of the New Yorker mattered little. Media far and wide trumpeted this rare public act by the author of "The Catcher in the Rye," while informing an entire generation that there were once artists whose goal in life was not making the cover of People magazine.

Then, without warning or explanation, Salinger halted publication.

"It was brilliant," explained a rather enthusiastic devotee who once chased Salinger's car down a New Hampshire back road for seven miles before hitting a tall tree on a sharp curve. "First he offered himself to the public and, just as they were ready to accept him, he pulled back. 'You don't own me'—that's what he was saying."

Pynchon followed Salinger's sally by quashing his publisher's plan to follow standard procedure and send bound galleys of his new book, "Mason & Dixon," to reviewers before the April 30 release date. Whether he was motivated by a fear of Communist Chinese copycats who have made millions pirating videos and compact discs or by a deeper, more mysterious force—possibly the post office—is not known. But one thing is clear: The man who made entropy as familiar to Americans as quantum mechanics in works like "Gravity's Rainbow" and "The Crying of Lot 49" was reminding Americans that he controls his art.

While the Paranoids played hit and run, the Exhibitionists struck back this week with a double whammy that lays everything on the table.

First came Leavitt—whose last book, "While England Sleeps," led the English poet Stephen Spender to accuse him of plagiarism. His new collection of stories, "Arkansas," includes a novella titled "The Term Paper Artist" that concerns a writer named David Leavitt who is accused of plagiarism. Chastened, this fictional character forsakes literature and begins writing term papers, which he trades to young men for sex.

Hot on the heels of this triumph of self-abnegation, the Exhibitionists played their trump card: Harrison's nonfiction account of the sexual relationship her estranged father began with her when she was 20. Combining unencumbered confession with unrestrained pathos, her book, "The Kiss," has become the topic of discussion in Literati, seeming to secure total victory for the Exhibitionists.

In a sign of Paranoid capitulation, Pynchon has allowed his publisher to release advance copies of "Mason & Dixon."

Privacy may be vanquished and Paranoia almost dead, said one highly unreliable source. But so is Elvis. Think about that.

March 16, 1997

No More Plain Brown Wrappers

Pornography used to be the province of scuzzy publishers such as Al Goldstein and Larry Flynt and barely talented film stars like John Holmes and Candy Samples who peddled their wares on the fringes of society.

But today's purveyors include Hollywood and Madison Avenue, the telephone company and television networks, Main Street business people and mainstream publishing houses such as HarperCollins, Doubleday and Little, Brown.

Lap dances are for sale in almost any American town. Phone books and magazines are replete with ads for "escort services." Prime-time has become porn-time as people casually utter obscenities and engage in lewd acts, just like in the movies.

It took Viagra to pull the mainstream press's attention away from the president's "distinguishing characteristics." And our local bookstores are awash in titles such as Lisa Palac's "The Edge of the Bed: How Dirty Pictures Changed My Life"; Bonnie Gabriel's "The Fine Art of Erotic Talk"; "Erotique Noire: Black Erotica"; "The Mammoth Book of Erotica" and "The Penguin Book of Erotica."

The marginal has become mainstream. Impulses once indulged at great risk have been de-stigmatized—as have mindless violence, unspeakable cruelty and gross deception. The days of shame and plain brown wrappers are over.

Thanks to the sexual revolution we are friskily freer as individuals and less oppressive as a society, especially in the treatment of gays and lesbians.

However, the price of this liberty has been the freedom to shape the world we live in. Few thinking people would suggest we return to the status quo ante, but who does not look at contemporary culture and shudder? Who feels that we can do something, anything, to correct it?

Societies have long used law, custom and taboo to rein in our naturally disruptive urges—Freud said the human mind has a similar filter built in as the paternal superego clamps down on the mischievous id. However, contemporary intellectual currents argue against our having any basis for making value judgments, for imposing restraint: Truth is seen as provisional, all claims of moral authority are interpreted as political assertions by groups seeking to dominate one another. "Perverted" and "deviant" are termed adjectives of repression while losing-side traditionalists who rail against naked reality are ridiculed as bigoted troglodytes. Make no mistake, for all their attention-getting bluster, the William Bennetts of the world have been routed.

In his provocative 1992 essay "Pornography and the New Puritans" the novelist John Irving gave voice to this victorious modern mindset: "No writer or publisher or reader should accept censorship in any form; fundamental to our freedom of expression is that each of us has a right to decide what is obscene and what isn't."

While this position affords maximum individual liberty, it diminishes our ability as a community to define our culture. Undoubtedly, past efforts to ban "obscene" works such as "Tropic of Cancer" and "Lady Chatterley's Lover" were dangerously misguided. But if we follow Irving's logic we can't even clamp down on child pornography.

Irving's position is especially perilous in these times of moral relativism. It is, of course, eminently sensible to walk in the other guy's shoes before judging him. But, as Roger Shattuk writes in his erudite book "Forbidden Knowledge" (1996), compassion is a tricky business: "Once we understand another life by entering it, by seeing it from the inside, we may both pardon and forgive a criminal action. We may not even recognize it as criminal. We are all guilty in some way. How can we ever judge anyone else, punish anyone else? [But] is there a point at which we must beware of such knowledge? Beware of empathy?"

As the French say, to understand all is to forgive all.

As our society has surrendered its moral authority, our culture is, by default, being shaped by corporate entities that traffic in instant gratification. Sure they are giving that mischievous id what it wants—who isn't fascinated by sex? But we also know that arousal is not completely satisfying. A culture that feeds our bodies but not our souls leaves us yearning.

Our immense challenge is to develop mechanisms that allow freedom while discouraging license, that encourage empathy while erecting compassionate limits that can help us a build a culture that does not make us shudder. We must do nothing less than fashion a persuasive new moral language, the first words of which have yet to be spoken.

July 5, 1998

When Culture Goes Raunchy

"What happens when hipster girls go wild?" asks the new issue of Rolling Stone. "Basically, the same thing that happens when sorority chicks go wild: They show off their ta-tas, make out with one another, and engage in a variety of behaviors they wouldn't normally dream of, just because there's liquor in their bellies and a camera in their faces."

If you doubt the magazine's claim, it offers a photo of two nearly naked young women pawing each other and directs readers to a Web site offering more of the same, LastNightsParty.com.

But why would you doubt it? Everywhere you turn, popular culture offers flashes of raunch. Flash: The slutty covers brandished by magazines from Vanity Fair to Maxim. Flash: The stratospheric success of the "Girls Gone Wild" video series. Flash: Mega-best-selling books such as Jenna Jameson's "How to Make Love Like a Porn Star." Flash: Health clubs offering "Cardio Striptease" workout sessions.

Final flashes: Paris Hilton, Howard Stern, "The Man Show" and the porn-saturated Internet.

The question is not whether raunch has gone mainstream, but why. New York journalist Ariel Levy tackles this question in her provocative yet disappointing book, "Female Chauvinist Pigs." Levy addresses the question from a fresh angle: Instead of plumbing the Neanderthal urges of men, she asks why women seem so eager to take porn stars as their role models. Why have they embraced "stripper chic"? Why doesn't anyone bat an eyelash when Rolling Stone refers to women as "girls" and "chicks"?

"Only 30 years (my lifetime) ago," Levy writes "our mothers were 'burning their bras' and picketing Playboy, and suddenly we were getting implants and wearing the bunny logo as supposed symbols of our liberation. How had the culture shifted so drastically in such a short period of time?"

That assertion belies a serious fault of Levy's book. Only a handful of women ever burned their bras or picketed Playboy. Only a tiny minority of women get implants or flash their breasts for the "Girls Gone Wild" cameras. "Women"—like "men"—are so varied by race, class and age that it is hard to make sweeping generalizations about them.

Almost all the people Levy interviews are a lot like her—white, well-educated and well-off. Almost all of them are perpetrators of raunch culture, including the female producers of the misogynistic "Man Show," and organizers of bump-and-grind, girl-on-girl parties in New York. As a result, she suggests that "women" are living *la vida* slut.

The true dynamic in play involves image, not substance. What's changed is not the action of most women, but their willingness to accept randy depictions of themselves in popular culture.

Levy reminds us this was not always the case in chapters that describe the wide movements of the 1960s and '70s to free Americans from our Puritan shackles. She details the feminist-led charge—which included powerful anti-pornography efforts—to wrest equality for women.

Some of Levy's sources claim that raunch culture is an empowering extension of the feminist agenda—that the gains of women are so wide and secure that they no longer need worry about being objectified. They have a point. But Levy's description of raunch culture as demeaning and pathetic is more persuasive. "It is worth asking ourselves," she writes, "if this bawdy world of boobs and gams we have resurrected reflects how far we've come, or how far we have left to go."

However, she is so intent on seeing raunch culture through a feminist lens that she is unable to explain its emergence. For example, she fails to align raunch culture with the general coarsening of the culture, with the decline of AIDS as a central fear of heterosexual life or the rise of the Internet, which has made hard-core pornography as accessible as tap water. These trends have little to do with the feminist project.

More problematic is her unwillingness to entertain ideas at odds with her feminist ideology. Levy compares women to Uncle Tom, the fictional slave who internalized his subjugation and sought to please his master. In fact, women are stronger and getting stronger—in 2003 41 percent of women and 34 percent of men ages 18 to 24 were enrolled in college. The notion that women are suddenly being forced to kowtow to men flies in the face of experience.

More compelling is the idea that women are choosing to accept raunch culture because of uneasiness with their new opportunities. By countenancing highly sexualized images of themselves, they may be signaling a retreat from the cultural forces that have urged them to define themselves through professional accomplishments—a recent New York Times article notes that increasing numbers of Ivy League graduates plan on becoming stay-at-home moms. By accepting a culture built on male fantasies of power, women are telling beleaguered men that they are still in charge.

To which this man can only say: If only.

"Female Chauvinist Pigs" is timely. It raises important questions; I wish it provided better answers. Raunch culture is all around us—and, sad to say, it isn't a flash in the pan.

October 9, 2005

Taking Aim at Graphic Concerns

The impulse to ban books seems so medieval that the subject fills the mind's eye with images of peasants jigging round a raging bonfire.

But the urge still burns today. The American Library Association reports that about 500 books are challenged every year, usually by parents disturbed over works discussing sex or containing language they deem offensive.

Book banning is an ancient issue—in "The Republic," Plato railed against "dangerous" works. But it has a new twist thanks to a publishing phenomenon: the rise of book-length, adult-oriented comics such as graphic novels and memoirs. This month parents in Marshall, Mo., demanded that their public library remove two graphic memoirs, "Fun Home" by Alison Bechdel and "Blankets" by Craig Thompson.

The complainants were riled not only by the substance of these works—which include salty discussions of hetero- and homosexuality—but also their style: They feared these comics would lure their children into a demi-monde of sharp tongues and sweaty bodies.

The book lover's knees jerk almost as quickly as the censor's: He instinctively dismisses all such objections as an attack on freedom. I share this concern, but the issue is far more than a clash between the close-minded and the enlightened. It also involves an issue that troubles both book lovers and book banners: The coarsening of American culture.

Ten minutes of TV is all it takes to witness how deeply violence, sex and offensive language have saturated popular culture aimed at children. A quick look at books aimed at children, such as "Walter, the Farting Dog," reveals how the crude has become mainstream. Video games have made graphic violence a staple of fun for millions of youngsters. And the Internet is a gateway to . . . everything.

Richard Krawiec, a novelist who teaches in the Raleigh schools, complained to me last week that video game culture is infecting his students' work. "It's taught them, boys and girls, that violence is not a moral issue but a normal part of life and the best way to solve their problems."

When parents seek to have certain books banned, they aren't just complaining about particular titles. They are also voicing deeper fears about the distasteful images and ideas bombarding their kids.

Why, then, are books often their target?

Three reasons. First, popular culture is such a vast and unyielding force that opposing it is tantamount to trying to stop the wind. A single book is a much more manageable target. Banning it will do no more to improve our children's culture than eating an apple after a Happy Meal will improve their health. But it is one of the few real actions parents can take to express their concerns.

Second, there are responsive mechanisms in place for attacking books. A few parents in Marshall joined forces and were given a respectful hearing before the local library's board of trustees. A thousand of them could write letters to Nickelodeon and have no impact on the channel's programming.

The third reason is the very special place that books occupy in America. TV, movies, video games and the Internet have tremendous influence, but they also enjoy the freedom of low expectations. Most people assume they will be lowbrow, aimed at baser instincts. Even though a dwindling number of Americans read books, most still consider them the embodiment of our highest aspirations. When our kids pick up a book, we expect them to be better people when they put it down. We want books to be a refuge from the world's ugliness.

When we discover that a work includes risqué material, we can feel helpless and defeated: Is there no safe place? This is not an entirely rational response—the best books often flirt with taboos—but if the world were a rational place, what would we talk about?

Sadly, Marshall's library board decided Wednesday to remove "Fun Home" and "Blankets" from their shelves until a "material selection committee" can set guidelines for determining whether works are appropriate. (Pity the tiny town's librarian, who may have to comb through every book for hints of subversion).

The good news is that such censorious acts are usually a bookseller's dream. Bechdel's and Thompson's works will almost certainly enjoy a spike in sales thanks to the good people of Marshall, and they deserve all the attention they can get.

Smart and moving, "Fun Home" and "Blankets" use words and images to explore one of literature's great themes: the challenging passage from youth to adulthood. They are rich, mature works, far too sophisticated for children under 13 to appreciate (kids who get their hands on them are more likely to be confused than corrupted). Teenagers fired up by the promise of these "controversial" books will be disappointed: Each contains only a few pages of mildly "graphic" drawings. Neither hardcore nor soft-core, they are best described as no-core.

Most adults who come to these books will be mystified by the kerfuffle they aroused. The "why" will become clear only when they lift their eyes from the pages and look around.

October 15, 2006

IDENTITY

RACE, GAY RIGHTS, AND 9/11

The History We Choose to Forget

If a great historical event occurs but no one remembers it, did it really happen? The question arose last fall as I read Timothy B. Tyson's stirring account of the race riot that ripped through Wilmington, N. C. in 1898.

"Despite their importance," Tyson wrote in the News & Observer's special section, "The Ghosts of 1898," "the events in Wilmington have remained largely a hidden chapter in our state's history."

The statewide campaign, centered in Wilmington, was engineered by North Carolina's ruling elite to destroy the powerful political alliance between poor whites and blacks. It ushered in a long and brutal era of white supremacy across North Carolina and the South. This epochal history was news to me and many of our readers. "Why didn't anyone tell us?" was their common refrain.

So I was more than a little surprised to learn that we had been told, repeatedly.

In the third and concluding volume of his magisterial biography of Martin Luther King Jr., "At Canaan's Edge," Taylor Branch reports that King made the white supremacy campaigns a centerpiece of the famous speech he delivered after the march from Selma to Montgomery in 1965.

In the late 19th century, King observed, poor whites and blacks recognized that the ruling elites were not serving their interests. Together they formed a fragile alliance to advance their economic and political interests.

"To meet this threat," King explained, "the southern aristocracy began immediately to engineer this development of a segregated society. . . . Through their control of mass media, they revised the doctrine of white supremacy. They saturated the thinking of the poor white masses with it, thus clouding their minds to the real issue involved in the Populist

Movement. They then directed the placement on the books of the South of laws that made it a crime for Negroes and whites to come together as equals at any level."

King did not uncover this history. Drawing it from C. Vann Woodward's seminal history, "The Strange Career of Jim Crow" (1955), King recounted the broad outlines of the history Tyson reported.

As I mulled this piece of "forgotten" history, I encountered another: that the American Revolution was fought in the name of tyranny as well as liberty. In his National Book Critics Award-winning work, "Rough Crossings," Simon Schama recounts how thousands of enslaved blacks escaped from their American masters to fight for the British on the Crown's promise of freedom.

"At the end of 1776," the British historian writes, "when the American army evacuated New York, an incoming British soldier saw 'black children of the slaves hugging and kissing each other' with joy and relief. . . . Wherever the British army went, in big battalions or small, in North Carolina and then in Virginia, slaves still continued to pour into their camps by the score, then in hundreds and finally thousands."

"Rough Crossings" is a disconcerting read—I never thought I'd root for the Redcoats. I never thought George Washington would make me feel ashamed; I did as Schama described Washington's pitiless efforts to deny life, liberty and the pursuit of happiness to enslaved blacks.

The most shocking fact is that Schama, like Tyson, is not breaking new ground. His history is based on a wide array of primary and secondary sources. His story has been told time and again. It startles us because we have chosen to forget it, time and again.

We have worked—willfully and insistently—to exclude it from the inspiring story we tell ourselves about the Revolution.

Tyson and Schama remind us that history is not a simple record of events. It is a dynamic process of selective memory whereby the dominant culture decides what to remember and how to remember it. History is made in the world, but it's forged in the mind.

Not too long ago, romantic notions of the "Lost Cause" informed Southern histories of the War of Northern Aggression. Until recently, most textbook histories of the United States glossed over the contributions of blacks, women, gays, lesbians and other marginalized minorities.

Americans have made great strides in acknowledging the complexity and richness of our past. By producing surprising works about major events, Tyson and Schama show us how far we have to go. That their efforts followed in the wake of so many others warns us of the difference between recording history and remembering it.

Let us hope that when future historians explore their fertile subjects, readers do not ask once more: "Why didn't anyone tell us?"

They might, however, because most people do not want an honest reckoning of history; that's why myths endure and painful episodes get buried. For every person who desires the truth, far more ask: "Why dredge up the past we cannot change?"

Such thinking asserts that history is only real when we acknowledge it, that we can erase darkness by denying it. But this approach works no better for history than it does in our personal lives.

It is far easier to suppress our memory of the past than its legacy. However much we celebrate our Revolution, it offered a raw deal to African Americans with dire future consequences. One of those was the white supremacy campaigns of the late 19th century, whose legacy haunts to this day.

John Lukacs observed that history is the fourth dimension of human experience. Invisible and ubiquitous, it guides and defines us. The only way we can see a brighter future is by looking the past square in the eye.

April 1, 2007

A White Man's View of Blacks

In his button-pushing memoir, "Black Planet: Facing Race During an NBA Season," David Shields suggests that white Americans think race inhabits two polar spheres. In one, Louis Farrakhan spews hate while Jesse Helms whistles "Dixie." In the other are the rest of us, who believe we judge people by the content of their character, not the color of their skin.

But if the vast majority of us are indeed committed to justice and equality, why is the legacy of slavery and segregation so palpable?

Shields fearlessly tackles this question in his over-the-top account of the season he spent watching the Seattle Supersonics. The author of four previous books, including two novels, Shields attempts to show how these two spheres overlap. Paradoxically, what his book lacks in scope—it's an intensely personal work that views race through the eyes of one man's relationship with one basketball team—it makes up for in raw ambition: exposing the profound sense of difference, of otherness, that separates even the best intentioned white and black Americans. As Kipling wrote, "All the people like us are We / And everyone else is They."

During 1994–95, Shields had Supersonics season tickets. He was a lifelong fan whose ardor intensified after his daughter's birth. My "obsession with the Sonics began just after Natalie was conceived, as if, on the verge of becoming a completely domestic animal, I needed to locate warrior-selves to identify with and glorify."

Seattle, Shields tells us, is a very white city, home to "have a nice day" and the man who invented the yellow smiley face. The predominantly black Supersonics are a group of gifted nonconformists, epitomized by their trash-talking star guard, Gary Payton. Talented, warriors, they eagerly defy their white coach. "To maintain the illusion that I'm some sort of potentially subversive individual," he writes, "the Supes are my surrogate subversives."

For Shields, "being bad is more interesting than being good." White fans, like himself, are stuck in a "middling, muddling, vanilla mediocrity." In response, they turn to funky and unfettered black men "to redeem our pale white lives."

Making love to his wife, "I feel like I am—I imagine that I am—as tall, thin, and muscular as Gary Payton. . . . I'm not him. I'm really not him. I wish I were him. I love him—the phantasm of him—to death."

These thoughts are, of course, a smorgasbord of stereotypes. Payton and his teammates never become full and complex people for Shields. They are icons, images and fantasies. Shields sees these black athletes as supermen; hatemongers cast them as subhumans: The result is markedly different, but both reduce African Americans into images painted by white minds.

The reader aches for Shields to break through, to get to know his subjects. But he never does. It would be easy to dismiss Shields as a pathetic narcissist, or worse. But that would deny us the useful insight he does offer. Often the best way to understand the mainstream is by confronting the extreme.

And as extreme as Shields's view of African Americans is, it highlights the fact that whites often understand blacks in ways that dehumanize them. His basic assertion is on target: While many whites have black friends, "the blacks" still exist as a group that spawns a host of thoughts and feelings. In fundamental ways, blacks are for whites the THEY, the OTHER. The result is a deeply colorized mind-set.

Shields extends this point by showing some of the smaller ways that he—like so many whites—tailors his responses when dealing with blacks. He watches what he says for fear of offense. He worries that a minding-his-own-business black youth will steal his briefcase. And "entering or exiting a store, I don't usually go wildly out of my way to hold the door open for the person behind me, but if the person is black, I never fail to. . . . Are black people conscious of how excruciatingly self-conscious white people have become in their every interaction with black people?"

That final statement encapsulates the power of Shields's book. It is an exploration rather than an indictment of white America. He reveals how many of us psychologically separate and segregate ourselves despite our best intentions. Our problem is not just hateful racism but the overwhelming sense of otherness that informs black/white relations.

Shields offers no solutions; he never reveals whether or how he was changed by his season of contemplation. But by throwing the ball back into our court, Shields forces well-intentioned people to examine our hearts, our minds, our complicity.

November 21, 1999

A Black Woman's View of Whites

What is bigotry? That question kept circling my mind as I read "Summer Snow: Reflections from a Black Daughter of the South." In fairness, only a few of the essays in this collection by Trudier Harris, a professor of English at the University of North Carolina at Chapel Hill, contain complaints about "white people." Most are loving tributes to Harris's mother, a resourceful, wise and loving woman and expert fisher who reared Harris and her eight siblings in Jim Crow Alabama.

Harris is far less interested in documenting the deprivations of her childhood than recalling her life with heartfelt nostalgia. She describes how her mother would prepare a pig: "Momma and the other women would clean the chitlins, cut and oven-brown the skin into cracklings or eating skins, and prepare the shoulders for grinding into sausage and the head for boiling down and making souse." Echoing a story my own grandmother told me about her youth in Virginia, Harris remembers the "wagonloads of watermelons that my father [a farmer] would drive up to the back porch of our house. He would hit a watermelon with his fist, thereby busting it open, pull out the heart, give it to one of his children, and toss the rest into the hog pen."

"Summer Snow" also includes evocative essays on "Porch-Sitting as a Creative Southern Tradition," the role and culture of black church choirs, the special challenges faced by well-educated African Americans and the cultural authority that comes from having picked cotton—whenever Harris or her siblings complained about having to do some "onerous" task, their elders would chide them, "You ain't never picked no cotton."

But race, like sex, is such a powerful issue that Harris's inflammatory comments stick with the reader at least as much as her finely nuanced remembrances.

Harris vents from the start with an essay about her distinctive first name. On the second page she complains that white men invariably mispronounce it. She tells them it is "Tru-di-er" but they continue to call her "Tru-dee-uh" or "Trudy." Harris says she is "always slightly surprised at how consistently white males do not listen to other people and how forcefully—and convincingly—they pass on their errors to other people."

On page three she says she is often called upon to explain her name's origin. "I fall into the role of potential entertainer," she writes, "that position in which white people are most comfortable with black folks."

Later she describes how white people routinely ignore her in Chapel Hill. "If I'm walking on the street at seven o'clock in the morning or at five o'clock in the evening, it's not unreasonable to assume that the white person coming toward me—similarly working out and sweating—is someone I might greet. Well, it's a hit-or-miss proposition that the white person will speak." They refuse to acknowledge her presence, she writes, because "I do not matter to them," because she is black.

When she attends a lecture or reception at the UNC campus, "I walk in and two or three white people—not a single one of them the host or the hostess—with eyes lit up in surprise, will walk up and say, 'Thank you for coming.' . . . The subtext is always 'This is our gathering. Be thankful that we let you in.'"

Admittedly, this is relatively mild stuff. And in an environment where racial matters are often larded so thickly in code that people rarely say exactly what they're thinking, Harris's honesty is refreshing. Yet it is the kind of thinking that leads to stereotyping and bigotry.

It is, of course, almost impossible to avoid generalizations. And in our racially charged world, many black people hold general ideas about whites, just as surely as many whites have fixed opinions about blacks. But if we have learned anything in the last half century it is that racism is underpinned by such sweeping statements. The fact that some whites have been rude to Harris tells us no more about "white people" than crime statistics do about "the blacks." Both phenomena can suggest avenues for deeper exploration; white rudeness and black crime can lead us to aching understandings of modern America. But the bald, unexamined opinions Harris repeatedly offers about whites are an intellectual dead-end.

Her assertions are particularly troubling because they come from a highly educated woman who displays a far more nuanced understanding of the racial landscape in other essays. Her piece on the lifelong dental problems created by white doctors doing charity work at her grade school—they pulled her decaying teeth instead of fixing them—is a surprising and powerful story about the complexities of race and class. Similarly, her essay about the white man who crudely propositioned her from his car, "Would You Go Out With a White Boy for Five Dollars?," is a provocative discourse on history, psychology and race.

Both of those essays—and Harris's remembrances of her youth—work because they ground their points in the particular. Instead of gross generalizations, they offer specific incidents that suggest larger patterns. Bigotry paints with a broad brush.

May 4, 2003

Imus's Sin Stains Many

If Don Imus collected his radio program's greatest hits, "nappy-headed hos" wouldn't make the cut.

His description of Washington Post reporter Howard Kurtz as "a boner-nosed, beanie-wearing Jew boy" would be a strong contender. So would this comment about Gwen Ifill, an African American reporter at the New York Times: "Isn't the Times wonderful? It lets the cleaning lady cover the White House."

Don't forget his characterization of Gloria Estefan as a "Chihuahua-looking ho," of New York Knicks players as "chest-thumping pimps," of Janet Reno as "that big fat lesbian" and of Native American Sen. Ben Nighthorse Campbell, R-Colo., as "the guy from 'F Troop.'"

Nevertheless, it was his description of the Rutgers University women's basketball team as "nappy-headed hos" that got Imus fired Thursday. The obligatory mea culpas he issued weren't enough to dampen the public outcry that forced advertisers to pull support from "Imus in the Morning."

There are always mixed feelings when someone sees his long career destroyed. This must be especially hard for Imus. Unlike Howard Stern and other shock jocks, Imus courted respectability through his generous support of charities, his cultivation of high-powered guests and his promotion of books.

But Imus's firing is well deserved; his chickens have come to roost. Racial and sexual stereotypes have long been the basis of his "humor," which some observers—particularly journalist Philip Nobile—have complained about for years.

I weighed in with a 1998 column that denounced his practice of "filtering world and personal news through the smeared lens of locker-room humor that relies on racial, ethnic and sexual stereotypes," and again in two columns in 2000. That year, the Pulitzer Prize-winning columnist

Clarence Page led Imus through an on-air oath: "I, Don Imus, do solemnly swear, that I will promise to cease all simian references to black athletes, a ban on all references to noncriminal blacks as thugs, pimps, muggers and Colt 45 drinkers . . . ." He broke that promise, and Page, who is black, says he was never invited back on the show.

Imus and his defenders have long insisted that he was an equal-opportunity insulter. "This program has been for 30 or 35 years a program that makes fun of everybody," he said Monday.

Nonsense. White men were often the targets of his scorn, but almost always as specific individuals criticized for particular actions. Well-heeled white men—who happened to be Imus's target audience—were never made to feel he was talking about them while he was lambasting Vice President Dick Cheney.

His mockery of blacks, gays, women and other minorities, by contrast, drew on such broad stereotypes that it was hard for them not to take it personally. Consider this "parody" of a Maya Angelou poem that Imus aired:

"Whitey plucked you from the jungle for too many years / Took away your pride, your dignity, and your spears . . . With freedom came new woes / Into whitey's world you was rudely cast / So wake up now and go to work? / You can kiss my big black ass."

Reports about Imus have referred to Mel Gibson's anti-Semitic remarks, Michael Richards's use of the N-word and homophobic insults from "Grey's Anatomy" actor Isaiah Washington. But Imus was different. Where Gibson, Richards and Washington were individuals whose conduct reflected poorly on themselves, Imus had legions of supporters.

When he wasn't denigrating minorities, Imus interviewed some of America's most powerful political leaders and opinion makers, including journalists Tim Russert, Frank Rich, Maureen Dowd and Howard Fineman as well as political leaders such as Sen. John Kerry, Sen. Chris Dodd and Sen. Joseph Lieberman. Until his firing, they happily supported him. Now these rats have jumped ship.

These high-powered enablers struck their deal with the devil long ago, when they decided to support Imus's program in exchange for the access he offered to his millions of listeners. Their actions revealed the soft underbelly of political correctness.

In theory, political correctness demands that we treat each person with dignity, that we eschew stereotypes because they demean and demoralize their targets. In practice, it has become a cudgel used against some perpetrators, some of the time. I doubt Russert bent over in laughter when an Imus henchman said "Jeopardy" doesn't have many black contestants because the show "doesn't recruit contestants in prisons." He and the show's other distinguished guests—and its advertisers and broadcast stations such as WRBZ in Raleigh—probably figured, he's getting away with it, so why worry?

The circle of culpability extends beyond Russert et al. Imus reached an audience of millions—people who, presumably, enjoyed his brand of humor. The problem was not just Imus, but all the people who enjoyed his ugliness.

Imus's enablers surely hope that his termination ends the matter, letting them off the hook. But if Imus deserves to be fired, then his famous guests need to explain why his words never bothered them—and his listeners should be encouraged to search their hearts.

Imus is no Klansman or segregationist. He is a comedian whose program relied on degrading stereotypes long used to separate "us" from "them." His popularity reflected the endurance of our darker impulses. Now that we've dealt with Imus, it's time to confront ourselves.

April 15, 2007

A Hard Look at the Slaveholding Fathers of Our Country

When the Founding Fathers were deciding whether to risk their lives and fortunes for their ideals, Benjamin Franklin remarked, "We must all hang together, or most assuredly we shall hang separately."

In the years after their bold gamble for freedom, the hangman's noose played a far darker role in our republic, becoming the lynch mob's weapon of choice for denying African Americans their inalienable rights.

Liberty and freedom, repression and racism—these warring yet braided strands form the Gordian knot of the American experience: A land of visionary light entwined in the darkest recesses of human cruelty.

Now comes Roger Wilkins like a modern-day Alexander to cut this knot, not with a sword but with his word processor.

In "Jefferson's Pillow: The Founding Fathers and the Dilemma of Black Patriotism," the civil rights activist and scholar offers a magnificent reckoning with our conflicted history. His rigorously researched, deeply felt meditation on American freedom combines knowledge, insight and compassion to show how our often divided house can face and ultimately embrace its common heritage.

Wilkins focuses his work on four Virginians who embodied the American paradox. Thomas Jefferson (the Father of the Declaration of Independence), James Madison (the Father of the Constitution); George Mason (the Father of the Bill of Rights) and George Washington (the Father of our country).

To Wilkins they are true heroes, bold and brilliant men who imagined a great nation. But they were also slaveholders whose comfort and station depended on human bondage.

Wilkins asks, "Can I embrace the founders who may have 'owned' some of my ancestors?" In response, he brandishes qualities all too rare in modern political writing: intellectual honesty and emotional empathy. His fierce anger toward the founders is infused with a profound understanding of how their humanity led them to act so inhumanely.

To understand these Southern men, Wilkins argues, we must understand their world. They were reared in a society of privilege, imbued by their fathers with strict notions of race and class. "White Christian Englishness was the only norm of civilization that such men knew or recognized," Wilkins writes. "Other people with different ways and different cultures could not possibly be understood as anything but inferior."

They even viewed "the poor whites at the bottom of their society as filth and scum." Commoners knelt when addressing the lords of Mount Vernon and Monticello, who each "ruled as a sovereign over" their estates.

Property, especially the slaves who worked their land to create their wealth, was the foundation of their privilege. It secured their status, defined their identity and worldview. Nowadays, we view this racist elitism as irreconcilable with their revolutionary pronouncements. But in a tour-de-force of psychological history, Wilkins reveals their limited understanding of the expansive freedoms they espoused.

These Virginians may have been kings in the colonies, but they believed that England's upper crust looked down on them. They chafed at the power the mother country held over them. "Taxes imposed without representation by a distant and arbitrary Parliament meant to the colonists that their property was always at risk," Wilkins writes. "Without property they would be rootless and without identities."

When they spoke of human equality, they aimed their words "at those who exercised power over them, not dropping down a welcoming cloak to enfold those over whom" they exercised power.

Ironically, slavery sharpened their understanding of freedom. "The fruits of subjugation ripened in the minds of our nation's founding fathers. . . . When they voiced fears that Parliament was trying to reduce them to slavery, this was no empty metaphor . . . they knew in their souls what real slaves were."

However, blacks served as far more than symbols during the revolution.

About 20 percent of the eventually victorious American army was black. This is a crucial, corrective theme in Wilkins's book, for it reminds us that our nation was not founded by white patriots only.

Blacks and whites have always been braided together; always living, always fighting, for the values of human dignity we all cherish. Wilkins offers another corrective when he describes the psychological toll the ideas of freedom took on these slaveholders.

They were brilliant men who were not, as some have argued, blind to the discrepancy between their words and deeds. Slavery troubled and haunted each of them. Wilkins feels a "rising rage" at their moral failure to extend freedom to all Americans. But he is also "acutely aware of [human] frailties." He understands what consistency would have cost them.

"The four founders might have freed all their slaves in their lifetimes and thereby lost enough status, wealth, and leisure to be rendered anonymous," he observes. "But financially—and probably psychically as well—they were incapable of such sacrifices. . . . they had been shaped, like all of us, by inherited culture."

He adds: "Privilege is addictive. The most natural thing in the world is for each human being to view the privilege he enjoys as, well, the most natural thing in the world."

Despite the continuing injustice that Wilkins ascribes to the founders' timidity, he honors them for their bravery. Though wedded to the status quo, they forged a nation built on democracy and freedom and dedicated to the proposition of change. "I love the opportunity this nation affords me to engage in the struggles for decency." he writes. "That, in my view, is the greatest legacy of the founders."

Books about our past are common; works that become part of our history are rare. To that small company that includes "The Souls of Black Folk" by W. E. B. Du Bois and "The Education of Henry Adams" we should now add "Jefferson's Pillow." Roger Wilkins has written a book that could help free us from the shackles of our dark history so that we might ride on its soaring wings.

July 11, 2001

Still the Same Old Same Old

'The problem of the Twentieth Century," W. E. B. Du Bois wrote in 1903, "is the problem of the color line."

As we stand on the far edge of this century, who would argue that his prophecy was not correct? As we hurtle and slouch toward the first edge of the next millennium, who would deny that the color line is as much a part of our future as our past?

The 20th century has witnessed sweeping progress toward legal equality and economic opportunity for blacks. Nevertheless, many African Americans are still denied some of the opportunities and dreams that other Americans take for granted.

Despite centuries of debate and discussion on race, there is still a color line in America. 1997 brought yet another presidential commission on race and the publication of dozens of thoughtful new books on the subject—including such standouts as Tom Dent's "Southern Journey," David K. Shipler's "A Country of Strangers" and Orlando Patterson's "The Ordeal of Integration"—we are still far from erasing this line.

It is a sign of the complexity of the problem but also its simplicity that Du Bois's classic 1903 work, "The Souls of Black Folk," remains perhaps the most perceptive and prescriptive book on race in America. As

Reginald F. Hildebrand, an associate professor of Afro-American studies and history at the UNC-Chapel Hill, told me, "If I could only use one book for Afro-American studies, 'The Souls of Black Folk' would be it."

The first African American to receive a doctorate from Harvard, a prolific author and a founder of the NAACP, Du Bois had the rare ability to write history that reads like philosophy. In lyrical and incisive prose, "Souls" finds in a particular moment of time—the years after the Supreme Court's 1898 decision in "Plessy vs. Ferguson," which legitimized the doctrine of "separate but equal"—enduring qualities of American character and society.

"Souls" is also pressingly germane because the issues Du Bois was grappling with are the same ones that bedevil us. African Americans of his day (and our own), Du Bois wrote, simply wish "to make it possible for a man to be both a Negro and an American . . . without having the doors of opportunity closed roughly in his face."

Today, some blacks, angry and disappointed, endorse separatism. But Du Bois noted that such a posture is a nonstarter because we are, inextricably, one nation, with blacks and whites "like a wheel within a wheel."

Likewise, many whites assert with oblivious dismissiveness that enough has been done for African Americans, who nevertheless remain largely on society's margins. The same tired argument was made in Du Bois's day as whites hoped to "shift the burden of the Negro problem to the Negro's shoulders and stand aside as critical and rather pessimistic spectators; when in fact the burden belongs to the nation, and the hands of none of us are clean if we bend not our energies to righting these great wrongs."

What is the answer? Du Bois tells us that "we cannot settle this problem by diplomacy and suaveness, by 'policy' alone."

In a nation where moral imperatives generally recede as the stock market rises, he reminds us that Americans have long sought to see race relations through the prism of economics. Most contemporary discussions of affirmative action, for example, are knotted up in the mathematics of quotas. But Du Bois knew that the real answer to changing people's stations is to change the nation's heart. Race, he wrote, is not a just a numbers game but a question of ideals, "the strife for another and juster world, the vague dream of righteousness, the mystery of knowing; but today the danger is that these ideals, with their simple beauty and weird inspiration, will suddenly sink to a question of cash and lust for gold. . . . What if the Negro people be wooed from a strife for righteousness, from a love of knowing, to regard dollars as the be-all and end-all of life? . . . Whither, then, is the new-world quest of Goodness and Beauty and Truth gone glimmering?"

After reading Du Bois's 95-year-old book, I saw America as a patient who has spent years on the therapist's couch: It understands the symptoms and causes of its problems, can see the path to a cure, but remains unable or unwilling to travel the distance.

February 22, 1998

For Men, "Straight" Label Is Inflexible

Can a man seem to seek sex with another man and not be gay?

No way, answered most Americans as scandal engulfed Idaho Sen. Larry Craig.

When the 62-year-old grandfather insisted "I'm not gay" after pleading guilty to charges that he sought sex with another man in an airport bathroom, his declaration was met with derision and disbelief.

"It's the tragedy of homophobia," Matt Forman, executive director of the National Gay and Lesbian Task Force, told the Associated Press. "People create these walls that separate themselves from who they really are."

In contemporary America, you can't be a little bit pregnant or a little bit gay. Just as our old racial caste system relied on the one-drop rule—a drop of black blood made you a Negro—a similar logic informs our culture's basic assumptions about male sexuality. Men who engage in any homosexual activity are considered gay. That's who they "really are."

Craig may have been married to the same woman for 24 years. An exhaustive investigation of his sex life by the Idaho Statesman may have uncovered just one man's claim that he had sex with Craig in a Washington bathroom. And the senator may have denied that story while insisting his arrest in Minneapolis was a misunderstanding.

No matter. The public concluded he was gay.

The thinking went: No heterosexual man would have placed himself in Craig's position—at a known cruising spot for gay men such as the bathroom at the Minneapolis-St. Paul International Airport, using a series of foot and hand signals that would lead an undercover police officer to decide he was soliciting sex. Since he did not appear to be acting straight, he must be gay.

Craig may be homosexual—that's his business (and it's shameful that Republican homophobes immediately pushed him toward the door). More interesting are the ways his case illuminates the rigid norms society imposes on straight men, especially the one-drop rule concerning sexual encounters.

Consider this: Almost half of all men who have sex with other men in public bathrooms consider themselves straight, according to William Leap, a professor of anthropology at American University, who has studied this behavior since the early 1990s.

"They insist, 'I'm not gay, I'm not homosexual, I'm straight,'" Leap told me. "The general description for these guys is they are married and they often talk about these encounters as recreational—fun, excitement, a break from the long workday."

One man told Leap that the encounters offered "dangerous excitement" in contrast to his emotionally dull second marriage. Another man said he would stop off at a known cruising spot after work, have sex, then pick up a quart of milk before returning home to his wife and kids. "It was almost like a scheduled activity he had in his day planner," Leap said.

Leap, who edited the essay collection "Public Sex, Gay Space," said the popular view that these men must be gay is simplistic. For starters, he said, that judgment defines these men by one aspect of their behavior, discounting, for example, their lives with their wives. It also presumes that society's general assumptions about how straight men should act are more accurate than their own conceptions of themselves as heterosexuals. Finally, Leap said, it defines homosexuality exclusively in terms of sex.

"Being gay is not just a sexual position," he said. "It also involves a self-acceptance and a public declaration, a willingness to say 'I am gay' and to make that clear to one's self. Perhaps these men are in denial, but if we just write them off as closeted or repressed, we limit our understanding of what straightness might entail."

I wasn't completely convinced. The taboos on homosexual activity are so strong that, it seems, only powerful urges could impel men to cross that line. At heart, it must be something they feel they must do to satisfy a fundamental need.

The issue, Leap countered, is not whether these men are gay but the constricted ways American society views straight male behavior. The rest of the population—women and gay men—are not bound by the one drop rule.

Few would suggest, for example, that a self-identified gay man who sleeps with women on occasion is secretly straight. Or consider the images of young women making out with each other in the "Girls Gone Wild" videos. I don't know anybody who immediately concludes that they are lesbians. Show Americans videos of men kissing, and most will instantly say they are gay.

A survey conducted in 2002 and 2003 by the National Center for Health Statistics found that 14 percent of women aged 18 to 29 said they had had at least one same-sex encounter; a little less than 10 percent of women 30 to 44 reported such activity. Yet only about 4 percent of women described themselves as lesbians. Would anyone explain this gap by arguing that 10 percent of American women are closeted and repressed lesbians?

This same survey found that 6 percent of men reported a same-sex experience; 4 percent identified themselves as gay. Clearly, cultural forces discourage men from exploring their sexuality—or from disclosing to pollsters that they have.

These differences highlight the fact that the sexual conduct of men is "heavily, heavily regulated," Leap said. "Power and authority in our society have long rested in the hands of men so there's heavy cultural pressure to define what it means to be a man. Women are afforded some room to experiment, whereas a man who plays around with other men is seen as walking away from his responsibilities, threatening the stability of his home and his country, challenging the specific images of masculinity our culture enforces."

Leap's findings are provocative. Although most political scandals do not deserve the attention they receive, I hope the questions raised by Craig's troubles linger, prompting us to consider the assumptions we apply to complicated questions of sexuality and identity.

September 9, 2007

Marriage of Our Hearts and Minds

Listen closely when straight people who support gay marriage discuss the issue. A few say yes, yes, yes; most just nod—of course, of course, of course.

Translation: Their heart is telling them one thing but their head . . . is not so sure.

This stance seems fine: Whatever road leads us to the right place is a good one. But the history of another American battleground, race relations, alerts us to its dangers.

There, political sensitivities have too often stifled the full and open discourse required to exorcise our demons. Discouraged from fully airing the attitudes ingrained through centuries of discrimination, many Americans find it difficult to express the truth of what they say they believe. Just as racist views wither in the light of reason, so too will resistance to gay marriage. Thinking and talking about the issue will forge a lasting bond between our heads and hearts.

A compelling place to begin this dialogue is Jonathan Rauch's new book, "Gay Marriage: Why It Is Good for Gays, Good for Straights, and Good for America." Rauch, a correspondent for the Atlantic Monthly, is a gay man. Although every argument against same-sex marriage is rooted in personal animus against gays, he shuns self-righteous invective.

Working to convince rather than condemn, Rauch displays the rarest of qualities: empathy. He understands that the bigotry in play is rooted deeply in human history. "Same-sex marriage," he writes, "is a big change. Advocates of gay marriage are trying to change the way things have been for—well, forever."

Oddly, most discussions of gay marriage focus on the concerns of heterosexuals, on the issues it might raise for them, rather than on the rich possibilities it would open for those most directly affected—gays and lesbians.

Rauch argues that same-sex marriage will benefit all Americans while strengthening the institution of matrimony. That is a bold claim and a smart one for it addresses fears that same-sex marriage will undermine one of the last pillars of tradition in a morally relativistic world.

Rauch makes his case by exploring the meaning of marriage. Most people might say that it is what it always has been—the freely entered union between a man and woman who love each other.

History and practice belie that belief. Arranged marriages and polygamy have been a norm through human history while interracial relationships were long taboo in America. Even today, married couples can be adulterous or celibate, loving or abusive; they can live together or apart. Procreation is not a factor as no state prohibits the infertile or the aged from marrying.

Rauch does not raise these points to cast marriage as meaningless. He uses them to focus on its essence, which is "two people's lifelong commitment, recognized by law and by society, to care for each other."

Same-sex marriage does not threaten this purpose. It fulfills it. It will not create more gays and lesbians—homosexuality is a biological fact, not a personal choice. It will allow citizens who can romantically love only members of the same sex to make the ultimate commitment. But wouldn't it open the door to polygamy and incest? No. The principle at stake is not whether we can marry anyone and everyone we would like to, but that each of us can wed one somebody. "Only homosexuals are barred, by law," Rauch observes, "from marrying anyone they love."

Some wonder: Why do homosexuals need marriage? The same question might be asked of heterosexuals. The answer is simple: For every reason it is good for you, it is good for them.

It is also good for America. Marriage stabilizes relationships and imposes obligations and responsibilities. It urges us to act like adults and thus be good citizens. "To say a neighborhood would be better off with fewer married gay couples and more gay singles or 'domestic partners' seems perverse," he writes.

Some may wish that homosexuals would just live their lives in silence. That, Rauch notes, is not an option. They are going to continue to press their claims for full citizenship. In response, companies and states have developed various alternatives, such as domestic partnership programs and civil unions, to provide some marital benefits to gays and lesbians.

But the law requires that such programs be made available to straights. Thus, to prevent homosexuals from tying the knot, we are inventing a series of alternatives to marriage.

Same-sex marriage, Rauch argues, would undercut these competitors by establishing a single standard: "If you want the benefits of marriage, get married."

My one quibble with Rauch is that he does not go far enough. Noting that same-sex marriage seems a radical proposition, he argues for a gradual approach. "Let the states try same-sex marriage individually," he suggests "if and when they are inclined to do so. . . . Let gay marriage take root at its own pace, in communities which are ready to accept same-sex couples into fellowship or matrimony."

This is the same argument heard during the civil rights era. While recognizing sensitivities, gradualism only lends credence to irrational fears. Because gay marriage also involves fundamental constitutional rights, it is one of those rare instances where it should be imposed on the nation by our courts and leaders.

We don't need time, but vigorous debate. We need to hear that same-sex marriage would not represent a turning point in American history, but another fulfillment of its promise. Our bedrock tradition is extending rights to marginalized groups—to immigrants, African Americans, women, etc. Gay marriage is our next great achievement. By opening our minds, we can change our hearts.

March 28, 2004

The Beginning of Dialogue

Panic and despair gripped America when tragedy struck Sept. 11. Sinew and synapse snapped into action. A navel-gazing people suddenly remembered that it possessed both a great army and a yawning ignorance about the world where that muscle might be flexed. The gentlest folk were riled to calls for revenge even as they rushed to televisions, newsstands, radio waves and bookstores to find out who? How? Why?

WHAT'S NEXT?

I was one of them. As night followed night my anger did not diminish. However, my understanding of what it means to be an American deepened. I have been reminded that our personal freedoms entail great obligations, our unsurpassed power saddles us with a tremendous responsibility: To learn. To think. To be engaged.

It seems profane to say that any good might come from this disaster. But it does present all of us—and each of us—with the opportunity to rise from our self-absorbed slumber. Enjoying peace and prosperity at home, we have for too long succumbed to the natural desire for oblivious comfort, casting life as entertainment. As we concerned ourselves with celebrity, scandal and the politics of personality, another world was roiling around us. A world that now commands our attention.

Since the morning of Sept. 11, I have been reading—to generate the sense of control information provides, and to begin to write a caption for the gruesome images seared in my brain. There is so much to consider: issues of war and peace and law, of commerce, politics and morality. I tried to learn about Muslims, not to provide a rationale for the insanity that drove the terrorists but to begin to understand the passions and concerns of the world from which they came. Karen Armstrong's "Islam: A Short History" proved an invaluable primer as did Ira A. Lapidus's more detailed survey, "A History of Islamic Societies." Most interesting was a brief but powerful work, "In the Name of Identity: Violence and the Need to Belong" by Amin Maalouf, a Lebanese writer driven from his homeland to France by his nation's devastating civil war.

Americans, who have rallied around the flag, do not need Maalouf to remind them of the importance of identity—the sense of belonging—to the human psyche. Our notion of ourselves as Americans, our connection with a strong and resilient culture, assures us that we will not simply endure, but prevail.

What Maalouf reveals is the flip side: how the triumphs that sustain and bolster us have created a crisis of confidence among others. He notes that until the late Middle Ages, Western culture was a backwater. After the fall of Rome, Europe was in shambles. The Muslim world was the home of human progress. But during the last 600 years, the West has reimagined, reorganized and reasserted itself. History provides lists of other empires, but none before has held power during an age when technology made true worldwide dominance possible. He is talking not only about the power of Western armies, though they have played no small part, but of Western ideas.

He writes: The West has "set physical and intellectual standards for the whole world, marginalizing all other civilizations and reducing their status to that of peripheral cultures threatened with extinction. . . . Its science became Science, its medicine, Medicine its philosophy Philosophy, and from then on that trend towards concentration and Standardization has not stopped. . . . Wherever on the planet one happens to live, all modernization is now westernization. . . . For the rest of the world's inhabitants, all those born in the failed cultures, openness to change and modernity . . . [have] never been adopted without a certain bitterness, without a feeling of humiliation and defection. Without a piercing doubt about the dangers of assimilation. Without a profound identity crisis."

This small snatch from Maalouf's broad work begins to suggest one aspect of the vast range of knotty problems that confront us. It is not simply the vices of America and its Western partners—especially the lingering legacy of colonialism in the Arab world and around the globe that breeds anger against us. It is also our virtues, our shimmering political ideals and miraculous technology that have fueled deep resentment among many, and murderous rage among a few.

Our vices must be addressed, but what of our virtues? What is the proper response when our greatest gifts to humanity, those very achievements which provide us with our bold sense of self, are sources of despair, and worse, for others?

Maalouf writes: "It would be disastrous if the current globalization were to be a one-way process, with 'universal transmitters' on one side and 'receivers' on the other, with the 'norm' set against the 'exceptions'; with on the one hand those who think they have nothing to learn from the rest of the world, and on the other those who believe that the rest of the world will never listen to them."

Sounds sensible. But how would one put such ideas into practice? Maalouf argues that we need to be more sensitive to and appreciative of cultural differences. At the same time, he says we must value "human dignity" and "work to ensure that every citizen is treated as a fully-fledged member of society, whatever his affiliations."

Again, a noble aim. But how to realize it?

I don't know the answer, which is the greatest lesson I have learned since Sept. 11. Americans have voiced strong opinions since the terrorist attack, but we should admit that two weeks of immersion is only the beginning of understanding. The world is so complicated, filled with so many people and ideas that even surface knowledge, much less definitive insight, seems beyond daunting. In recent years we Americans have heard a lot about "information overload" while enjoying peace and prosperity. In response, we have been content to focus on our own small worlds, figuring everything else would take care of itself.

It hasn't.

On Sept. 11 we were reminded that no man or nation is an island. Even as we watch our leaders formulate a response, we must remember that we are not just a great power but a democracy. We citizens must do what we can: learn, think, engage. It is a burden we have begun to carry these past two weeks as the nation has immersed itself in a long overdue dialogue not just about what was done to us but our place in the world.

Even as we rightly begin to turn some of our attention back to baseball and other pastimes that make life sweet, I hope that our discourse does not dissolve. A nation of the people and by the people cannot perish from the Earth when it takes its responsibilities seriously.

September 23, 2001

The Age of the Fear of Terror

In 2001, about 30,000 Americans committed suicide, roughly 18,000 were killed in drunk driving accidents, and 14,000 were homicide victims.

But the statistic that mattered most was 2,977—the number of people murdered in the terrorist attacks of Sept. 11, a tragedy that spread panic across the country. In response, Americans sent a clear message to our leaders: This can never happen again. If it does, we will hold you responsible.

President Bush acknowledged our mood through actions as big as our anger and fear, launching a "war on terror" that "will not end until every terrorist group of global reach has been found, stopped and defeated."

Though America has not suffered another direct attack on our soil, Bush's popularity has plummeted amid a series of difficulties and miscalculations. Yet even as a string of critical books—including "Fiasco," "Hubris" and "Imperial Hubris"—document his failures, the basic narrative of our times, felt by the American people and articulated by the president, remains unchallenged: We are fighting a powerful, shadowy enemy ever willing and able to destroy us.

Five years after 9/11, Americans will accept all manner of death, except by the hands of terrorists. For that we have zero tolerance. John Kerry learned this lesson in 2004, when he was pilloried for suggesting that we will never vanquish terrorism, that our goal should be to render it a "nuisance" like prostitution or illegal gambling.

Since then fearful Democrats have castigated Bush's prosecution of the war on terror, rather than his description of it. They have depicted Iraq as a diversion from that effort, without challenging his basic assumptions about it. As a result, the global struggle has become a hostage to domestic politics. We argue over "Who's stronger?" and "Who's to blame?" instead of pursuing the crucial question raised after 9/11—"What are we up against?"

Our collective failure to focus on the motives, methods, capabilities and aims of our enemies has exacted a steep price. "If anything, we appear to know less about the nature of our adversaries in the war on terrorism than we did when we began," Louise Richardson writes in her vital new book, "What Terrorists Want: Understanding the Enemy, Containing the Threat."

A senior lecturer at Harvard University who grew up in Ireland when the IRA was at its peak, Richardson reminds us that Osama bin Laden and his acolytes did not invent terrorism. Their motives and methods fit a wider tradition of terror—from the Zealots who attacked Roman soldiers, to medieval period Assassins to today's Tamil Tigers in Sri Lanka. She also argues that America's response to 9/11 corresponds to actions taken by other governments facing strange and deadly foes.

"The first reaction," she writes, "is almost always to demonstrate resolve by the adoption of a draconian response that goes largely unchallenged by the public."

Just as we found it hard to believe that a lone gunman had killed President Kennedy, we couldn't accept that a small, relatively weak band of ideologues could have produced such damage, whose impact is better measured by its psychological blow than its body count.

"In responding to the attacks of 9/11, Americans opted to accept al-Qaeda's language of cosmic warfare at face value and respond accordingly," Richardson writes, "rather than respond to al-Qaeda based on an objective assessment of its resources and capabilities relative to their own."

As a result, we elevated al-Qaeda, making it seem a worthy adversary. Bin Laden may be as evil as Hitler, but he lacks the dictator's resources. We defined the battlefield on the terrorists' terms, turning their weakness into a strength. "By dispatching any operative into any Starbucks, subway station, or shopping mall in the country and blowing it up," Richardson writes, "a terrorist group could demonstrate that the most powerful country in the history of the world has not been able to beat it."

Americans must accept that such low-level attacks ever loom. Richardson notes the difficulties Israel has faced battling terrorist attacks and the failure of Britain, despite deploying up to 30,000 troops and spending $5 billion a year, to defeat the IRA, which had only a few hundred members.

As for the truly apocalyptic weapons that have received so much attention from politicians and the media—biological or chemical agents, nuclear weapons or "dirty" bombs—the threat is minuscule, Richardson maintains, because those weapons are extremely difficult to deploy and develop.

While urging us not to overestimate our adversaries' abilities, Richardson says we must pay greater attention to their motives. Even suicide bombers are not crazy extremists, she writes. Most seek glory and revenge, including the Iraqi man, radicalized by the sight of U.S. soldiers, who shot into a crowd of demonstrators, and the 40-year-old Palestinian mother determined to avenge her son's shooting by Israeli soldiers.

Suicide bombers do not believe their sacrifice will change the world. Neither, Richardson argues, do the people who train and dispatch them nor the larger communities that glorify their acts. Terrorists have smaller ambitions: to strike back any way they can, to even the scales and provoke a response that will bring more death to their side but also more converts to their cause.

Richardson makes no apologies for terrorists who, by definition, kill innocent civilians. But she reminds us that America's response to the injustice of 9/11 was revenge on a massive scale—a series of military actions that have inevitably (if unintentionally) claimed the lives of thousands of civilians.

Apart from suggesting that we work more closely with our allies, honor the Geneva Conventions and address the root causes of terrorism, Richardson does not offer an alternative plan for combating terror. Instead, her book urges us to think more clearly about the threat we face: We may never destroy global terrorism, but it cannot destroy us. We do not live in the Age of Terror so much as the Age of the Fear of Terror.

September 10, 2006

What's Up with the Muslims?

"What's up with the Muslims?" my friend asked as the pope was being pressured to recant what most Westerners see as a statement of fact—that there is a link between Islam and violence.

For many of us, Islam does not conjure images of peace and love but of terrorism and suicide bombs, of honor killings and arranged marriages. Its adherents place bounties on the heads of novelists (Salman Rushdie), murder filmmakers whose art challenges its beliefs (Theo van Gogh) and summon angry mobs to protest cartoons that criticize it.

A spokesman for Pakistan's foreign ministry seemed to say it all by responding to the pope's words with this statement: "Anyone who describes Islam . . . as intolerant encourages violence."

What is up with the Muslims?

Scores of books and thousands of newspaper articles and columns have tackled that question since 9/11. Some of the more stimulating works I've read include "Jihad: The Trail of Political Islam" by Gilles Kepel, "The Clash of Fundamentalisms" by Tariq Ali, "What Went Wrong?" by Bernard Lewis, "Murder in Amsterdam" by Ian Buruma and "What Terrorists Want" by Louise Richardson.

These books do not offer simple answers to our question. Instead, they tell us why it is so unhelpful. About 1.5 billion Muslims are scattered in every nation across the globe, and any generalization about "the Muslims" is a stereotype, as useful as those made about "the blacks" or "white folks." Boiling down Islam to its most shocking practices or equating all Muslims with its most extreme followers prevents us from seeing the world in a clear light.

Many of us engage in such reductionism because of fear. We see a threat and focus on that—most Americans never gave a thought to Islam until it became associated with violence against us. Recent history suggests this is a rational response. Nevertheless, we can be a lot smarter about managing our fright by determining precisely who is and is not a threat. As a first step, my reading suggests that it is useful to think of Muslims as falling into three general categories.

First are the Muslims we tend to ignore, the overwhelming majority who pose no danger. This group belies the canard that Islam is an engine of anger, hatred and terror. Undoubtedly, violence is not anathema to Islam and some commit murder in its name. But most Muslims do not take up the sword. This suggests that while religion may influence those who do, it is not their primary spark. If every Islamic leader called for peace tomorrow, we would still have terror.

Instead we should ask what leads some Muslims to embrace violence? What's up with those Muslims?

These questions lead us to focus on those who deserve our attention, the relatively small number of hard-core ideologues whose lives revolve around murder. All may pledge allegiance to Allah, but they commit murder for a variety of reasons.

Most suicide bombers from Gaza or Iraq are driven by political goals, not religion. The 9/11 hijackers wanted to strike a symbolic blow against

American power while the "homegrown" terrorists who struck London's subways were apparently protesting British policies. The Dutchman who murdered Theo van Gogh was seeking vengeance against the film-maker for his short film challenging Islam's attitudes toward women, "Submission."

Taking President Bush's lead, we tend to lump these terrorist attacks together, casting them as part of an Islamic crusade against the West. However, scholars such as Louise Richardson argue these vicious attacks are usually launched in response to specific cultural and political griev-ances.

While terrorists pose the greatest threat, they are not our greatest chal-lenge. Our vast military and intelligence resources will always be able to limit, though probably never eliminate, the actions of Osama bin Laden and his ilk. We may have a harder time developing strategies for dealing with the third group—the millions of Muslims who feel burning rage to-ward the West. These are the people who would never strap on a suicide belt yet celebrate those who do, who protest perceived insults to their faith (whether they be Danish cartoons mocking Muhammad or scholarly com-ments by the pope) even as they disparage other religions in vile terms.

Many sources of their anger—including Western policies in Muslim nations, Europe's problems integrating its Muslim immigrants, wide-spread misinformation about the West and bigotry—can be addressed. The bedrock issue, the true "clash of civilizations," seems intractable. We in the West fought centuries of bloody wars to loosen the relation-ship between church and state, to create secular cultures where faith is respected, but subject to often biting criticism. Most Muslim nations are just that, Muslim nations. What we see as free speech, they see as crimi-nal insults to the faith—some Turks are calling for the pope's arrest when he visits the country this fall.

Mobs calling for murder in response to political cartoons or critical speeches are incomprehensible to most Westerners. While they are dis-turbing, they are not a threat to us—yes, some zealot may seek vengeance against the "infidels," but such acts are rare.

Finally, while my reading urges us to make fundamental distinctions when thinking about whom and what we are facing, one generalization is useful: Most Muslims are different from those of us who do not follow the faith. As we stand by and defend our beliefs, we should not expect them to do the same. We must separate real dangers from cultural differences, combatting the former while working to understand, if not fully accept, the latter.

September 24, 2006

Assimilation and Its Discontents

I hailed the emergence of "African American" during the 1980s. Journalists hate to repeat words. Now, I could refer to blacks or African Americans.

Without much thought, I accepted the notion that this was how my fellow citizens wished to be identified.

Recent events have forced me to rethink this.

Two months ago, I attended diversity training at work. The leaders asked us to describe ourselves. Nearly all of the dozen or so whites called themselves Americans; one said he was a Southerner. Tellingly, seven of the eight blacks said they, too, prefer the label American, rather than African American.

The result of this small, unscientific survey surprised me. Still, I didn't give it too much thought until riots erupted across France. News reports identified most of the perpetrators as Muslim youths whose anger was driven by economic distress and deep alienation from their adopted home. Many were born and reared in France but felt they would always be considered outsiders, not French.

Los Angeles Times reporter Terry McDermott illustrated the darkest result of this phenomenon in "Perfect Soldiers: The 9/11 Hijackers: Who They Were, Why They Did It." He notes that several of the terrorists had spent long years studying in Germany. Instead of being embraced by their new land, they felt unwelcome. Feeling rejected by Germans, they took a hard turn toward radical Islam in a search for identity.

Of course, few Muslims turn their faith into a vehicle for violence. But, as Bruce Bawer notes in his forthcoming book, "While Europe Slept: How Radical Islam is Destroying the West From Within," the failure of European societies to integrate their swelling ranks of Muslim immigrants is creating an oppositional culture. Unable to be seen as Dutch, French, German or Spanish, many Muslims turn to religion as a source of identity. Simultaneously, many of their leaders see the West's sexual, religious and political freedoms as a threat to traditional Islamic beliefs.

Bawer—a gay American living in Europe whose earlier books include a critique of fundamentalist Christians, "Stealing Jesus"—also notes a powerful paradox: Europe has been unable to integrate immigrants in part because it largely denies the notion of difference. Nations proclaim that everyone is the same: We are all French, all Dutch, all Germans. This dangerous idealism, Bawer argues, prevents European nations from recognizing the differing needs and mores of its citizens. This failure makes it harder to forge respectful paths toward a shared identity.

France and other European countries are not truly multicultural states—where differences are celebrated under the umbrella of unity—but bi-cultural societies in which entrenched families and relatively recent immigrants occupy separate spheres.

What has gone wrong in Europe sheds light on what has worked right in the United States. James Baldwin underscored this difference in the 1970s, when he explained why he was returning to the U.S. after years abroad. "America has found a formula to deal with the demon of race," the great writer explained, while Europe was set to "explode" under its weight.

Baldwin was no Pollyanna. He knew that our history was littered with racial violence that makes the Paris riots seem like kid's stuff. The American story is filled with the brutality of anti-black and anti-immigrant mobs and of oppressed groups taking up arms in defense.

But as historian David R. Roediger writes in "Working Toward Whiteness: How America's Immigrants Become White," the nation made strides to accept and integrate Italians, Greeks and other European immigrants during the first half of the 20th century. The civil rights movement of the 1960s started the ongoing effort to welcome blacks into the American mainstream.

Only a fool or a demagogue would claim that America has become a colorblind society. Despite the great strides made by black Americans, they lag as a group in nearly every indicator of economic and social well-being.

Nevertheless, America is no longer gripped by the racial violence plaguing Europe. After 9/11, attacks on Muslims were relatively rare. That we have not been hit again suggests that new immigrants do not feel isolated or under siege.

Various forces have helped Americans shape a multicultural society —especially the limited but still-effective willingness to own up to and remedy past failings, to live up to the high ideals that sparked our revolution. Above all, there is the bedrock belief that one becomes an American by living in America, that your status is not defined by your lineage but your mailing address.

And so I began to wonder whether the term African American is useful. It's a question I still can't answer. On the one hand, the American system works because it respects differences. We are not a homogeneous society but a gorgeous mosaic of hyphenated Americans.

Paradoxically, our greatest strength lies in the dropped hyphen. Our greatest achievement is that so many Italian Americans, Irish Americans, Iraqi Americans and African Americans also see themselves as plain old Americans.

Still, the ethnic and sectarian tensions we see in Europe and around the world suggest the fragility of this civil compact. No people are immune from the failings of the human heart. Through hard work and open hearts we have built a road of progress—but it is one that necessarily rests on a slippery slope. If we don't continue to forge ahead, we may fall back.

November 20, 2005

No-Brainers Meet the Brainwashed

Initially it was a no-brainer. The decision by Muslim cabdrivers in Minneapolis to refuse passengers carrying alcohol because they were violating the Quran struck me as a gross repudiation of American values. The city's plan (since rejected) to accommodate the drivers by affixing lights on their cabs alerting passengers to their rules struck me as craven kowtowing.

My rule of thumb: When in Minneapolis, do as the Minneapolitans.

Ian Buruma has made me reconsider this response through his provocative book, "Murder in Amsterdam." Starting with the murder of filmmaker Theo van Gogh by a Muslim extremist, Buruma raises larger questions about what may be the crucial social issue of the 21st century: how Western nations deal with the massive wave of immigrants who don't feel the need to adopt their customs or beliefs.

Buruma is a professor at Bard College and a frequent contributor to the New York Review of Books. He is also an immigrant who left his native Netherlands in the mid-1970s and eventually settled in the United States.

This background provides him with an interesting perspective when he returns to his homeland to assess the impact of Muslim immigrants on Dutch society. Both a scholar trained to empathize with marginalized groups and an immigrant, Buruma is able to see the Netherlands as an insider and as an outsider.

Van Gogh, a direct descendant of the Dutch painter, was murdered in 2004 by a Dutch-born Muslim extremist incensed by his short film, "Submission" (itself a translation of the word "Islam"), which challenged his faith's treatment of women. While condemning van Gogh's murder, Buruma uses the crime to explore the nature and limits of tolerance.

The Dutch pride themselves on having "the fairest, freest, most civilized, perfect multi-culti paradise," Buruma notes. But that attitude is being tested by the influx of immigrants, especially to major cities such as Amsterdam, where almost half the population is foreign-born.

"Slowly, almost without anyone's noticing," he writes, "old working-class Dutch neighborhoods lost their white populations and were transformed into 'dish cities' linked to Morocco, Turkey, and the Middle East by satellite television and the Internet. Gray Dutch streets filled up, not only with satellite dishes, but with Moroccan bakeries, Turkish kebab joints, travel agents offering cheap flights to Istanbul or Casablanca, and coffee-houses filled with sad-eyed men in *djellabas*."

Many native Dutch feel like strangers in their own land. Nativist groups have emerged, with a harsh message for newcomers. Leader Pim Fortuyn once declared, "This is our country, and if you can't conform, you should get the hell out, back to your own country and culture."

Buruma sharply illuminates the mind-sets of the old-line Dutch and the new immigrants, revealing pressure points epitomized by their differing views of faith. The Netherlands is a largely secular nation where faith is fair game for challenge or mockery. To many Muslims, including van Gogh's assassin, faith is sacred, its disparagement taboo.

Buruma writes: "At first sight, the clash of values appears to be straightforward: on the one hand, secularism, science, equality between men and women, individualism, freedom to criticize without fear of violent retribution, and on the other, divine laws, revealed truth, male domination, tribal honor, and so on."

Here Buruma offers his most jarring analysis. He knows that most of his readers not only support that first set of values but also see them as the expression of universal desires. For them, everybody wants freedom; those who do not are ignorant, brainwashed or both. Yet devout Muslims, Buruma observes, believe their faith is universal. For them, those who do not embrace Islam are ignorant, brainwashed or both.

Rather than choose sides or make judgments, Buruma casts these ideologies as flip sides of the same coin. Westerners may see their demand that immigrants embrace their values as a cultural upgrade, but to Buruma it is no less coercive than the demands of some Muslims that nonbelievers honor their faith.

To my mind, this is moral relativism run amok. History and personal reflection have convinced me that "secularism, science, equality between men and women" are better than "divine laws, revealed truth, [and] male domination."

Buruma embodies those Enlightenment values more than I do. He espouses an open-mindedness of which I am incapable. That's what makes his perspective so challenging. When he argues that assimilation is a form of coercion because it limits the ability of newcomers to shape their own identities, I can see his logic. When we ask Muslim cabdrivers to violate their beliefs and serve passengers carrying alcohol, we force them to subscribe to our beliefs.

However, his prescription strikes me as a one-way street. Essentially, he expects Westerners to practice their values—e.g. tolerance—while devout Muslims follow theirs, which include intolerance. In theory, this approach makes sense. In practice, he avoids the knotty questions surrounding accommodation. In the real world, "mutual respect" requires not only the honoring of one's highest values, but also give and take.

Buruma's flight from reality is also apparent in his dismissive approach to the notion of national culture, to the idea of when in Rome, do as the Romans. Yes, assimilation may be coercive, but the desire to preserve one's culture, to expect newcomers to accept the core customs of their adopted lands, is powerful and persuasive.

Though Buruma does not settle these questions, he does challenge those who reflexively dismiss newcomers' demands. In our jet-fueled global world, where it is far easier to change your country than your culture, these issues will only intensify. As Buruma reminds us, the questions they raise are anything but no-brainers.

November 12, 2006

NEW DIRECTIONS IN A CHANGING LANDSCAPE

The Perils of the Luckiest Generation

When the news broke that former Sen. Bob Kerrey led a 1969 raid in Vietnam that took the lives of 13 women and children, I hit the books. I revisited Michael Herr's "Dispatches," Neil Sheehan's "A Bright Shining Lie," and two books, one good, the other great, about the war by Tim O'Brien, "If I Die in a Combat Zone, Box Me Up and Ship Me Home" and "The Things They Carried."

I read so much because the story raised serious and complicated issues. I figured I had time to learn, to think, to decide.

I was, as Bogart put it in "Casablanca," misinformed.

Two weeks later, the Kerrey revelations seem like ancient history. The news has cycled on. The deep questions that story raised evaporated like morning dew off a stagnant pond.

We might chalk this up to the ADD reportage spawned by CNN—in the era of 24-hour news, media attention mimics the sharp rises and precipitous declines of dot-com stock prices. We could also attribute it to the problems of establishing with any certainty what happened one night in Vietnam 32 years ago. And there is, of course, the natural aversion to scratching old wounds.

But relying on those reasonable explanations blinds us to the larger cultural shift that makes it difficult for Americans to grapple with complex national issues. At the root of it all is the blithe spirit that allows us to purchase bigger cars and larger homes while global warming intensifies; that enables us to act as if we live in a colorblind society, while racism and its legacies persist; that permits us to fill our death houses even as it becomes clear that capital punishment is more a roll of the dice than a mechanism of justice. This blithe spirit makes us incapable of confronting the knotty moral questions raised by Kerrey's wartime conduct.

The irony is that this dangerous mindset stems from dumb luck. Fact is, we, today, are the Luckiest Generation in American history. Here's why.

Darkness, death and despair defined the daily reality of our immediate forebears. The Great War was soon followed by the Great Depression, which gave way to World War II, the most frightening days of the Cold War, the civil rights movement, Kennedy's assassination, Vietnam and Watergate. For 60 years this unrelenting torrent of momentous gutchecks forced our predecessors into national life. Their lives were entwined with, shaped by, the roiling currents of American history.

Then, about a quarter century ago, a worn-out nation said, "Enough." President Nixon's resignation in 1974 marked the end of a "national nightmare" in more ways than we could have expected. National life entered a state of suspended animation. Peace and prosperity, desire and circumstance propelled the Luckiest Generation inward. We ceased seeing ourselves as citizens. We were individuals—of ourselves, by ourselves, for ourselves. We no longer asked what we could do for our country; but what our country was going to do for us.

No event proved powerful enough to pull us, as a people, out of our shells. The Berlin Wall fell, the Gulf War raged, a president was impeached, but most Americans—if they thought about it at all—considered themselves merely witnesses to this history, which seemed to occur beyond the boundaries of their lives and which required nothing of them. History seemed benign, a take-it-or-leave-it proposition.

I was born in 1962. As a charter member of the Luckiest Generation, I have never been called upon to make a sacrifice for my country. I care about certain issues out of interest, not necessity.

It is hard to overestimate the great blessings of the Luckiest Generation. We take comfort and self-determination for granted. We have been afforded the luxury of defining and understanding our lives with a freedom our beleaguered forebears never would have imagined. Allowed to believe the world will take care of itself, we've been able to focus on the complexities and challenges of domestic life.

It's said there are no atheists in a foxhole—but that's a lousy place to find God. Similarly, if the absence of war and want have denied the Luckiest Generation a full reckoning of the meaning of citizenship, that's a bargain most rational people would gladly accept.

The pendulum has swung too far. Our sweet liberty has fostered a collective paralysis. Our quest for quiet and self-fulfillment has rendered us incapable of truly engaging in national life. The profound disconnection Americans feel from politics, and each other, is the price of years of retreat. We've talked so little about so much for so long that we have lost the art of national conversation. We can still recognize looming threats—such as global warming, lingering racism and a deeply flawed criminal justice system—but we cannot, we will not, address them.

Years from now, our progeny may look back on us and say "They were the Luckiest Generation." They might also call us the most irresponsible one.

May 13, 2001

Friendly, from Afar

Earth Day isn't my favorite holiday. A born and bred Gothamite, my idea of roughing it is hiking to the store, hunting for bargains or fishing for something to wear.

The thought of sleeping outside on the ground (I believe that's called "camping") seems an absurd affront to progress: Why do you think we invented houses? If I had a slingshot, I'd probably use it against those %$@#@*!& birds who ruin my rest each morning.

And yet, it is precisely because I am a modern man (and a bit of a cheapskate) that I try to recycle and reuse my household items and limit my use of water, gas and other natural resources.

In this spirit, I was almost happy to join my youngest daughter's Indian Princess tribe last weekend as they cleaned up Raleigh's Fallon Park for Earth Day.

While we collected muddy cigarette packs, sticky candy wrappers and submerged beer cans, my initial reaction, yuck!, was replaced by larger environmental questions, especially about our regional drought and global warming.

I wondered what impact eco-friendly but nature-free people like me will have on our ability to confront environmental challenges. Must one know and love Mother Earth to protect her?

This question is becoming pivotal as Americans increasingly turn away from the great outdoors, choosing malls over mountains, couches over cold streams, cyberspace over open spaces. During the past two decades, the number of people who visited national parks or went camping or hiking declined between 18 percent and 25 percent, according to a study published by the National Academy of Sciences.

Applications for fishing permits fell by 25 percent between 1981 and 2005. The number of hikers on the Appalachian Trail dropped 18 percent between 2000 and 2005. Since 1987, the study notes, "time spent in nature dropped by about one percent annually" with no signs of improvement.

This retreat from nature has many causes. But the study pays special attention to the rise of the Internet and video games.

Echoing a Kaiser Family Foundation survey that found that kids between ages 8 and 18 spend an average of 6.5 hours a day with electronic media, the authors asserted: "The replacement of vigorous outdoor activities by sedentary, indoor videophilia has far-reaching consequences for physical and mental health."

As a denizen of the concrete jungle, I haven't given much thought to these developments. So I spoke with two people who have pondered the environmental implications of our fraying relationship with nature, writers Richard Louv and Bill McKibben.

Louv focuses on how our disconnection from nature is affecting kids.

In his book "Last Child in the Woods," he coined the term nature-deficit disorder to describe the myriad ill effects of our shut-in culture.

While many of these consequences involved health, including rises in obesity, attention disorders and depression, Louv also explored the troubling paradox our retreat from nature has created as we grapple with environmental issues.

On the one hand, Americans are more ecologically aware than ever.

"When I was a boy growing up in the 1950s, I played in the woods, loved the woods, without understanding how they were connected to a larger world," he said. "I'd never heard of climate change, acid rain or holes in the ozone layer."

Nowadays even elementary school students recognize how our ecological fate is tied to what's happening in the Amazon, the Arctic, China and India.

On the other hand, this rising awareness is largely abstract. Like a blind person trying to understand colors, we know facts and figures about nature but not the thing itself.

"Our view of nature is primarily intellectual," Louv said. "It is based on news and information, rather than experience. We are increasingly carrying environmentalism in our briefcases rather than our hearts."

And that knowledge, he continued, is wrapped in doom. We often define nature as a threat, a force of destruction and death; it is a problem we must confront rather than a source of sustenance and renewal.

"It's important to address the problems, but if all we do is paint portraits of disaster, it will be harder for us to solve them," Louv said.

Scratch an environmentalist, he continued, and you will invariably find someone who had a "transcendent" experience in nature, usually during childhood while playing outside.

"If kids aren't developing a relationship with nature," he said, "how deeply will they care about it when they're grown and responsible for dealing with it?"

Louv's concerns are echoed by McKibben, whose books include "The End of Nature" and "Deep Economy: The Wealth of Communities and the Durable Future." We can't fix the environment, he said, without repairing our relationship to nature and one another.

McKibben noted that our retreat from nature is a monumental shift. Since the dawn of humanity, almost everyone worked and played in nature.

"In the last few decades in America, we've seen the virtual disappearance of this way of life," he said. "Not only have we fallen into a consumerist pattern that isolates us from each other and the world around us, but we've come to see this completely abnormal state as normal."

As a result, we define environmental challenges as engineering and political problems to be solved through cleaner technologies and smarter policies. Without discounting the importance of those efforts, McKibben said they may not be enough.

To develop the will to save Mother Earth, we must also get to know her better, enjoying the pleasures and lessons she offers, especially about our connections to one another and the world.

So I got my answer.

Eco-friendly but nature-free is only a halfway approach as we face our environmental problems.

Our retreat from nature may be as much of a concern as the carbon we pump into the air and the resources we use at breakneck speed. Our heads may be in the right place, but what about our hearts?

Honestly, I don't know if I can rise to this challenge and kindle a love of nature in my concrete-jungle soul. I don't know if I have the capacity to help my children meet it.

But thanks to McKibben and Louv, I'm thinking about it. And thinking is the first step toward action.

April 27, 2008

Feeling All Righteous

I'm no eco-saint. But since the drought, my motto has become "it's the least I can do so I do it."

My lawn is turning brown, just like my once-white car—don't touch! My children think I'm a poet because of my flushing credo, "If it's yellow, let it mellow."

You may be glad to know I still shower every day. But I do collect that first gallon of cold water in a bucket for other household uses; I turn off the spout as I wash my hair and, like Roger Bannister, try to finish before the four-minute mark.

These minor steps pay a major dividend: They let me experience that ecstatic rush of self-esteem known as the Prius Syndrome. First observed among owners of hybrid cars, it describes the virtuous glow that suffuses every fiber of one's being after making a small contribution to the environment. I feel noble when I fill my toilet with shower water and fill my light sockets with energy efficient bulbs! I can only imagine how good I'll feel when I finally remember to bring my canvas bags to the market!

While unleashing warm and fuzzy feelings, the Prius Syndrome can make one judgmental. I was filled with righteous indignation on Dec. 4 as I read the N&O article about a Knightdale man who spent $6,000 for a private well to keep his lawn lush. "It was an expensive deal," Joe Kanze explained, while I played the world's smallest violin in sympathy for his bank account. "But you know what? I'm retired and this is my avocation."

There's been a spike in applications for irrigation wells since watering restrictions were put in place. But, local officials said, such wells are unlikely to have any impact on municipal water supplies.

"That," I screamed at my paper (it didn't answer; it never does) "is beside the point." Our response to the drought is not just a matter of lake levels and water tables. It is also a moral question that involves our sense of community and sacrifice.

As a practical matter, my water-saving strategies will have as much impact on our situation as those wells. I do what I can, in part, because my neighbors are doing the same. But if they began drilling wells, I might be inclined to engage in a little nocturnal watering. If they aren't pitching in, why should I?

That's the dangerous question raised by the well diggers among us. It's the same one people ask when wealthy environmentalists defend their large homes and fuel-guzzling private jets by noting that they purchase offsets to erase their carbon footprints.

Their argument recalls the medieval-era Christians who bought indulgences from the church to remove the stain of sin, and Civil War-era Americans who bought their way out of military service. They, too, found a way to play by the rules while breaking the spirit of them.

Even as I decried these actions, I had to admit that they reflect the spirit of our times. In contemporary America, the notion of cutting back and doing without in the name of some larger communal purpose has gone the way of the horseless carriage. For some people, flying commercial or enduring a wilting garden is too heavy a demand. For others, buying a hybrid car or collecting shower water is a sign of great moral rectitude. Both show us how far removed we have become from the notion of genuine sacrifice.

And, truth be told, that's not a bad thing.

Sacrifice does not stem from choice but necessity. Think back to the last time Americans came together in the name of sacrifice, the Great Depression and World War II. You don't need me to tell you, those were not exactly salad days. Who would want to relive those desperate years?

Since then, most Americans have enjoyed tremendous prosperity, obviating the need for sacrifice. The two W's, worry and want, have been replaced by the three C's, convenience, comfort and consumerism. Instead of struggling to decide what we must forsake, the vexing question of our age has become "what should I buy next?"

Ideology, like prosperity, has also undercut the idea of sacrifice. Since the rise of the counterculture in the 1960s and Ronald Reagan's conservative revolution of the 1980s, America has embraced the idea of radical individualism. In their own way, these strange bedfellows spoke with a single voice: Do your own thing, they counseled. Imagination and initiative, they argued, are the wellsprings of happiness, not the government or traditional institutions.

One result has been the fusion of personal happiness and the common good. Rather than all of us working together, they suggested that society works best for the greatest number of people when we all pursue our own self-interest. We're better off if each of us guides our own rowboats rather than thinking of ourselves as passengers on a single ship.

On the whole, I agree with this logic. Yes, our civic ties have frayed in recent years, but the gains in personal choice and freedom have been worth it. Since World War II, our history has been marked by expanding wealth and freedom. We are a happier, healthier nation.

Considering those blessings, it doesn't seem much to ask that everyone let their lawns turn brown when the rains don't come and that none of us confuse ourselves with Mother Teresa when we do the least that we can.

How lucky we are that that's what passes for sacrifice these days.

December 16, 2007

Hiding from the Silence of the Mind

Wolf Blitzer here. Wolf Blitzer there. Wolf Blitzer everywhere.

The CNN anchor's voice was inescapable as I waited for my flight at Raleigh-Durham airport. After the Larry Craig kerfuffle, I decided against reading my book in the bathroom. So I just sat at the gate, my ears burning as my thoughts turned to that Zelig of modern life: noise.

From the moment our eyes pop open to the second our head hits the pillow, we're cocooned in cacophony: buzzing alarms, blaring traffic, howling leaf blowers and mind-numbing Muzak piped into elevators, stores, outdoor malls and telephones as we wait on hold, forever. Restaurants can be as loud as rock concerts, and if you plan on bar hopping, bring earplugs.

Stewing in these aural juices, I made a disquieting observation: I only have a problem with other people's noise. Truth is, I'm always surrounding myself in sound. I'm awakened each morning by my radio. I leave it on while I dress. On the drive to work, more radio. In the office, I run a fan for its soothing whir. Back home, I pop on the radio while doing the dinner dishes. I turn it off only when my wife sighs, "Do you have to have that thing on all the time?" Then I fire up my stereo.

That's only a sample of my sonic world, which includes TVs, computers and, every so often, conversation. I like 'em all, even the roar of my leaf blower.

There is one sound that I rarely hear: the sound of silence. When I catch a snatch, I move to fill it, as unthinkingly as Pavlov's dogs responded to their master's bell.

Sure, I'm the captain of my own ship, but I'm also sailing on the S.S. America. On this carnival cruise, constant stimulation is the name of every port of call. Passengers fret that if we aren't cramming every minute with exciting experiences, we're missing out. When the world isn't bombarding us with sounds and images, we're doing it to ourselves. It's how we remind ourselves that we're alive. On these roiling seas, boredom is the great white shark, to be feared and avoided at all costs.

The result is a war on silence. Noise is only the loudest weapon in an assault that has also diminished its meaning and value.

For much of human history, silence was a virtue. In fact, it was golden. Lao-tzu taught, "Silence is a source of great strength." A Hebrew proverb instructed, "If a word is worth a coin, silence is worth two." More recently, Mother Teresa said, "We need to find God, and he cannot be found in noise and restlessness. God is the friend of silence."

People knew the power of silence because it was inescapable. Until the 20th century brought us radios, TVs and personal stereos, it was mighty hard to fill the quiet air. As technology enabled us to vanquish actual silence, political movements challenged our metaphoric understanding of the term.

Since the 1950s, when marginalized groups demanded to be heard, silence has been cast as a problem. Martin Luther King Jr. asserted, "Our lives begin to end the day we become silent about things that matter." The feminist poet Adrienne Rich stated, "Lying is done with words and also with silence." As AIDS activists declared that "Silence=Death," abortion rights opponents produced a horrifying film called "The Silent Scream."

The growing recognition that people should not suffer in silence is a healthy development. And it is not hard to find a direct causal link between the rise of the confessional culture and the blaring noise that defines our sonic landscape.

Nevertheless, these forces have combined to depreciate the value of silence. Long regarded as a path to enlightenment, silence is now seen as a force of social control or boring nothingness. Practiced by mystics, monks and meditative lay people as a window to deeper understanding, silence now seems like a door that closes us off from the real world.

And yet, even as we prize self-expression, we steadily diminish the silence that can lead to knowledge.

Karen Armstrong underscores this point in her new introduction to "A Time to Keep Silence," Patrick Leigh Fermor's 1957 memoir about his stays at European monasteries: "Many of our problems spring from thwarted egotism. We resent the success of others; in our gloomiest, most self-pitying moments, we feel uniquely mistreated and undervalued; we are miserably aware of our shortcomings. In the world outside the cloister, it is always possible to escape such self-dissatisfaction: we can phone a friend, pour a drink, or turn on the television. But the religious has to face his or her own pettiness twenty-four hours a day, three-hundred and sixty-five days a year. If properly and wholeheartedly pursued, the monastic life liberates us from ourselves incrementally, slowly and imperceptibly."

Despite the urgent pleas of friends and family, I am not planning to take a vow of silence. Still, Armstrong seems on target when she suggests that we are silencing silence to avoid the hard questions that often arise when we are alone with our thoughts. As Bob Dylan observed, "Experience teaches us that silence terrifies people the most."

The hullabaloo of our hurly-burly world provides many passing pleasures, but it is also a powerful tool of distraction. Silence countervails such absent-mindedness. It leads us to think, to question. That can be scary. T. S. Eliot wrote, "And they write innumerable books; being / too vain and distracted for silence: seeking / every one after his own elevation, and / dodging his emptiness."

As a sonic addict, I have lost touch with silence. Since that day at the airport I have resolved to listen to the world a little less and to myself a bit more. But still my hand reaches out to flick on the radio, stereo or TV.

Noise is a hard habit to break.

November 18, 2007

Parents Give Traditional
Names Creative Twists

Exotic baby names are like violent crimes. They demand far more attention than they deserve. So forget Apple, Moxie CrimeFighter, Kal-el and all the other crazy names celebrities have given their little bundles of joy. All an expectant parent needs to know is this one simple name: Aidan.

Easy, right?

Now think of every possible way you can spell it, including Aden, Aedan, Aidyn, Aydan, Ayden, Aydin and Aiden. After that, imagine every possible rhyme with every imaginable spelling. Your short list might include Braden (and Bradyn, Braeden, Braedon, Braiden, Brayden, Braydon), Caden (and Caiden, Cayden, Kaden, Kadin, Kaeden, Kaiden, Kayden) and Haden (and Haiden, Hayden).

Welcome to the brave new world of baby names. Call it the Age of Tweak. Instead of inventing names out of whole cloth, parents are shifting and reshaping traditional names so their children will stand out—just not too far.

"There's a real push and desire by parents to avoid names that are popular or ordinary," says Laura Wattenberg, author of "The Baby Name Wizard." "Parents say they want to find a name that's different but not too different."

The dynamic was reflected in list of popular baby names for 2006 released last month by the Social Security Administration. Though Jacob and Emily again topped the list, the real news was that, swaddled together, the eight most common spellings for Aidan made it the most popular name for boys. Indeed, more parents chose a newfangled spelling of the name—Aiden—over the traditional Aidan. Just as telling was that Zayden made its first appearance on the list of the top 1,000 (at 871).

"The hundreds of parents who came up with the name Zayden thought they were coming up with something new, but hundreds of other parents had the same bright idea because we're all playing with the same set of pleasing sounds," Wattenberg said. "Parents are trying to hit two very different targets: They want a name that nobody has but that everybody likes."

This challenge has led many parents on far-flung searches, said Cleveland Kent Evans, associate professor of psychology at Nebraska's Bellevue University and a past president of the American Name Society. Place names—especially Brooklyn, Savannah and Paris for girls, Memphis for boys, London for both sexes—are increasingly popular. So are mellifluous words—Serenity and Destiny—and commercial monikers, including Armani, Lexus and Nautica; one family named their son ESPN (pronounced Espin) as an homage to the sports network.

Specific sounds, especially strong vowels sounds at the beginning and softer vowels at the end, seem particularly pleasing. Seven of the top 10 names for girls start with strong vowel sounds—Emily, Emma, Isabella, Ava, Abigail, Olivia and Hannah—and seven of those top ten names end with an "a" sound: Emma, Isabella, Ava, Olivia, Hannah, Sophia, Samantha.

"Today's hard-charging parents like to start strong," Wattenberg says, "to grab attention from the start."

Other sounds clang on modern ears, Wattenberg noted, citing the decline of names with consonant clusters such as Mildred and Elmer.

Nevertheless, overarching trends explain only so much. About 75 percent of the 4.3 million American babies covered by the Social Security Administration's survey were given one of the top 1,000 names for boys or girls. That means that more than 1 million babies were given names even more obscure—though some of these, such as Tzipora, which is popular among religious Jews, reflect America's diversity.

Though the name game has accelerated in recent years, the trend began in the mid- to late 19th century. Previously, names were a matter of custom, says Harvard sociologist Stanley Lieberson, whose books include "A Matter of Taste: How Names, Fashions, and Culture Change." Anchored in the past and tradition, they were often family names handed down from one generation to the next.

"Back then, naming your child was probably less of a decision," Lieberson says. "Naming your child after an ancestor, especially for males, just wasn't an issue."

As a result, popular names were extremely popular. Consider the Lost Colony established by Sir Walter Raleigh in 1587. Of its 99 men and boys, Lieberson said, 23 were named John, 15, Thomas, and 10, William. In the Massachusetts Bay Colony between 1630 and 1670, 53 percent of girls had one of three names: Mary (21 percent), Elizabeth (17 percent) and Sarah (15 percent).

During the 19th century, names started becoming a matter of fashion, Lieberson says. The days of Juniors and Roman numeral names (James Jones III, IV or V) were numbered as parents increasingly favored names that pleased their ears instead of their own parents. By 1946, only about 5 percent of American baby girls and boys were given the most popular names—James and Mary. In 2006, the top selections, Emily and Jacob were given to a little over 1 percent of newborns.

This break from the past was fueled by a growing aversion to the aging process, Lieberson adds. Names popular in the early part of the 20th century—Helen, Dorothy, Mildred, Ronald and Howard—not only came to sound old-fashioned but also conjured unpleasant images for some of the elderly people who carried them.

However, if a name stays unpopular for a long enough period, it can get a fresh start, as the newly fashionable Hazel and Adelaide suggest.

While acknowledging the name game's long history, Evans and Wattenberg note various trends pushing parents away from traditional names. These include the Social Security Administration's list of popular names, which has made parents aware of such trends since it debuted in 1997; mass media, which exposes them to innumerable names they wouldn't encounter in their local communities; and search engines such as Google, which allow them to test the popularity of their choices.

Google, Wattenberg warns, is a two-edged sword.

"When your baby becomes a teenager and posts something embarrassing under her unique name," she says, "it will follow her the rest of her life."

June 5, 2007

An Old-Fashioned Icon in a Fragmented Culture

Harry Potter is a throwback freak, the residue of a faded age, the likes of whom we may never see again.

I don't mean the archaic fantasy world of Muggles and wizards that author J. K. Rowling has created through seven novels, the last of which, "Harry Potter and the Deathly Hollows," goes on sale Saturday. I'm talking about the real world of Harry hoopla, where the Potter books have sold more than 325 million copies, inspired five hit movies and dizzying numbers of doodads big (a Potter theme park being built in Florida) and small (lunchboxes, action figures, banners, bookends, watches, magic wands . . .).

That blockbuster success makes Harry part of a dying breed, a once-dominant species whose members ruled our culture with their lips, hips and light sabers. Elvis, Marilyn, the Beatles, "I Love Lucy," the "Star Wars" films—like Harry, they weren't just hits. They were icons.

Icons and hit makers have taken a beating over the past two decades in a bloodless revolution that has transformed our cultural landscape. The chief weapon was not the mighty sword but sophisticated technologies, from the Internet and 500-channel cable systems to TiVo, the iPod and other gadgets that let us decide when we will watch and listen to the proliferating content available.

We still have hit TV shows, records and books; every week we're told that some movie is No. 1 at the box office. But as Chris Anderson documents in his must-read book, "The Long Tail: Why the Future of

Business Is Selling Less of More" (2006), "Hits are starting to, gasp, rule less. Number one is still number one, but the sales that go with that are not what they once were."

Among the reams of supporting data, Anderson notes that "most of the top fifty best-selling albums of all time were recorded in the seventies and eighties (the Eagles, Michael Jackson), and none of them were made in the past five years." In 1954, he writes, 74 percent of households with TVs watched "I Love Lucy." Today fewer than half of all TVs in use are tuned to programs on the major networks. Glamour events that once commanded large national audiences—the Grammys and Oscars, the World Series and the Olympics—attract ever smaller numbers of people.

The one area where this phenomenon does not hold is books, where Danielle Steel, John Grisham, Stephen King, J. K. Rowling and other best-selling authors enjoy far higher sales than their popular predecessors. Of course, a book that sells a million copies is a runaway hit, while network TV shows with the same audience are quickly yanked off the air. Anderson's point about big culture still applies.

On one level, this is happy news, because the new culture has been driven by the proliferation of choice. Everyone used to watch "I Love Lucy" because there were few other options; today there are hundreds. Instead of being limited to the few movies playing at local theaters, Americans can choose from more than 80,000 titles offered by online companies such as Netflix.

Where the largest mega-bookstores carry about 100,000 titles, online retailers such as Amazon offer more than 10 million choices. Absent the increasingly rare blockbuster, such as "American Idol" and "Harry Potter," nobody's on the same page anymore.

What we have witnessed is broad democratization of the marketplace. Instead of having to choose from a relatively small menu of options, consumers can customize selections to their own tastes. They are in control. Consumers, Anderson writes, "are scattered to the winds as markets fragment into countless niches."

This power and freedom have wider ramifications. In profound ways, they undercut the traditional aims of civil society. Culture, at bottom, is an instrument of coercion. Where our instincts urge us to do as we please, society pushes us toward cooperation. Like watchful parents, it tries to rein in our selfishness by reminding us of our ties and obligations to others.

A world of niche consumers upends this. While liberating us from small menus of forced choices, it also loosens our bonds to one another. It encourages us to think of ourselves and our tastes in isolation, to see ourselves as distinct individuals, not as members of the larger community. Our parents may have had few alternatives to "I Love Lucy," but they did have something to talk about around the water cooler.

If this trend were limited to pop culture, it would just be a curiosity. But it has ramped up at a time when scholars have documented a breakdown in bonds to family and community, the most famous being Robert Putnam's 1995 article "Bowling Alone: America's Declining Social Capital."

I feel conflicted about these developments.

The great economic abundance Americans now enjoy, along with the loosening of social strictures that began in the 1950s and empowered blacks, women, gays and others, has bestowed great blessings. America has long been known as a nation of reinvention, the place people come to lose the shackles of the past and define themselves for themselves. Today we have this on steroids.

It's no wonder, then, that Americans are embracing this radical individualism, which has arisen at a time when America has become a far richer and fairer nation. But I wonder if has eroded our ability to confront problems that demand collective action—from global warming to health care reform.

I fear we may be nearing a tipping point where our individualism vanquishes our sense of community.

I don't know if we'll see the likes of Harry Potter again, but I hope so.

July 15, 2007

If Mother Superior Speaks, Listen

Be outrageous; defend the indefensible; try to convince me that fat-free tastes as good as the real thing.

As a first response, I'm a regular Sally Jesse Raphael—sans the satellite dish glasses. I'll listen, really listen, withhold judgment, and try to see your point of view. But just when I'm ready to say, "I understand," my Mother Superior kicks in. Instead of patting you on the head, I'll smack your knuckles with a wooden ruler and say, "Cut that out."

Gender issues aside, none of this worries me. In these loopy times, when the word "inexcusable" has become archaic, a split personality is the best defense.

So I approached two new books, Tony Horwitz's "Confederates in the Attic" and Donald McCaig's "Jacob's Ladder," with an open-mind. Though Horwitz is a journalist and McCaig a novelist, both of their works try to find what was noble, admirable and courageous about the Confederate soldiers who shed their blood to insure that millions of innocent men, women and children would remain in bondage.

Whoops, there's Mother Superior talking—pipe down, sister; you'll get your chance.

Thwack!

"Ow."

"Jacob's Ladder" is McCaig's epic tale of the interlocked lives of slaves and slave owners whose lives are forever changed by the Civil War. In a recent phone interview, McCaig told me that as a "Northern liberal"— he'd been an ad man in New York before moving to Virginia 25 years ago—he had to clear a big moral hump in order to write the empathetic portrayal of Confederate soldiers that lies at his book's center. They seemed unfathomable to him: horrible and evil. "I must have spent two years on false starts with this book," he explained. "Then, one day I was at a 'deer-beer party' down by the river near my home. Willie Nelson was blaring out of some pickup truck speaker, and I looked around at all my neighbors and I thought, if this were 1861, I'd be going to war with them."

Reminding me of Hannah Arendt's classic work on Nazi Germany, "Eichmann in Jerusalem: A Report on the Banality of Evil" (1964), McCaig continued: "What I learned as I researched my book was that a good many honorable and decent men and women in the South were slave owners. Slavery was a great sin, a great wickedness, but they weren't any different from you or me—how could they be? They didn't wear the mark of Cain on their arm. They were, for the most part, decent people doing the best they could in a tragically flawed system."

Horwitz underwent a similar conversion while writing "Confederates in the Attic," which depicts the black and white world of modern-day men who spend their days dressed in blue and gray (mostly gray). For these Civil War reenactors, the Lost Cause is not a blood-soaked crucible. Instead, it is a nostalgic portal, Horwitz writes, to "a time when the South seemed a cohesive region upholding Christian values and agrarian ways . . . [when] larger-than-life men like Stonewall Jackson, Robert E. Lee and Nathan Bedford Forrest" walked the earth. It is a balm that blows them back to a simpler era when people knew who they were and what they were."

As Horwitz crisscrossed the South, he watched strange birds who soaked their uniform buttons in urine to give them that real old-time look and starved themselves to achieve that gaunt appearance that was all the rage at Andersonville. He marveled at one gifted shape-shifter who could make himself look bloated and sallow like an authentic corpse on an ersatz battlefield.

We might dismiss these men as historically impaired yahoos as long as we include Horwitz, a Pulitzer Prize-winning reporter, among their ranks. As his book marches on, the lines fade between the writer and subject as he gradually cottons to the reenactors' illusory certainties: "It restored my appreciation," Horwitz writes, "of simple things: cold water, a crust of bread, a cool patch of shade."

What do these two books tell us? It is that too much understanding, like too little knowledge, can be a dangerous thing. Undoubtedly, it is useful to acknowledge that slavery's defenders were not anomalies of evil and that their modern-day doppelgangers are not simply pathetic. But we must also heed Mother Superior's warning: Do not allow that empathy to obscure your moral vision. People may display nobility and courage in the name of evil. Others may derive comfort from that cause. But, the failure to understand the evil that lay at the heart of the Confederacy is inexcusable.

April 26, 1998

You Are at Your Service

I'm not just a humble reporter. On any given day—often in the space of a single hour—I also work as a bank teller and a travel agent, a gas station attendant, a supermarket checkout clerk and a waiter. Thanks to the good people at Regal Entertainment Group, I may soon add another title to my resume: movie usher.

The Tennessee-based company said the job once held by pimply faced lads will now be performed by paying customers. Fulfilling the dream of every frustrated hall monitor, the chain will issue wireless devices to celluloid sheriffs in 114 theaters. If the projector malfunctions or a fellow moviegoer misbehaves, a press of a button will summon the Regal posse.

The company has not said whether it will provide night vision goggles or red dot lasers so its newly commissioned ushers can point out miscreants, or whether other customers will serve as bodyguards for them when the path to their cars is blocked by ejected cell phone yakkers and popcorn throwers.

Welcome to modern America, where customers may not always be right, but they're increasingly busy. From automated teller machines to online flight reservation systems to do-it-yourself supermarket scanners and movie ticket kiosks, service has given way to self-service. Though Oprah Winfrey is widely credited for spreading the gospel of self-help, American business is making it our way of life.

Free labor has always been capitalism's Holy Grail. Automation has allowed corporations to shed those high salaries once commanded by telephone operators and salesclerks. But the self-service economy is the Grail beyond the Grail, as businesses not only get customers to do the work once handled by paid employees but also charge them "service fees" for helping themselves.

Beautiful!

Through doublespeak worthy of George Orwell's classic novel "1984," businesses say they are getting rid of bank tellers and movie ushers in order to improve customer service. The help desk is closed, so that we can better help you.

Best of all, no one is complaining. Who didn't feel the thrill of progress upon spying their first self-checkout lane at the supermarket, at least until the scanner—swipe, swipe, SWIPE—failed to read the bar code on that feminine hygiene product: Assistance needed on Checkout Line 7.

Who doesn't believe they're getting extra value when they get to play waiter at all-you-can-eat restaurants—until the tailor sends you her bill for letting out your pants.

And isn't it fun to book your own plane reservation at Air.com—so long as your plans never change.

Even as we celebrate business for creating the self-service economy, we must admit that there is still much work to be done—by us. What's to stop department stores from turning loyal customers into salesclerks, "Show off your knowledge to fellow shoppers." Restaurants could let diners prepare their own meals, "Just the way you like it!" Can't you see pharmacies allowing patients to fill . . . maybe that's going a little far.

And crime won't be a problem at those self-service operations. I'm sure the ushers at Regal theaters would be delighted to pursue new opportunities in the growing field of law enforcement.

Yes, the self-service economy offers exciting possibilities for everyone willing to ask: May I help me?

June 1, 2007

Nowadays, It's Easy to Hear Women Roar

Feminism is often portrayed as a portal—a movement that afforded women access to the corridors of power.

Achieving that, feminists are also pushing a broader claim: that American culture reflect the sensibility of women. They demand that we address the issues of particular interest to women (abortion, for example) and discuss a range of other issues—from politics to entertainment—in language that speaks to their concerns.

What is the language of women? It is a language of feelings, of personal dynamics. We are edging toward stereotype when we say women are interested in people and men care about things, that men are from

Mars and women are from Venus. Examples to the contrary abound. Nevertheless, the broad-brush descriptions ring true.

Admitting these gender differences is essential if we are to identify one of the most important yet least recognized accomplishments of the women's movement: the feminization of American culture.

Consider a few profound developments from the last 40 years: The deep interest in the personal lives of our leaders; the rise of a confessional culture (hello, Oprah); the preference for personal anecdotes over cold data; the celebration of feelings. Nowadays we talk about everything— usually in the most personal terms.

Many factors have fueled these trends. It is hard to imagine them without Freud or the rise of mass media, especially TV. But it is impossible to explain their ascendancy absent the rise of women. Men may partake of feminine culture, but they never would have built it.

A confession: As a 20th century American man, I still feel more comfortable talking about things rather than people. Our let-it-all-hang-out style is not my style. I don't know that I will ever reach the point where I will embrace it completely.

As a critic, however, I have a deep admiration for the changes women have wrought. It also seems clear that even as the female sensibility has suffused our culture, it has not received the respect it deserves. It is not simply a culture of feelings, but a deeply intellectual exercise from which men have much to learn.

I'll cite one example. A few months ago I began stockpiling books for a column on Mother's Day. Soon my desk was overflowing with works that praise and parse motherhood from a variety of angles. Many were lovely love letters, such as "Mama: Latina Daughters Celebrate their Mothers" by Maria Perez-Brown and Julie Bidwell and "Rise Up Singing: Black Women Writers on Motherhood" edited by Cecelie S. Berry.

The more provocative ones addressed the tensions many mothers feel between the demands of work and home. These included novels such as "From Here to Maternity" by Kris Webb and Kathy Wilson, memoirs like "You Make Me Feel Like an Unnatural Woman: Diary of a New (Older) Mother" by Judith Newman and works of social criticism including "The Mommy Myth: The Idealization of Motherhood and

How It Has Undermined Women" by Susan J. Douglas and Meredith W. Michaels.

If you've browsed your local bookshop recently, you know there are hundreds of others. What's clear is that women are writing and buying these books because of the modern challenge to be both a breadwinner and a bread baker. The women's movement has provided great liberties and hard choices.

What often gets lost in the discussion of these books—which are too often dismissed as whiny and self-indulgent (though some may be)—is the intellectual process at work. Women aren't simply expressing their feelings, they are studying them. They aren't overwhelmed by emotion; they are figuring out how to conquer life. They are answering philosophy's highest call: to live an examined life.

Another recognized yet largely under-addressed fact is the great changes the women's movement has wrought in the lives of men. In numerous and obvious ways, our traditional roles as boyfriends, husbands and fathers are being rewritten.

Despite these sea changes, the literature of the new man is relatively paltry. The world is making new demands. Yet, we are responding in the same old way: we're winging it. Though most of us happily devour books on baseball, technology, history and other pressing matters, we have little interest in exploring the forces shaping our personal lives. It seems we still have a hard time asking for directions.

Perhaps we still consider that women's work. But thinking about your life so that you might respond to its challenges with a smidgen of informed reason is a noble human endeavor.

May 9, 2004

Men Peek Out from the Cave

Men are working overtime to give masculinity a bad name.

In the 1980s and '90s, male fantasies fixated on cigar-chomping gazillionaires in shiny Armani suits and colorful Ferragamo ties. In the new millennium, masters of the universe have been replaced by a coarser, more populist ideal: the beer swilling, tail-chasing Neanderman.

Evidence of this new icon are as plentiful as mosquitoes. Hip-hop music has few women but plenty of hos. Lad mags such as Maxim and Gear draw millions of readers with a primal mix of submissive women and swaggering men. Films like "Old School," in which a group of men address their midlife crisis by starting an "Animal House"-type fraternity, have given guys something to watch while they wait for their "Girls Gone Wild" videos to rewind. All-sports radio stations including Raleigh's 850 the Buzz have tapped the male psyche by mixing balls and babes.

But network television, the hearth of modern culture, is ground zero for the Neanderman sensibility. Beer commercials are built around male fantasies of catfights between scantily clad bimbos. "Reality" programs like "Joe Millionaire" and "The Bachelor" imagine a world where every chick digs you. The Neanderman ethos is pithily grunted in the theme song to Comedy Central's popular program "The Man Show": "Grab a beer and drop your pants / Send the wife and kid to France / It's 'The Man Show!!!'"

Because there's a little Neanderman in me—on more than one occasion my remote has stopped working after taking my TV to "The Man Show"—my guess is that he galumphs around in most men. The mind may say no, but other parts of the body say yes, Yes, YES! to a dreamy world that is just as we'd hoped it would be when we were 13.

The rise of the Neanderman would be funny if it weren't so pathetic. The male desire to regress is a direct response to female progress; men are clinging to the fantasy of power precisely because it is slipping from their grasp in the real world. Yes, most CEOs and high ranking government officials are men, but most men aren't CEOs or senators. Nevertheless America women are on the ascent. In a nation where education is the gateway to success, roughly six out of every 10 recipients of bachelor's or master's degrees are women, and the gap is widening.

Men today are looking back at 40 years of feminist sensitivity training and asking, "What has it got me?" Ever more confident women no longer feel the need to keep men in line, so they don't raise much of a peep when men act like boys. They recognize that male sexism is, in some ways, good for them, because it limits men's ability to compete in the real world. In the big picture, it is, of course, ruinous for all.

The broad societal forces that encourage men to behave badly will not be overcome easily. But glimmers of hope for a Neanderman backlash are appearing on bookstore shelves. They are the male version of the confessional novels women have been devouring since Bridget Jones hit the scene. Imagine any priapic pun you want to describe this male version of chick lit—being a family newspaper, we'll call it Richard lit. But a raft of novels featuring male narrators obsessing over their love lives suggests a willingness among some members of the hirsute set to admit they have . . . feelings.

These works include "Love and Other Recreational Sports" by John Dearie, which describes a 35-year-old New York banker's efforts to find true love after being dumped at the altar; "Man and Wife" by Tony Parsons, whose protagonist is a recently remarried father juggling his new family and his old, and "Flabbergasted" by Ray Blackstone, a light comic novel about a single man's plan to find love at his local Presbyterian church in Greenville, S.C. In August we'll see "Love Me" by Garrison Keillor, which tells of a man who renews his life by writing a lonely hearts column, and September will bring "Swagbelly: A Novel for Today's Gentleman" by D. J. Levian, whose protagonist is a divorced pornography mogul who learns that rafts of money and centerfold sex do not always bring happiness.

No one will confuse these early examples of Richard lit with chick lit. Their narrators do not gush emotion but work to dam the floodgates of feeling. Keillor's narrator tells us, "Communication is an injurious thing in marriage," a point that is echoed by Levian's hero: "What I want, always wanted, and always will, is to become rich enough not to have complicated feelings."

These books have not come to praise Neanderman, though, but to bury him. They cast traditional male traits as a problem, and use them as a source of ridicule. After one incredibly brief exchange, the hero of "Flabbergasted" deadpans, "I suppose, for two single males, we'd just had what amounts to a deep conversation."

Of course, these Richard lit authors are playing off the same stereotypes as "The Man Show"—if you ever have the occasion to talk to a walking/talking man, you'll find he can do more than grunt. But as much as the images of popular culture may diverge from reality, they also have the power to shape it. Today the ubiquitous Neanderman rules the male imagination, but the emergence of Richard lit suggests men are still evolving.

July 6, 2003

My Children's Bookshelf
Is a Battleground

Each night, my older daughters, ages 3 and 4, pick books for me to read. As they snuggle into my lap, I inhale the sweet scent wafting from their downy heads and revel in their squeals of anticipation.

We open a cover. "Once upon a time" spells abracadabra as we are transported to a magical land filled with dysfunctional parents and disobedient children, cruel neighbors and gleeful little murderers, casual violence and situational ethics.

Listening to "Hansel and Gretel" my daughters hear their father tell them that parents sometimes abandon their children in the woods to die. In "The Story of Babar" they learn that mothers can be murdered by wicked hunters. They watch the roistering little fellow who shouts "run, run as fast as you can you can't catch me I'm the Gingerbread Man" meet a quick end as the fox's snack—the same fate met by Chicken Little and his friends Henny Penny, Cocky Locky, Ducky Lucky, Drakey Lakey, Goosey Loosey and Turkey Lurkey.

I watch my 3-year-old shout in glee, "Down, down into the river!" as the evil troll in "The Three Billy Goats Gruff" is killed because he wouldn't let our heroes cross his bridge.

Am I a great father, or what?

But these are not the only books we read. In fact there is a sharp divide on my children's bookcase. While classic tales tend toward the macabre, more modern stories for little kids are all peaches and cream. The only threat offered by "Goodnight Moon" and "Guess How Much I Love You?" is that multiple readings might induce diabetic shock. Dairy products are all that bite the dust in "The Very Hungry Caterpillar" and "Sidewalk Trip" ("I'm splashing through a puddle / with a splish, splish, splish. / Ice cream! Ice Cream! Ice Cream! / is my wish, wish, wish.").

Arthur, the immensely popular aardvark, seems edgy only when you compare him to Clifford the big red dog. "Farm Friends Clean Up" features a mean wolf, but all he does is chase "his farm friends, scaring them with his big teeth." And the big softy agrees to make nice if the other animals promise to teach him how to brush his teeth—even though we haven't seen him DEVOUR A THING!

These stark differences between older and more modern books made me see my children's bookshelf for what it really is: a battleground of fear. In one camp stand the contemporary tales that address the fears of parents who do not want to expose their children to unsettling images and ideas. We like to think of our kids as blank slates whose thoughts and feelings are shaped by their experiences. Surround them with happiness, we think, and they will become happy. Teach them the right and true and they will know no other path.

In the other camp stand the classic tales that allow children to confront primal fears in direct and often brutal ways. They view youngsters as complicated maelstroms of strong emotions. As Bruno Bettelheim argued in his groundbreaking study of classic fairy tales, "The Uses of Enchantment" (1976), these stories do not introduce children to the discomfiting idea of monsters and abandonment. They provide, instead, a way for kids (and adults, to whom these tales were also addressed) to articulate and defeat their lurking demons. He wrote: "A struggle against severe difficulties in life is unavoidable, is an intrinsic part of human existence—but . . . if one does not shy away, but steadfastly meets unexpected and often unjust hardships, one masters all obstacles and at the end emerges victorious. . . . Morality is not the issue in these tales but rather assurance that one can succeed."

The irony is almost palpable. We moderns like to think of our forebears as a bunch of repressed squares who never met an emotion they couldn't swallow. We revel in facing dark truths and exposing terrible secrets. In our therapeutic culture, no feeling is unworthy of obsession. And yet, it is the dusty old classics that are filled with vim and vinegar and psychological insight while our more modern tales seem quaint, innocent and, well, old-fashioned.

Why do we treat our little ones with almost Victorian gentility and reserve?

I suspect that it is the very nakedness of contemporary adult culture that pushes parents to button up our children's world. To be alive today is to be bombarded by images of dysfunction, violence, cruelty and despair. It is natural that parents should seek to carve out a sanctuary of sweetness for their children.

I also suspect that the solipsism that drives our confessional culture is pushing parents to put their own needs ahead of their children's. Rather than selecting works that help children confront their fears, parents seek books that allay their own. It is easier to feel good about ourselves when we provide our kids with wholesome, toothless entertainment than when we expose them to discomfiting situations and ideas. But if modern culture—and the Brothers Grimm—have taught me one thing it is that fears cannot be wished away. I can offer my daughters no more protection nor better sanctuary than to allow them to face life's demons from the safety of my lap.

April 8, 2001

Peter Pan Literature Takes Flight

Once there was a book columnist who had a very exciting day. In the morning, the mailman brought him four children's books written by famous authors who, until now, had only written for grown-ups: "A Perfect Friend" by Reynolds Price, "The Giggler Treatment" by Roddy Doyle, "The Boy Who Ran to the Woods" by Jim Harrison and "The Very Persistent Gappers of Frip" by George Saunders.

"Yippee," he thought, "a trend."

His mind did loop-de-loops, because trends are to columnists what dough is to bakers or politicians. A brand new development! One that no one else had noticed!! That's the cat's pajamas!!!

But then he had second thoughts. Four books weren't much of a trend. And besides, lots of famous writers, like John Updike, Toni Morrison and Margaret Atwood, have written children's books.

Just as he started to pout, fortune smiled on the columnist. He saw a note attached to the George Saunders book from a "publicity manager"—these are very pleasant people who always have nice things to say about others. It said that "Gappers" wasn't a kids book at all, but an "adult fable."

So, the columnist read "Gappers." He was perplexed—not because it was a hard book. It was a simple story about a tiny town of goat-herders whose selfish inhabitants refuse to help each other in times of trouble. In the end they learn that the best way to help themselves is by helping each other. The columnist saw how this book could be read as a critique of the breakdown of community that so many people lament nowadays. But he couldn't figure out why a book written at an elementary school level would be marketed to adults.

Then, like Jack's beanstalk, his trend grew and grew. He thought of "The Boomer" by Marty Asher, a short novel about modern angst written like a comic book. He recalled the glowing reviews given earlier this year to Tony Earley's novel, "Jim the Boy," which was another "adult" book written at a child's level. And, of course there was Harry Potter, the series of children's novels that has gained millions of adult fans.

The columnist thought: When I was growing up (which didn't seem so long ago to him), my friends and I read lots of the same books that adults did, like "Adventures of Huckleberry Finn," "Robinson Crusoe" and "The Hobbit." Now the process seems reversed. Adult readers are becoming interested in childlike books, and literary authors are increasingly interested in writing in the style of children's books.

He gave this trend a snappy name—"the rise of Peter Pan literature." But he still had to answer the biggest question of all: "What does it mean?" Newspaper people call the answer to that question a "nut graph"; the columnist didn't know why exactly, except that sometimes the explanations people come up with to describe human affairs are pretty nutty.

He definitely didn't want to be a nut, or a legume.

He thought about how modern literature teaches adults that life is not just complicated but downright undecipherable. The smart set insists there is no reality or truth, just perception and opinion. He also thought about how preoccupied modern writers—and people who make movies, TV shows and records—have become with "dysfunctional characters," a.k.a. weirdoes.

He knew there were lots of good reasons for this; in fact, some of his favorite books were darker than midnight and at least as complicated as algebra. But it struck him that the really weird thing was that most people are a lot more normal than the way modern artists represent them. And sure, he thought, life is tricky, but it's also pretty straightforward. At least that's what parents always tell kids when they teach them to do "the right thing." Adults must believe there are moral truths, 'cause they wouldn't lie to children, would they? And yet, adults seem afraid to communicate with one another with the same conviction they use to address their children. In their world, sincerity and earnestness have become intellectual sins; the hippest writers use a device called "postmodern irony" to distance themselves from genuine feelings.

The columnist thought that Reynolds Price was suggesting just this in "A Perfect Friend," his story about a young boy who misses his dead mother as much as he loves elephants. Price could be describing modern writers when he says his hero, Ben, is someone who "understood that he was the kind of person who saw and felt things that he couldn't mention or people would laugh and think he was crazy."

Like what? In one scene, "[His mother's] eyes met Ben's and they felt so kind that he was reminded of what he'd nearly forgotten since she left—how she'd almost never said a mean word to him in his whole life with her. And now he realized how she'd been the finest human being he'd known or might ever know in the long years to come."

That, the columnist thought, is exactly how many people feel about their mothers. But, had Price written with such sweet eloquence in an "adult" novel, critics would have dismissed him as "mawkish" and "saccharin."

Maybe, the columnist thought, more adults like to write and read books written at a child's level because it remains the one safe space to express the simple lessons and moral truths that many adults believe but do not dare utter. Maybe, the columnist thought, his little trend might be signaling the birth of a new kind of literature, one that allows for sincerity, earnestness and conviction. Sometimes the simplest language is also the most honest.

At least that's what he believed that one very exciting day.

September 17, 2000

Happy Days in a Grumble-Free Land

Has any generation been more blessed than ours?

Low interest rates, low unemployment and a soaring Dow; these must be the salad days of civilization. If you have any doubts, just turn on the news. Pick up a glossy magazine or colorized newspaper. They'll tell you how the mega-companies that own them are making the economy purr, leaving happiness and freedom in their wake.

But good numbers are only part of the explanation for these good times. For the first time in our history, the American economy and American culture are in perfect alignment, like Ginger Rogers and Fred Astaire in a clean, well-lighted ballroom. Business tells us what we want, and we want nothing more than big business can offer—except, of course, more of it. The result is a grumble-free America.

This wasn't always the case. In the 1920s, when Calvin Coolidge said that the business of America was business, a slew of critics shouted, "No!" There's more to life, they yelled, than what mass consumer culture had to offer.

Slow to respond, business took a drubbing during the next half century. The 1950s produced stinging critiques of The Company Man, such as "The Man in the Gray Flannel Suit" and C. Wright Mills's "White Collar," while the '60s brought an all-out assault against "corporate tools" and "capitalist pigs." For us today, who live in a world where Bill Gates, Michael Eisner and Sandy Weill are hailed as visionaries and kids dream of becoming venture capitalists, it is hard to imagine the disdain with which business leaders were once held.

What changed?

Business wised up. First, it realized that the best way to quiet its critics was to own them. During the last decade, big business snapped up many of the nation's most influential newspapers, magazines, book publishers and television networks. Wary of biting the hand that feeds them, the media have increasingly exchanged their traditional role as cultural critics for the safer position of corporate shill. Hence the celebritization of CEOs, the decision by NBC affiliates to devote more than half of their 11 p.m. news broadcasts to the last episode of "Seinfeld," and CBS's move to outfit its Olympics announcers in hats, parkas and gloves bearing the Nike swoosh. The traditional line between church and state—between the business and news sides of media organizations—is vanishing.

With the watchdogs at bay, business next had to find a way to win over an increasingly skeptical American public.

No book distills this strategy better than "Commodify Your Dissent," a collection of essays from a small, Chicago-based magazine called "The Baffler." It begins by laying out the basic tension between modern business and modern Americans. "The Establishment demands homogeneity; we revolt by embracing diverse, individual lifestyles. It demands self-denial and rigid adherence to convention; we revolt through immediate gratification, instinct uninhibited and liberation of the libido."

Brilliantly, "Commodify" notes, corporations resolved this conflict by making conformance to the consumer culture the pathway to individuality and self-fulfillment: Every buying decision is a personal statement; the way to make a personal statement is through our buying decisions. "Turn on the TV and there it is instantly: the unending drama of Consumer Unbound and in search of ever-heightened good time, the inescapable rock n' roll soundtrack, dreadlocks and ponytails bounding into Taco Bells, a drunken, swinging-camera epiphany of tennis shoes, outlaw soda pops, and mind-bending dandruff shampoos."

Business has decided, if you can't beat 'em, join 'em. No commercial captures this truth-in-advertising approach better than Sprite's new spot featuring basketball star Grant Hill. As Hill touts the soft drink's appeal, cartoon likenesses of him clutching fistfuls of dollars pop up on the screen. The message: He is endorsing the product because he's being paid to. At the close, we're told that we should drink Sprite because it tastes good, not because a celebrity tells us to.

Through its dense levels of irony, the commercial makes a critique of advertising its sales pitch. With a sly wink, it lets us know we're too hip, too tuned-in to buy the very line we're falling for.

The genius of this approach is that it satisfies our need to rebel against mainstream culture while remaining part of it. Unwilling to take itself seriously, it boxes out those critics who might. Who can complain? And complain about what? Oh, happy day.

May 31, 1998

When Our Lives Become iMovies

Charles Bronson murdered my father. He hid a bomb inside a bottle of red wine, and when it exploded, he gave my old man everlasting life. For this, I am eternally grateful.

The fateful moment occurred in 1987, about halfway through that woefully underappreciated masterpiece, "Death Wish 4: The Crackdown." Dad, who had spent his career working behind the scenes in TV and film, was the picture's production manager. When the director needed an Italian-looking man to a play a doomed Mafioso, one look at my father's Roman profile told him he'd found his victim.

So there he is for a few glorious minutes and two short lines, "Kid, kid, get back in the kitchen," and, "What the hell?" They cut his other dialogue, Dad said, because "I was stealing the scene." When American Movie Classics (I told you it was a great film) began showing "Death Wish 4" recently, I gathered my three daughters around the TV. There, in living color, they saw their late grandfather, whom they faintly remember and only know through still photos and family lore.

"He's only acting," I assured them. "If he was really a gangster, we'd be rich!"

As I replayed the scene (isn't DVR grand?) I thought about my dad, of course. But I also considered the mind-bending breakthrough that this snippet of celluloid represents. We haven't found Ponce de Leon's Fountain of Youth, but we can enjoy the next best thing to virtual immortality. All of us!

Not only will my children always have those few minutes of film of their Papa John, but so will their children, grandchildren, great-grandchildren and so on down the line. Ten thousand years from now, our descendants will be able to see and hear him, wondering, no doubt, why he came to such a nasty end.

I'll have to film a little segment explaining the circumstances and include it among the boxes of DVDs chronicling my girls' lives: their earliest words and first steps, their toddler talents and elementary school view of life. Pure gold!

Here's the amazing thing: As our video cameras whirr away, we take it all for granted. In fact, our ability to preserve the past is nothing less than a radical transformation of history, a profound empowerment of memory that has been fueled by ambiguous scraps since the dawn of time.

Through most of history, only the famous were immortalized. They endured through written accounts; that's how we know of Cleopatra and Alexander the Great, Charlemagne and Joan of Arc. Sculptures and paintings gave inklings of what dignitaries and a few anonymous plain-folk looked like. But these renderings were arbitrary, as much a reflection of their creators' eye as their subjects' countenance.

Even for history's stars, the gaps are wide. Scholars hold that we have no firsthand accounts of Jesus. We certainly don't know what he, Buddha or the Prophet Muhammad actually looked like.

And consider Shakespeare, whose 37 plays continue to shape how we look at the world and ourselves. Through his work, we understand his artistic mind. But we know little about the man.

Until the 1820s, we couldn't see what people truly looked like because there were no photographs. Until the 1860s and '70s, we couldn't hear what they sounded like because there were no recordings. Until the 1880s, we couldn't watch how they moved because there were no films. Before the 20th century, we had shards of knowledge about a handful of figures. Of the vast majority, zilch.

My great-grandparents exist for me as a few snapshots taken in their sunset years. I don't know what they looked like when they dared to leave their homes in Italy, Sweden, Denmark and England and come to America. I don't know what they sounded like, how they lived, what they thought, their favorite books, foods or sports. Their parents are only names on birth certificates.

For much of the past century, technological preservation was largely the reserve of the privileged few. We have extensive film and sound recordings of every president since Theodore Roosevelt. Where Washington's farewell to his troops and Lincoln's Gettysburg Address are only glorious words on the page, we can hear FDR's fireside chats and watch Richard Nixon resign.

We're told that the 19th-century star Edwin Booth played a mean Hamlet, but we can watch Laurence Olivier play the part forever. We can hear Bessie Smith sing, see Robert Frost read his poems and watch Martin Luther King Jr. deliver his "I Have a Dream" speech.

For the rest of us, there are few records. The only film of me taken before I bought a video camera in 1997 when my first child was born is a few minutes from a silent home movie my aunt made when I was 4. I'm the tow-headed nut punching the clown.

Imagine if you could watch films of your ancestors from 100, 200 or 300 years ago: walking, talking images of people we know only through unreliable family stories or simply as names and dates on silent tombstones.

We can't. Thanks to affordable video cameras, we don't have to suffer the fate of the forgotten. Like ageless gods, even the humblest can live on in hi-def glory.

Next time you break out the camera, look good, sound smart, try to crack a joke. And don't be like my mother, who's always turning her head, putting her hand over her face.

Get ready for your close-up, it's going to last.

May 11, 2008